Lincolnshire History and Archaeology ̄ ̄
Society for Lincolnshire F̈ ̈
historic county of Lincolns

Jews' Court, Steep Hill, Lin

The journal is issued free t
purchased by non-members.

Contributions should be sent to the Editor, Jews' Court, Steep
Hill, Lincoln LN2 1LS, info@slha.org.uk. Typescripts should
be prepared in line with recommendations of the **Modern
Humanities Research Association Style Book** (which can be
downloaded from the Modern Humanities Research Association
website, http://www.mhra.org.uk/). 'Notes for the guidance of
contributors' are available from the Editor and from the Society's
website.

Books for notice or review should be sent to the Reviews Editor,
Jews' Court, Steep Hill, Lincoln LN2 1LS.

Editor:	Mark Bennet
Editorial Board:	Wendy Atkin, Mark Bennet, Adam Daubney and Ken Redmore
Reviews Editors:	Ray Carroll and Claire Hubbard-Hall
Designer:	Ros Beevers

Cover:
Horkstow Roman Mosaic, 1799, by William Fowler. Engraving.

Horkstow Roman villa was discovered in 1796 close to Horkstow
Hall when this mosaic was found by labourers laying out a new
kitchen garden. The mosaic was drawn by William Fowler who
lived close by in Winterton and his drawing was later engraved
and published. The mosaic probably dates to the mid fourth
century. The western end of the mosaic (top of the image) depicts
Orpheus charming various birds and animals. The eastern panel
(bottom of the image) shows a chariot race in progress. There are
some errors in this engraving. Fowler has rearranged the figured
scenes and the central roundel is somewhat flattened. These
changes were probably made so that the image would fit the sheet
of paper that was available to Fowler. There is a discussion of this
mosaic in David S. Neal and Stephen R. Cosh, *Roman Mosaics of
Britain, volume 1, Northern Britain incorporating the Midlands
and East Anglia* (2002), pp.148-59. A contemporary engraving by
Samuel Lysons of the discovery of the mosaic was published in
1801 and used on the front cover of *LHA* 31 (1996). The surviving
parts of the mosaic are now on display at the Hull and East Riding
Museum, Hull, having been transferred there from the British
Museum in the 1970s.

William Fowler (1761-1832) was born in Winterton in
Lincolnshire. The son of a builder, he became an architect and
builder in Winterton and from about 1796 drew several Roman
mosaics that had been found in north Lincolnshire, at Winterton,
Roxby and Horkstow. He went on to publish coloured engravings
of twenty-five mosaic pavements in his lifetime.

Reproduced courtesy of Lincolnshire County Council, The
Collection: Art and Archaeology in Lincolnshire.

Lincolnshire History and Archaeology

Volume 48, 2013

Contents

The presentation of, and the views expressed in, the various contributions are those of the authors and reviewers and not necessarily those of the Society.

Articles in this journal refer to sums of predecimal British currency. The currency changed to the present decimal system in 1971. The predecimal coinage used pounds, shillings and pence (£.s.d.). There were twenty shillings in one pound and twelve pence in one shilling. One guinea was twenty-one shillings or one pound and one shilling.

ISBN 978 0 903582 52 0

ISSN 0459-4487

Printed by J W Ruddock & Sons Ltd, 56 Great Northern Terrace, Lincoln LN5 8HL

Obituary

Rex Russell, 1916-2014

Rex Russell, historian, teacher and family man lived his entire long and varied life with the constant ethics of his left-wing intellectual background. He was no bigot, no stick-in-the-mud, and viewed every aspect of human behaviour with a measured eye and (mostly) with benign tolerance. He was a solid, kind, honest, generous man who inspired a huge following amongst Lincolnshire historians.

Rex was an active member of the Society for Lincolnshire History and Archaeology for many years and members have enjoyed his input to the society, and to the study of Lincolnshire's history, in the form of organised outings (particularly to deserted medieval villages), talks and publications.

It was a surprise to some members of the Lincolnshire Methodist History Society to learn that Rex, a founder member of the Society, was not a Christian. Rex would not pretend to a faith he did not have but he saw in the history of Methodism a massive contribution to the progression of the working man towards education and equality. He saw the opportunities offered by Methodism as a great enhancement of trust earned by the working populations of two centuries ago.

Rex was fond of telling people that he was born in Hackney Workhouse in London during a Zeppelin raid; his parents were Master and Matron of the workhouse. The Zeppelin raid dates his birth to another world beyond the memory of most people now alive. He could remember the vast complex of buildings that surrounded him in infancy and spoke of the workhouse bakery and butchery, the offices and the infirmary. As a child of five or six Rex moved to Yorkshire with his mother and three brothers as his father sought other employment in London. Holme-on-Spalding-Moor in Yorkshire became the background to Rex's childhood. His great-grandfather had been head teacher of the village school there and the four clever Russell boys all attended that school. Rex won a scholarship to a minor public school (Bancroft's, a Drapers' Company School) which meant that he became a boarder and enlarged his horizons far from the village school.

As a teenager Rex chose to be a commercial artist and he trained for this work by winning an Essex County Scholarship to art school. He later used his graphic skills to enhance his many history publications, particularly as a cartographer, and he produced wonderfully drawn and lettered maps showing pre-enclosure and post-enclosure parishes. In 1938 Rex married Eleanor – 'Froude' as she was known – and, for a time, they both worked on the land which gave Rex that sympathy with farm workers, and their low pay, which he always held. Rex served in the Royal Navy during the war between 1941 and 1946. After the war, as a mature student, he gained a degree in History and Education at Durham University

(1947-51) and it was at Durham that he found his true vocation in teaching. In 1951, he was appointed Workers' Educational Association tutor organiser in North Lindsey and he and his family moved to Barton-upon-Humber. In 1964, he was appointed staff tutor in local history in the Hull University Extra-Mural Department and remained in this post until retirement in 1981.

Rex's teaching was never one-sided; he preferred dialogue and discussion. He prepared carefully and spoke clearly; it was a delight to attend his classes. Most of all he gave encouragement on a generous scale and gave helpful suggestions and detailed information on sources. Many of his publications were a joint effort with students and, invariably, his students wanted to do more work on the subject of local history which they were learning with enthusiasm from primary sources under Rex's guidance. He published numerous articles and books on subjects such as enclosure; allotments; headstones; labourers' movements, Methodism, friendly societies, water drinkers (tee-totallers, which Rex was not); education in north Lincolnshire; homes of the poor; deserted medieval villages and the effect of the French Revolution on Lincolnshire. His last publication, in 2002, was on changes in popular culture in Lincolnshire: *From Cock-Fighting to Chapel Building*. Hundreds of students benefited from Rex's knowledge and enthusiasm and in 2010, when he was a resident in Nettleton Manor Care Home, he was honoured with a personal achievement award, made to him by the British Association of Local History, for his enormous contribution to local history as a tutor and writer.

Rex and Eleanor had two children, Kleta and Adrian, and they spent most of their married life in Barton-upon-Humber. Eleanor died in 1989. In 1994 Rex surprised his friends by marrying Joan Mostyn-Lewis when he was nearly eighty years of age. Joan was, like Rex, an artist and so began, late in life, another happy phase for Rex. Fifteen years later, with Rex and Joan no longer able to look after each other, Joan and later Rex went into care homes for their last years, Joan died in 2012. Rex was cared for in Nettleton Manor where he died aged ninety-eight on 15 December 2014 of extreme old age.

Jean-Jacques Rousseau in Spalding, May 1767

Michael Honeybone and Diana Honeybone

In early May 1767, a post-chaise drew up at the entrance to the White Hart Inn in the Market Place of Spalding, Lincolnshire, and from it descended two passengers and a small brown dog, accompanied by very little luggage. The arrival of travellers at the White Hart was not unusual; this large inn and posting-house had been receiving visitors for centuries. What was particularly striking on this occasion was the identity of the travellers. The man, aged fifty-four and wearing a slightly old-fashioned coat cut in the French style, was an international celebrity: no less than the famous philosopher, composer and author Jean-Jacques Rousseau (Fig.1), whose books were read in the original French or in translation across Europe, and whose ideas had stirred controversy across the reading world. He was accompanied by his *gouvernante* (housekeeper), Thérèse Levasseur, who had been his companion for over twenty years, and his dog, Sultan.

Their arrival raises a series of questions. What had brought this famous man, after fifteen months in England, to the small Fenland market town for a ten-day stay in the spring of 1767? What did he do during that time and why did he take his departure as abruptly as he had arrived? His visit to Lincolnshire is among the less well-known events of his well-documented and widely researched life, which was internationally celebrated in 2012, three hundred years after his birth. The reasons for Rousseau's journey lie in the events of his past, some of them going back for years and others of more recent origin.

So, who was Jean-Jacques Rousseau? On all his books he proudly called himself *A Citizen of Geneva,* where he was born on 28 June 1712. He was born a Swiss Protestant and he had no formal schooling, being brought up by his father, a watchmaker who taught him to read, and then by his aunt, who sang to him. In 1718, when he was sixteen, he walked out of Geneva, became a Catholic and spent ten years travelling, much of which was spent playing and singing music in the household of the rich Baroness de Warens near Chambéry, then a part of the Kingdom of Sardinia. He also spent some months in Turin, developing a great enthusiasm for Italian music, which influenced his own compositions. This came to a climax with the performance of his very agreeable operetta, *Le Devin du Village (The Village Soothsayer)*, before Louis XV

Fig.1. Jean-Jacques Rousseau, wearing his Armenian costume, by Allan Ramsay, 1766 (Scottish National Portrait Gallery).

at Versailles in 1752. As Rousseau himself said, '*The Village Soothsayer* brought me completely into fashion' and indeed it was to be performed in England in 1766.[1] It was in the 1750s that Rousseau was busy writing his twelve articles on music for his friend Diderot's *Encyclopédie* and he earned a living wage by copying music, particularly during the last decade of his life from 1767 to 1778.

Rousseau had moved to Paris in 1742 in order to present to the Académie des Sciences a new system for musical notation he had invented. It was not accepted, but Rousseau became an enthusiastic member of the Republic of Letters whilst teaching music, tutoring young scholars and beginning to write essays. His friends were the *philosophes*, in particular Diderot and d'Alembert. Diderot suggested in 1750 that Rousseau might write an essay for a prize established by one of the main French provincial societies, the Académie de Dijon. Here we find a real difference between England and France: at that time very few English towns had prosperous intellectual societies. One of the few outside London was the Spalding Gentlemen's Society, founded in 1710. In France such societies were widespread, encouraged by the government, with prizes often being offered by the societies. Rousseau won first prize for his essay for the Académie de Dijon and his career as a philosopher took off.

Fig.2. Thérèse Levasseur (1721-1801), Rousseau's companion and gouvernante *(housekeeper), by E. Charryère after a sepia by Naudet, late eighteenth century (image in the public domain, Wikipedia).*

By the middle 1760s, England and France were at last at peace after a series of wars lasting years. Many British people were visiting Paris, perceived as the cultural centre of Europe. King Louis XV, during a long reign, consolidated the cultural authority of France and maintained the Versailles court, where the aristocracy were able to shine. Louis generally tolerated the rather outspoken philosophers of his reign, but he could not accept Jean-Jacques Rousseau because of his free-thinking about religion. There was a threefold audience in Europe for writings such as Rousseau's. The highest stratum in France represented *le Monde*: aristocratic gentry and salon-based ladies who insisted on *la politesse*, enjoyed civilised conversation and avoided controversial argument. They either attended the court at Versailles, dominated by the King, or they lorded it over their home establishments, controlling local government absolutely in the way the Crown absolutely controlled national government. In Britain, the House of Lords and the House of Commons controlled politics, so here it was the aristocrats and MPs and their wives who formed *le Monde*.

The next stratum of the audience in France was the Republic of Letters: the French intellectuals, *les philosophes* as they were known, could not participate in government, so they tried to act politically by inventing a new audience – public opinion. They wrote extensively about every known topic. Their best-known product was *L'Encyclopédie*, published from 1751 and derived from Ephraim Chambers' *Cyclopedia* of 1728. *L'Encyclopédie* was edited by Diderot and d'Alembert, with thirteen articles by Voltaire and twelve by Rousseau, including one on political economy. One reaction of the French Crown was to imprison Diderot for a short time. However, *L'Encyclopédie* and Chambers' *Cyclopedia* were popular and, along with the newspapers and novels of the period, they created a new branch of society: the reading public. This was the politically aware group which was developing across Europe in Italy, Poland, Germany, France and particularly Britain. The reading public read newspapers, popular books and novels, notably Rousseau's *Julie ou La Nouvelle Héloïse* (1761), and pamphlets of all sorts.

Rousseau himself was a great reader. Not having undergone conventional schooling, he was free to read whatever he wanted and he found that his most-loved author was the classical Greek writer Plutarch. He read Plutarch's *Lives* to see how great men governed and he was most impressed by Sparta, a state controlled by a powerful ideal, where the citizens lived without luxury. In his book about the ideal education, *Émile* (1762), Rousseau wrote: 'Plutarch is my man' and 'I would prefer to begin the study of the human heart with the reading of lives of individuals.'[2] After his first successful essay, Rousseau wrote a second in 1754: *A Discourse on the Origins of Inequality,* in which he claimed that 'all the inequality which now prevails ... becomes at last permanent and legitimate by the establishment of property and laws'.[3] He longed for original man in a 'state of nature in its first purity' and he hated 'civilised man', whom he accused of every crime possible, which he listed in amazing and readable detail.[4] Finally, he pinpointed the essence of this civilised man: the desire for *luxury,* 'the causes of all the miseries, into which opulence at length plunges the most celebrated nations'.[5]

This extraordinary outburst distressed Rousseau's fellow philosophers and was one of the origins of his troubles, to escape from which he eventually fled to England, ending up in Spalding. Voltaire became his greatest enemy, and the Republic of Letters henceforth became a battleground. Voltaire replied to Rousseau's *Discourse*:[6]

> Never has anyone so brilliantly tried to convert us into beasts. One feels the urge to walk about on all fours when one reads your work. But as it has been more than sixty years since I've lost the habit, I regret it would be impossible for me to regain it.

When Rousseau spelt out all his objections to modern political society, and thus the French Crown, in *The Social Contract* (1762) he began with the world-famous words: 'Man is born free; and everywhere he is in chains.'[7] Had he stopped there, he might not have been so viciously attacked, but he published *Émile* in the same year, in which he included a plea for natural

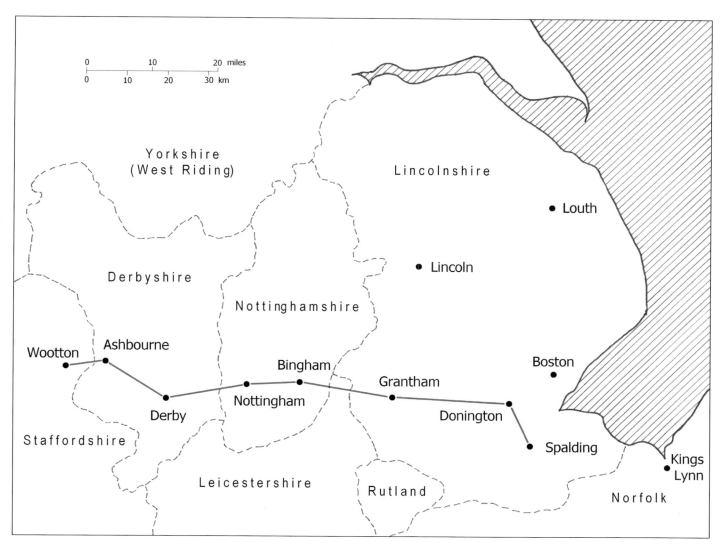

Fig.3. Conjectural route taken in 1767 by Jean-Jacques Rousseau and his housekeeper, Thérèse Levasseur, from Wootton (Staffs) to Spalding (Lincs), based on known posting routes (Ken Redmore).

religion: 'my profession of faith such as God reads it in my heart.'[8] He made a strong attack on organised religion and the Church, saying 'I would be less attached to the spirit of the Church than to the spirit of the Gospel, in which the dogma is simple and the morality sublime, and in which one sees few religious practices and many works of charity.'[9] Thus by 1762 Rousseau had totally upset his fellow philosophers, the French Crown and the French Church. He was henceforth *persona non grata* in France, Italy and most Swiss cantons. In particular, he was attacked in his home city of Geneva. It was this bitter persecution which strongly disturbed him and which was the origin of his paranoid view that, wherever he was, he was being plotted against. He tried to find refuge in Frederick the Great's Swiss principality, Neuchâtel. There he lived with his *gouvernante*, Thérèse Levasseur, whom he had taken up with in 1745 and with whom he lived for the rest of his life; but even in Neuchâtel he was hated for his apparent irreligion, and a stone was thrown at his house. He had to run for his life, pausing briefly in Paris, where he arrived on 16 December 1765, en route for England.

The French Crown allowed Rousseau to stay in Paris for three weeks to sort out his affairs and arrange his departure to England with the great Scottish philosopher, David Hume, with whom he had been in touch for several years and who now became a close friend. Whilst in Paris, Rousseau paraded in his strange Armenian outfit, which he wore as his protest against luxury. It also helped him to cope with a permanent and distressing medical condition involving a catheter. He attended the salons of *le Monde*, where a most unfortunate joke began to circulate around Christmas 1765. The celebrated satirical wit, Horace Walpole, who found Rousseau's solemn parading of his sensitive sufferings rather excessive, composed a joke-letter purporting to come from the Prussian King, Frederick the Great, which appeared to offer Rousseau sanctuary, but which concluded with an unkind satirical comment:[10]

> My dear Jean-Jacques, You have renounced Geneva, your native soil. You have been driven from Switzerland, a country of which you have made such boast in your writings. In France you are outlawed: come then to me. I admire your talents, and amuse myself with your reveries; on which however, by

the way you bestow too much time and attention. It is high time to grow prudent and happy: you have made yourself sufficiently talked of for singularities little becoming a truly great man: show your enemies that you have sometimes common sense: this will vex them without hurting you. My dominions afford you a peaceful retreat: I am desirous to do you good, and will do it, if you can but think it such. But if you are determined to refuse my assistance, you may expect that I shall not say a word about it to anyone. If you persist in perplexing your brains to find new misfortunes, chuse such as you like best; I am a King and can make you as miserable as you can wish: at the same time I will engage to do that which your enemies never will, I will cease to persecute you, when you are no longer vain of persecution. Your sincere friend, Frederick.

Rousseau does not appear to have heard of this joke until it was published in the English newspapers, including the *Stamford Mercury* on Thursday 10 April 1766, but the Walpole letter, originally written in French, had already become a huge success in Paris in December 1765. As a result, Walpole became very popular amongst *le Monde*; after all, he was the son of the late British Prime Minister.

Rousseau came to England on extremely good terms with Hume in January 1766, and Thérèse joined him later. In London he took part in the social life. He had cousins there, possibly including John Rousseau (married there in 1767), whom Rousseau later accused of helping in the plots against him. After a few days in London, Hume arranged for Rousseau to go to rooms out in Chiswick, where he stayed for some weeks, visiting Chiswick Hall and returning to London from time to time. Whilst this was going on, Hume was doing two outstandingly helpful things for Rousseau. First, he was in close touch with Lt-General Conway, Secretary of State and leader of the House of Commons, who was arranging the establishment of an official pension for Rousseau from King George III. Second, he was organising a permanent home for Rousseau at a house owned by a rich Cheshire gentleman, Richard Davenport, at Wootton in Staffordshire. All was going well for Rousseau in early 1766.

The house in Wootton, which Richard Davenport lent to Rousseau, fitted perfectly into his belief about the ideal conditions for human life, with its emphasis on rustic solitude. It was deep in the countryside of the Peak District and was ideal for two things: his writing and his latest passion, which was botanising. Wootton had a staff of servants, who would relieve him of the problems of daily life. He was now occupied in writing his *Confessions*, which he stipulated were not to be published until after his death and which thereupon became incredibly popular, starting the fashion for private autobiographies, which have been popular ever since. In the *Confessions* he wrote about his new major interest:[11]

> Botany – as I had always considered it and as I still did when it began to become a passion with me – was exactly the kind of idle pleasure to fill the void of my leisure, leaving no room for the wildness of the imagination or for the boredom of total inaction.

During his thirteen months at Wootton, Rousseau, who spoke little English, met several Derbyshire gentlemen who spoke excellent French. He was able to attend musical soirées and discuss opera, in particular with Bernard Granville, who lived nearby at Calwich Abbey and was a friend of Handel.[12] Brooke Boothby, whom Rousseau met and corresponded with in Derbyshire, recorded that Rousseau passed his time 'chiefly in botanising upon the hill in his armen[i]an dress'.[13] It is significant to the town of Spalding that Rousseau met another local gentleman, Erasmus Darwin of Lichfield (Staffordshire), grandfather of Charles Darwin and an important botanist. Erasmus Darwin's father was Robert Darwin, who had been a close friend of the first Secretary of the Spalding Gentlemen's Society, Maurice Johnson, and was himself a member of the Society earlier in the eighteenth century. Another correspondent and companion on his botanising walks was the Duchess of Portland, a significant natural historian, and Rousseau called himself '*l'herboriste de la Duchesse de Portland*'.[14] She sent him a copy of John Ray's famous book on plants, *Synopsis Methodica Stirpium Britannicarum*.

Unfortunately, the weather was not kind during the thirteen months Rousseau spent at Wootton and his *gouvernante* was never happy in England (Fig.2). She spoke very little English and did not get on with her fellow servants or the English food – she had enjoyed introducing the English to French food when they were at Wootton.[15] Rousseau was also reluctant to learn and speak English. A further problem was that, during the year, the relationship between Rousseau and Hume collapsed. Brooke Boothby records that in April 1766, while at Wootton, Rousseau learnt from the newspapers of the existence of the joke-letter, falsely claimed by its author, Horace Walpole, to have been sent to Rousseau by Frederick the Great. Boothby said, 'I found him in extreme agitation in consequence of a pretended letter... a bad joke of Horace Walpole's'.[16] Rousseau could not take a joke, particularly if he was the butt, and completely lost all sense of proportion over it. He accused Hume, the friend of Walpole, of a plot against him and he was convinced that all the *philosophes* of France and England were ganging up against him. Many of the letters which passed between Hume and Rousseau found their way into the newspapers and so every member of the reading public in England knew about the quarrel and no doubt loved every moment of it. Rousseau did not and when it showed no sign of abating, he decided he could no longer remain in England. So began the final story of his English exile: the Spalding episode.

On 1 May 1767, Rousseau and Thérèse hired a post-chaise in Ashbourne in Derbyshire, just over the border from Wootton. On 5 May Rousseau wrote a letter from the White Hart (the post inn at Spalding) to Lord Camden, the Lord Chancellor, asking for a guard to protect him on

Fig.4. Spalding Market Place by Hilkiah Burgess, 1822. A coach can be seen outside the White Hart Inn, where Rousseau stayed in May 1767 (Spalding Gentlemen's Society).

his journey to Dover.[17] What happened in the intervening four days and why his journey paused in Spalding is open to conjecture. Rousseau wanted to return to France, but was determined not to travel via London if it could be avoided, as he was convinced that his enemies were concentrated there. Brooke Boothby suggested in a letter written some time later that Rousseau, 'looking at the map ... saw Boston the nearest port'.[18]

There may be another reason why Rousseau came to Spalding. He had a correspondent in Louth, Maximilien Cerjat, a rich Swiss gentleman and the High Steward of Louth, now naturalised English and married to an Englishwoman. Rousseau had written to him earlier in the year, asking if they could meet in order that Cerjat could help with the transport or storage of his papers. Some historians have suggested that Rousseau wished to leave his precious manuscripts with Cerjat, as he did not trust the English post. Whatever happened, we know he left three large trunks of his possessions with Davenport at Wootton and they were sent on to Rousseau later. He probably never went to Louth, as the journey was too complicated and time-consuming. A much more likely suggestion for his route through Spalding would be posting by post-chaise from Ashbourne via Derby, Nottingham, Bingham and Grantham, all of which had post inns where he could

change horses and chaises (Fig.3). He most probably arrived in Spalding on 4 May and took rooms at the White Hart (Figs 4 and 5), from where on 5 May he wrote to Lord Camden, the first of several letters, which are the main evidence for his Lincolnshire residence.

We can easily imagine Rousseau and Thérèse arriving in their hired post-chaise with no idea as to exactly where they were. The purpose of the trip was to return to France as soon as possible, but how? There were no boats via Boston, they discovered. They must have found that out on their journey, possibly at one of the posting inns on their route through Lincolnshire. Maybe they arrived at Donington to change horses and learnt that they could not get a boat at Boston, so went south to Spalding. Perhaps it was the port of Spalding that drew them: was Rousseau hoping to find a boat there for France? Did he give up hope of travelling from an eastern port and pause there to consider the route via Dover? He may have investigated the possibility of taking ship at King's Lynn. However, no evidence for any such enquiries remains.

What was Spalding like at the time of Rousseau's visit? The town was still an active river port for trading vessels, with constant schemes for dredging the channel of the Welland to allow easy access to the sea. As the

Armstrong map of 1778 shows, trade in Spalding was good and merchants were building great houses along the eastern bank of the River Welland.[19] The Market Place was a hub of activity, with regular weekly markets for produce and animals. Town government was carried out and the Quarter Sessions were held in the seventeenth-century Town Hall to the west of the Market Place. This had recently had new oak doors, paid for partly by Maurice Johnson, the founder of the Gentlemen's Society. For a provincial town, there was no shortage of entertainment: apart from assemblies in the Town Hall, especially at the time of the local races, there was a recently established theatre in Crackpool Lane used by touring companies. During the 1760s, the doctors, clergy, lawyers and merchants met together weekly on Thursdays at the Spalding Gentlemen's Society in its meeting-place, which at that time was in Cox's Rooms (Fig.6) by the western bank of the river near the High or Great Bridge. Their meetings were typical of the polite society of Europe: they discussed a wide range of topics, including new books, ancient coins and artefacts, and they collected botanical specimens and fossils and carried out scientific observations using the latest equipment, such as microscopes and telescopes. In Spalding, the gentlemen of the Society were a little more serious than most of the reading public: they read *The Spectator, The Tatler* and *The Rambler,* though to avoid quarrels their rules insisted that they could not discuss religion and politics. There is little doubt that the average Spalding reader of novels would have thoroughly enjoyed J-J. Rousseau's popular sentimental novel *Julie, or the New Héloïse: Letters of Two Lovers in a Small Town at the Foot of the Alps.* This was translated into idiomatic English by William Kenrick in 1761 and went into nine editions in England, rapidly becoming the most popular novel in Europe during the eighteenth century. The newspaper devoured by every member of the reading public in Spalding was the *Stamford Mercury.*

There are three things Rousseau did in Spalding for which we have documentary evidence: shopping for new clothes, letter-writing and long conversations with the gentlemen of the town. Rousseau had left his Armenian dress in Wootton, giving it to the family of one of the maids. He contacted a local tailor's shop in Spalding (there were several in the Market Place) and the tailor prepared a new blue suit for him, ready for his return to France.[20] Four of the letters that Rousseau wrote from Spalding have survived. Reading them, we can gain an understanding of the dichotomy of Rousseau's mental state. In a letter to the Lord Chancellor he said he was in danger and needed the personal protection of the Lord Chancellor's man to travel anywhere. David Hume's response to this letter was that Rousseau was 'plainly mad, after having been long maddish'.[21] Whilst he was in Spalding, Rousseau wrote two letters to his Wootton host, Richard Davenport. An important element of his

Fig.5. Blue plaque at the White Hart Inn, Market Place, Spalding, unveiled 28 March 2012 to replace missing original plaque commemorating Rousseau's stay there in May 1767 (W. J. Atkin).

terrible worries is explained by the length of time (six days) his letter of 11 May took to get from Spalding to Davenport at his home in Calveley, Cheshire.[22] Fearing that his supposed enemies in London would steal and open it, Rousseau sent the letter by the much slower country cross-posts. He wrote that he preferred liberty to the kind of captivity he was experiencing in England. He evidently felt he was in extreme danger of death and that people, both French and English and led by David Hume, were permanently plotting against him. These sensations were the result of his paranoia caused by the publication in the newspapers of his letters, both private and public, and by his conviction that his letters were opened and read by the people plotting against him. In his second letter to Davenport, dated from Spalding on 14 May, Rousseau wrote that if he was able to have at Wootton his 'absolute liberty as much for my person as for my letters, there is no other place on the earth I would prefer to your house at Wootton'.[23] He also said that he was going to Calais and asked Davenport to be ready to take action regarding the forwarding of his three big trunks of possessions which were at Wootton and to send them to Rousseau, as he would instruct him. These letters at least allow us to date more closely Rousseau's stay in the town: the evening of 4 May to some time on 14 or 15 May.

The third aspect of Rousseau's stay in Spalding for which we have evidence arises from his association with those gentlemen he met or had correspondence with in the town. His main conversations were with the Revd John Dinham, Vicar of Spalding from 1758 and President of the Spalding Gentlemen's Society from 1759 to his

Fig.6. Cox's Rooms by the High Bridge, where the Spalding Gentlemen's Society met, by Hilkiah Burgess, 1827 (Spalding Gentlemen's Society).

death in 1782. Dinham later told a friend that 'he had passed several hours every day with Rousseau, while he was in that place; that he [Rousseau] was cheerful, good-humoured, easy, and enjoyed himself perfectly well, without the least fear or complaint of any kind.'[24] This offers an interesting contrast to statements in Rousseau's letters, which were either gloomy or frantic.

We do not know whether Rousseau attended the Thursday meeting of the Spalding Gentlemen's Society on 7 May 1767 as, unless they became members, visitors were not named in the Treasurer's accounts, which were the only surviving record of meetings at this time. What we do know is that it was a very flourishing society in the later years of the 1760s. Although the founding members were now all dead, the Society was being well run by its President, John Dinham, and its Operator (today called the Curator), Dr Edmund Jessop, the Assistant Operator, Mr Calamy Ives, the Librarian and Secretary, the Revd Mr John Rowning (a significant natural philosopher and master of the Grammar School), and the Treasurer, Walter Johnson J.P. (second son of Maurice Johnson and who had taken over his father's legal business).

In May 1766, Dinham borrowed from the Society's library the *History of England* by Rousseau's former friend David Hume. The library's main user was Dr Edmund Jessop, who also borrowed Hume's book in July 1767. One book Jessop kept on borrowing was Ainsworth's *Latin Dictionary*. We now know one use to which he put this dictionary: in order to write a letter in Latin to his philosophical hero, J-J. Rousseau, who had just arrived in Spalding.[25] His letter was effusive in its praises of Rousseau's literature and philosophy, although the actual quality of the Latin, that of an educated medical doctor rather than a Classical scholar, makes it rather difficult to translate. Jessop chose Latin as a compliment to a man of learning; earlier in the eighteenth century it had been in quite common use as a means of communication between educated men of

different nationalities. Indeed, some correspondence from abroad to the Spalding Gentlemen's Society, including that with a Norwegian astronomer, had been conducted in Latin.[26] It was by now, however, a little old-fashioned to use Latin, but perhaps Jessop's French was not of a quality to undertake a letter to a well-known author.

Jessop wrote effectively about Rousseau's view that it is civilisation that has caused the problems mankind finds in this world; indeed, a careful translation of Jessop's letter reveals an unusually thoughtful reaction and a clear view that Rousseau was the most significant philosopher of the time: 'It often grieves me greatly that you, the greatest and, in my opinion the unique philosopher of this age, have received injuries from both political and religious tyrants ... I greet you as a hero of Truth!' Rousseau responded in a totally negative manner. His reply in French was needlessly antagonistic to someone who was writing to express thanks to Rousseau for his books:[27]

> You speak to me on literary subjects as you would to a man of letters; you load me with praises which are so pompous that they appear ironic and you believe that you are intoxicating me with such flattery. Sir, you deceive yourself on all these matters.

Clearly, Rousseau wanted to escape from the literary works which had caused so much controversy and difficulty; he now saw himself as a botanist and he became angry with anyone who referred to the works which had actually caused his alienation from the Republic of Letters, in particular from his main enemy, Voltaire.

It appears that Rousseau's stay in Spalding had both positive and negative aspects. Clearly he had good conversations with some Spalding gentlemen, but equally clearly he was not able to escape from the negative side of his personality, which led him to attack unnecessarily anyone who in any way upset him.

By 18 May 1767, Rousseau was in Dover. He had taken the fastest coach available, probably the regular service from Boston to London, which passed through Spalding, and had travelled through London, as far as we know without stopping. He was scared of London and so he pressed on to Dover with all speed. At Dover he wrote his final letter in England, to the secretary with responsibility for foreign affairs, Lt-General Henry Conway, in which he promised never to write about 'the miseries that have happened to him in England and that he will never write about Mr Hume', provided that he could have a safe departure.[28] Rousseau actually kept this promise: his *Confessions* end in 1765 with his departure from Switzerland for Paris and England.

By 22 May 1767, Rousseau was happily established in Calais. Hume wrote on his behalf to Turgot, the leading French politician and philosopher, asking that Rousseau should be left in peace.[29] That is exactly what happened. Rousseau spent the rest of his life botanising, being looked after by varied admirers in France at their estates and writing works of less controversial philosophy up to his death in 1778. It was only with the outbreak of the French Revolution in 1789, after his death, that he was so magisterially raised to the heights of philosophic splendour as someone he would not have expected to become, an inspirational hero of the Revolution.

Note: All quotations that were originally in French or Latin have been translated for the purposes of this article.

Notes

1. J-J. Rousseau, *The Confessions,* trans. by J. M. Cohen (Penguin Classics, 1953), p.344. A CD recording of *Le Devin du Village,* Intermezzo in One Act by J-J. Rousseau is available: CPO777 260-2, Classic Produktion Osnabrück.
2. J-J. Rousseau, *Émile or On Education,* trans. by Allan Bloom (Penguin Classics, 1991), p.240.
3. J-J. Rousseau, 'What is the origin of inequality among men and is it authorised by Natural Law?' in *The Social Contract and Discourses,* trans. by G. D. H. Cole (1913), p.238.
4. *Ibid.,* p.235.
5. *Ibid.,* p.244.
6. Cited in Daniel Gordon, *Citizens Without Sovereignty* (1994), p.188.
7. Rousseau, *The Social Contract and Discourses,* p.5.
8. Rousseau, *Émile or On Education,* p.310.
9. *Ibid.,* p.310.
10. Quoted in Gavin de Beer, *Jean-Jacques Rousseau and His World* (1972), p.80.
11. Rousseau, *The Confessions,* p.592.
12. Simon Manby, *Owd Ross Hall: The Story of Jean Jacques Rousseau in Wootton* (2012), pp.25-26.
13. *Correspondance Complète de Jean-Jacques Rousseau,* edited by R. A. Leigh, vol.XXXIII (1979), p.277.
14. Manby, *Owd Ross Hall,* endnote 38.
15. Manby, *Owd Ross Hall,* p.24.
16. *Correspondance,* p.277.
17. *Ibid.,* p.44.
18. *Ibid.,* p.277.
19. Lincolnshire Archives, LCM/13/4, Map of Lincolnshire comprehending Lindsey, Kesteven and Holland, surveyed in the years, 1776, 1777 and 1778 by Captain Andrew Armstrong – engraved by Stephen Pyle.
20. Manby, *Owd Ross Hall,* p.24.
21. *Correspondance,* p.62.
22. *Ibid.,* pp.54-55.
23. *Ibid.,* pp.60-61.
24. *Ibid.,* note at the top of p.46.
25. *Ibid.,* pp.51-53. The date of the letter is rather confusing; Jessop presumably made a mistake in calculating the Latin date, which he gave as '*Die quarto Nonarum Maii*', that is literally, the fourth day before the Nones of May [the 7th of the month in the case of May]. This would date the letter to 4 May, when Rousseau was just arriving and Jessop was unlikely to know of his presence in the town. The most probable version of the date would be 'four days after the Nones', making it 11 May, a much more likely timing, as news of Rousseau's presence would have spread around the town and the Society.
26. *The Correspondence of the Spalding Gentlemen's Society, 1710-1761,* edited by Michael Honeybone and Diana Honeybone, Lincoln Record Society, vol.99 (Lincoln, 2010), pp.5, 48-49, 60.
27. *Correspondance,* pp.55-57. The original letter in French was translated into English for Dr Jessop by the Revd Mr Rowning, the Secretary of the Spalding Gentlemen's Society, thus confirming that Jessop knew little, if any, French.
28. *Ibid.,* pp.63-68.
29. *Ibid.,* pp.80-82.

Lincolnshire History and Archaeology Vol. 48, 2013

Margaret Skipwith of South Ormsby: A Lincolnshire Mistress to Henry VIII

Elizabeth Norton

Margaret Skipwith of South Ormsby, a native of Lincolnshire, was first suggested as a possible mistress of Henry VIII in the 1980s. This identification has remained largely unchallenged in subsequent years with little investigation carried out to substantiate it. The available evidence is analysed below, together with the surviving evidence of the affair that Margaret's mother-in-law, Elizabeth Blount, who was another resident of Lincolnshire, had with the king, in order to demonstrate that Margaret Skipwith can be considered to be one of the last mistresses of Henry VIII.

Mary or Margaret Skipwith?

Direct evidence of Margaret's affair with Henry VIII is scant. In a letter of 3 January 1538 to his employer, Lord Lisle, John Husee, who was resident at court commented that:[1]

> The election lieth betweixt Mrs Mary Shelton and Mrs Mary Skipwith. I pray Jesu send such one as may be for his Highness' comfort and the wealth of the realm. Herein I doubt not but your lordship will keep silence till the matter be surely known.

Muriel St Clare Byrne, in her commentary on the Lisle letters, suggested that the recently widowed king, who was already searching for a fourth bride, was casting an appreciative eye on both ladies, looking to make one of them either his mistress or his wife.[2] This is very probable. Mary Shelton, who was referred to in the letter, was a cousin of Anne Boleyn. There is some confusion over which sister was referred to in the letter as both a Margaret and a Mary Shelton were resident at court and the name Margaret, when written as an abbreviation, resembles Mary. A 'Madge' Shelton, who is generally identified as Margaret had already filled the role of royal mistress during the king's marriage to Anne Boleyn. It may be that the Mary Shelton of January 1538 was the second sister or, more probably, both ladies were the same (whether actually Margaret or Mary). Henry VIII's interest in Mistress Shelton in 1538 was widely known, with his ambassador to the court at Brussels commenting on Christina of Denmark, whom the king was hoping to marry, that she resembled the English lady.

There is some evidence that it was Mistress Skipwith, rather than Mistress Shelton, who succeeded in winning Henry VIII's affections. In his letter, John Husee identified Mary Skipwith as the subject of the king's interest. Like the Sheltons, there were also two Skipwith sisters named Mary and Margaret who could be identified as the lady. The sisters were the daughters of Sir William Skipwith of South Ormsby and his second wife, Alice Dymoke.[3] They came from a solid Lincolnshire family of gentry status who were locally very prominent.

The lady in question is usually identified as Margaret Skipwith, although it is necessary to consider this in more detail. In a recent study, it was claimed that it was likely to have been Margaret rather than Mary since Mary married George Fitzwilliam of Mablethorpe around 1550, suggesting that she was too young to have been considered as a potential royal mistress or bride in 1538.[4] There is, however, evidence that Mary's marriage was somewhat earlier than 1550, something that is suggested by documents relating to the Fitzwilliam family.

Mary's husband, George Fitzwilliam, inherited Mablethorpe and other family lands in the mid-sixteenth century.[5] He was described as being thirty years and more in the *Inquisition Post Mortem* taken for his father, John Fitzwilliam of Skidbrook, in August 1547, suggesting that he was born in about 1517.[6] Mary Skipwith bore her husband four sons and four daughters. In his Will dated 13 January 1560, her husband named all eight of the children, with the eldest son, William described as being under the age of twenty-one.[7] None of the daughters were then married, although the eldest, Frances, was betrothed to the son of Thomas Massingberd Esquire, with the terms of her father's Will implying that the marriage was imminent, something that would suggest that she was already approaching, or over, fourteen – the age of consent for girls. Whilst it would have been just possible for Mary Skipwith to bear her husband eight children in around ten years of marriage, given the likely older age for Frances in 1560, coupled with high infant mortality in the sixteenth century, it is improbable that this was the case. It is to be expected that a family of eight children would have seen the loss of some children as infants, something that must push the date of Mary's marriage back some years earlier than 1550.

This can also be seen from the surviving evidence of later generations of the family. The second youngest daughter, Mary, had, by 1591, married three husbands, something which suggests that she may have been born some years before her father's death in 1560.[8] She survived until 1607. Stronger evidence is provided by the family of Mary Skipwith's eldest son, William. William's first wife bore eight children. Whilst the couple's youngest child was baptised in 1589, an elder daughter, Hester, was baptised on 15 May 1566.[9] Whilst it is possible that

William was the eldest child of his parents and produced a child in his mid teens, it was more common for men to marry somewhat later than women and his age is more likely to have been around twenty to twenty-five at Hester's birth, giving a birth date of about 1541 to 1546. William's daughter, Mary, married on 12 October 1590, whilst her sister, Bridget, may have married as early as 1587. Assuming that both women married at around twenty, this would support an earlier birth date for their father and, thus, also an earlier date of marriage for his parents. It is entirely possible that Mary Skipwith was old enough to be considered as a potential mistress or wife for the king in 1538.

Mary and Margaret Skipwith were both the daughters of their father's second marriage to Alice Dymoke, with his first marriage, to Elizabeth Tyrwhitt, producing one child, another Sir William Skipwith.[10] In addition to this, the sisters had four full brothers and two further full sisters. Their half-brother was knighted in 1547 and also served as a member of parliament for Lincolnshire in that year, dying in 1586.[11] His parents married in 1505 and, whilst the date of death for his mother is not recorded, the fact that the marriage produced only one surviving child, coupled with the fact that Elizabeth Tyrwhitt chose to be buried with her birth family in Bigby, rather than at South Ormsby, suggests that there may have been an estrangement.[12] It has been estimated that she died in around 1520, something that, given that Margaret Skipwith married in 1539 and Mary in about 1541 to 1546 must suggest that both sisters were relatively young in 1538 with, perhaps, Margaret being born in about 1520 and Mary a year or two younger. Both would, however, have been potentially old enough to have been the mistress of Henry VIII in 1538.

The usual reason for discounting Mary Skipwith as the mistress of Henry VIII in 1538 is therefore incorrect. However, there is still strong evidence that the royal mistress was indeed her sister, Margaret. With the exception of John Hussee's letter, there is no surviving evidence to place either sister at court in 1538, but Margaret was there by at least the early months of the following year, implying a possible earlier arrival.

Margaret remained resident at court for the remainder of Henry VIII's reign. In a sixteenth-century biography of her second husband, Peter Carew, the *Life and Times of Peter Carew*, it was recorded that he first came across Margaret after returning to England from Calais where he had been sent, with her then husband, George Tailboys, to welcome the new queen, Anne of Cleves:[13]

> At his return home, he still continued at and about the court, being wrapped in Venus bands, and stricken with Cupid's darts: for he had been, and was, a suitor to a lady in the court, being the widow of a baron deceased.

Margaret remained at court following the death of her first husband in September 1540, something that suggests that she may have had long-standing connections with the court and that her presence there was not merely due to the position of her husband.

In all probability, therefore, the reference to Mary Skipwith by John Husee, in fact refers to Margaret. It is now necessary to consider the evidence for whether she can be considered to be one of Henry VIII's mistresses.

Mistress to Henry VIII

Henry VIII has been described as 'a model of husbandly temperance'.[14] Although he has a lascivious reputation, this largely rests on the fact of his six marriages, rather than extra-marital affairs. His two most well known, and longest lasting, affairs were with Elizabeth Blount, who bore him his only acknowledged illegitimate child, and Mary Boleyn, the sister of his second wife. Elizabeth Blount makes a particularly interesting point of comparison with Margaret Skipwith as, when the king had tired of her, he arranged for her to marry Gilbert Tailboys of South Kyme, with the couple settling in Lincolnshire. Less than twenty years later, Margaret Skipwith was married off to Elizabeth Blount's son, George Tailboys.

The strongest evidence that Margaret Skipwith was a mistress of Henry VIII is found in the arrangements made for her first marriage. The affair obviously only lasted a few months, with the king taking steps to marry Margaret off by April 1539. On 17 April 1539, Margaret's uncle, Sir Thomas Heneage, wrote to Thomas Cromwell to confirm that the king had given his consent to a match between Margaret and the sixteen-year-old George, Lord Tailboys. Tellingly, the king commanded Sir Thomas that it would be well to have them married as soon as possible, something that suggests that he was anxious for matters to be concluded.[15] Arrangements were made with some secrecy, with John Husee informing his master on 26 April 1539 that 'it hath been shewed me that Mrs Skipwith shall marry the Lord Tailboys. This it shall please your lordship to keep secret till you hear more'.[16] The reason for this secrecy, or even Lord Lisle's interest in the match, is pertinent, particularly as on 15 May 1539 Husee deemed it important enough to inform Lady Lisle that 'the Lord Tailboys is married' with no further comment.[17] The suggestion must be that Margaret, as the king's most recent love, was newsworthy.

Dr St Clare Byrne speculated that the reference to Margaret Skipwith as a potential love interest for Henry, coupled with the king's interest in her marriage and the secrecy with which it was conducted 'perhaps justify the suspicion that the youthful George was happy to follow obligingly in his father's footsteps for the sake of an attractive young wife and the enjoyment of his own inheritance at sixteen, instead of having to wait until he was out of wardship at the age of twenty-one'.[18] This is highly probable, as the evidence of George's parents' marriage shows.

The Tailboys family settled in Lincolnshire in the fifteenth century when they acquired South Kyme and other manors in the county through marriage.[19] Gilbert Tailboys' father, Sir George, contracted an illness known as the 'land evil' in 1499 and was widely considered to be a lunatic. He was only able to avoid having his lands and person taken into royal wardship by making a payment to Henry VII of eight hundred marks.[20] Although Sir George made a partial recovery, the questions over his sanity were enough, in 1516, for an inquisition to be held into his mental state at Lincoln.[21] The following year, he and his lands were placed in the custody of Cardinal Wolsey and eight of George's relations and neighbours, on account of 'the said Sir George being a lunatic'.[22] George's heir, Gilbert, who had by then reached his majority, but had no position in society given his father's continued survival, passed into the Cardinal's custody at the same time, as a member of his household.

Gilbert Tailboys was very conveniently placed in early 1522 when the king had decided to discard his established mistress, Elizabeth Blount, a woman who had borne him a son and, perhaps, also a daughter during an affair that had lasted approximately five years.[23] The price of Gilbert's marriage to Elizabeth was freedom and, within a few months of his marriage, he was able to act largely free of the cardinal's influence in Lincolnshire, building his own powerbase. Gilbert was regularly appointed to commissions of the peace in his home county, for example.[24] He was also often appointed as one of the gentlemen commissioned to collect the king's subsidies in Lincolnshire, a role that may, perhaps, have made him less than popular in the local area.[25] In 1523, the year after his marriage, Gilbert received the first of three nominations as sheriff of Lincolnshire.[26] He may also have sat in parliament that year. He was certainly a member of parliament by 1529, in the year that he was also created Baron Tailboys of Kyme.[27]

In addition to this, Gilbert and Elizabeth received grants of property from the king, such as the manor of Rugby as a wedding present.[28] More significantly, they were given access to Gilbert's inheritance, in spite of his father's continued survival. In 1523 an Act of Parliament was passed in Elizabeth's favour, ostensibly following a petition by Gilbert and his father, the incapacitated Sir George:[29]

> Humbly shewith unto your most excellent Highness your true and faithfull subjects and servant Sir George Tailboys Knyght and Gilbert Taylboys son and heire apparent to the said Sir George, That where the said Gilbert hath married and taken to wife Elizabeth daughter of John Blount Esquyer, by which marriage aswell the said Sir George Taylboys Knyght as the said Gilbert Taylyboys have received not alonly great somes of money, but also many benyfitts to their right mych comfort. In consideration wherof and for the great love favour and affection that aswell the said Sir George Taylboys as the said Gilbert Taylboys his son have and towerd the said Elizabeth, your said

> Oratours moost humbly beseecheth your Highness that by thassent of the Lordes Spirituall and Temperall and the Commons in this present parliament assembled and by authority of the same, to ordeyne establish and enacte that the said Elizabeth maye have holde and enjoye for terms of her lyfe naturell without empechement of any waste this Lordshippes Manours Londes Tenements and Hereditaments hereafter ensuing which be of thenheritaunce of the said Sir George Taylboys, that is to saye; All the Houses Londes and Hereditaments that the said Sir George Taylboys or Gilbert Taylboys his son or any of theym or any other person or personnes to their use or thuse of any of theym have or hath in possession or revercion or otherwise in the Citie of Lincoln; and the Manours of Skeldyngthrp Bamburgh Freskeney Sotby and Faldyngworth in the Countie of Lincoln.

In addition to this, Elizabeth received a life interest in her father-in-law's Yorkshire and Somerset manors. The grant enriched Gilbert and Elizabeth at his parents' expense, with the value of Gilbert's lands rising rapidly during the 1520s from £66 13s.4d. to £343: a vast increase given that his father was still very much alive.[30] In addition to this, the claim that Gilbert and his father 'have received not alonly great somes of money, but also many benyfitts to their right mych comfort' from the marriage hints at the negotiations that must have gone on between Wolsey, the king and Gilbert in order to secure the young man's consent to his marriage. That these grants were solely for the benefit of Gilbert and Elizabeth are clear from surviving letters written by Gilbert's mother complaining that the couple were attempting to put pressure on her and her incapacitated husband to relinquish further lands, with the elder lady's suspicion being that her daughter-in-law was directly making suit for them with the king at court.[31]

By agreeing to marry Elizabeth Blount, Gilbert Tailboys received access to his inheritance during the lifetime of his father. He also received a peerage and grants from the king. It was also hardly a misfortune to marry Elizabeth Blount, who was reputedly one of the most beautiful women of her generation, albeit one with a reputation tarnished enough for one contemporary to write that:[32]

> We have begun to encourage the young gentlewomen of the realm to be our concubines by the well marrying of Besse Blont whom we would yet by sleight have married much better than she is and for that purpose changed her name.

Elizabeth's reward was a higher status husband, wealth and continuing friendship from the king.

Matters followed a similar pattern with Elizabeth Blount's likely predecessor as the king's mistress, Elizabeth Carew, who later wrote that 'all that I have had in my life hath been of his grace, and I trust that his grace will not see me lack; but whatsoever his grace or your lordship shall appoint me, I both must and will be content'.[33] The estates mentioned by Elizabeth Carew in her letter written after the execution of her husband, Sir Nicholas Carew, in 1539, had been settled on the couple by Elizabeth Carew's father-in-law at the time of their marriage.[34] It appears that it was common for the king to provide for a former mistress through grants from her new husband's family estates. This can be paralleled in the case of Margaret Skipwith.

Soon after her marriage, Margaret's financial future was safeguarded by an Act of Parliament, which recited that the king was in possession of George's lands during his minority and that he had granted his wardship to Sir William Fitzwilliam, Earl of Southampton. According to the Act, the king, at the request of the earl, who was a kinsman of Margaret's, and in gratitude towards the 'good and faithfull' service given by Gilbert Tailboys, had:[35]

> Pondered and considered that the saide George nowe lorde Tailboys hath not ne can have by thorder of his laws any parte or porcion of the rentes or profittes of his saide inheritance to support and mayntayne his convenient and reasonable lyvinge during his saide mynoritie, but only by the appointment and assignement of his said most gracious highness; and also considering that the saide George lorde Tailboys, by thorder of his saide lawes, during his saide mynority cannot make any effectuall feoffament, ne estates or jointer, to the saide now lady Margarett, wife to the saide George lorde Tailboys, towards her necessarie living.

As a result of the Act, George and Margaret were granted the right to make use of a number of their Lincolnshire manors, as well as Tailboys lands in Somerset. George, like his father, was, by his marriage, able to circumvent the usual laws governing inheritance in order to enter into estates before they were due to him. Given the value of the Tailboys family lands, it is unlikely that the king would have entered into the agreement as an empty gesture. More probably, this Act of Parliament, like the earlier Act made for the benefit of Elizabeth Blount and the grants to Elizabeth Carew can be taken as firm evidence that Margaret Skipwith, like her mother-in-law before her, received a rich marriage as her reward for an intimate relationship with the king. It is interesting to note that South Kyme, the home of the Tailboys family, isolated as it was in the early modern period with poor roads in winter,[36] was used by Henry VIII as the repository for two of his cast off mistresses and as a means of rewarding them for their services rendered.

Margaret Skipwith and Henry VIII

Although no details of the actual affair survive, Margaret remained in high favour with the king, a position that parallels the respect in which her mother-in-law, Elizabeth Blount, continued after the ending of her own affair with Henry VIII. At New Year 1541, Margaret was one of a select number of favoured ladies who gave the king a gift, with her servant receiving 13s.4d. for his pains, the same sum that had been given to Elizabeth Blount's servant for delivering a gift in 1529.[37] Whilst

details of the gifts made by the king do not survive, it is highly probable that he reciprocated. Lists of Henry VIII's New Year's gifts are fragmentary, but it is clear that he often honoured former mistresses with a present, as both Elizabeth Blount and Mary Boleyn found, for example.[38] In addition to this, on 16 June 1543, Margaret was granted the wardship of Charles Tottoft, the son of a substantial Lincolnshire landowner, taking custody of the boy's lands until he came of age.[39] It may be Margaret to whom the king's letters were directed in 1546, for which a receipt survives confirming that they were addressed to 'Lady Talboys'.[40]

Further evidence that Margaret Skipwith was the king's mistress can be found with regard to Peter Carew's courtship of her. When the widowed Elizabeth Blount was courted by Lord Leonard Grey in 1532, her suitor petitioned Thomas Cromwell to ask the king to intervene on his behalf.[41] He also took steps to ascertain that the king would not be displeased if he proposed marriage to Elizabeth.[42] A very similar approach was followed by Peter Carew whose suit was met as lukewarmly by Margaret as Grey's was by Elizabeth. According to his biography, Carew attempted for some time to woo Margaret:[43]

> But having used all the means he could to obtain his purpose, and minding not to have the repulse, he went unto the king, and opening unto his grace his suit, did most humbly beseech his highness to stand his good lord. The king at first seemed to strain courtesy at the matter, neither would have any good liking thereof: nevertheless, in the end, he did so consider of the worthiness and nobility of the gentleman, that he did not only grant his request, but also wrote his most earnest letters unto the lady in his behalf, and promised also to give with that marriage a hundred pound land to them and to the heirs of their bodies.

Henry's intervention and his promise to dower Margaret suggests a connection between the pair. In this he went even farther than he had done when Leonard Grey had asked him to intervene on his behalf – perhaps due to Margaret confirming that she was content to take Carew as her husband. The couple married on the day of Edward VI's coronation in 1547, suggesting that pressure from the old king was not Margaret's only motive in accepting the match given that she could have allowed the matter to have dropped when he died if she had wished.

Margaret Skipwith was evidently a desirable woman as Carew courted her for some years, in the face of her refusals.[44] Whilst no surviving portrait of Margaret is known, given Carew's affection for her and her evident relationship with the king, she must have been attractive. As a member of the court, she is also likely to have been accomplished. In a letter written on 4 August 1539 Margaret, along with a number of other court ladies, wrote to Henry VIII to thank him for arranging a trip for them all to see his fleet at Portsmouth.[45] The ladies were able to assure the king that, whilst they were disappointed that he had not been present, the ships were 'so goodly to behold that in our lives we have not seen (excepting your royal person and my lord the Prince your son) a more pleasant sight'. The king laid on entertainments and gifts for the ladies and invitations to the event must have been highly sought after. The fact that Margaret was one of the ten women appointed to attend hints strongly at her close relationship with the king. She had probably already been promised a place in the household of Anne of Cleves, with whom marriage negotiations were then busily being conducted on the king's behalf. When Anne arrived in England at the end of December 1539, Margaret was one of the ladies appointed to receive her.[46] This was a prestigious appointment given that England had then been without a queen for more than two years and is evidence that Margaret was indeed well known to the king.

Conclusion: Margaret Skipwith of South Ormsby, Mistress to Henry VIII

The evidence strongly suggests that it was indeed Margaret Skipwith to whom John Husee referred in his letter of 1538 and that, in the months that followed, she was involved in a love affair with the king. If John Husee's comments are reliable, it appears that Henry VIII even considered making Margaret his bride, as he would do with four other Englishwomen during his reign. Lincolnshire therefore came close to producing a queen of England although, ultimately, the relationship proved a brief, albeit profitable one for Margaret Skipwith of South Ormsby. The association with the Tailboys family of South Kyme and Henry VIII is an interesting one as both Gilbert Tailboys and his son, George, were prepared to marry the king's cast off mistress in return for their independence.

Notes
1. *The Lisle Letters*, five volumes, edited by M. St Clare Byrne (1981), vol.V, no.1086.
2. *Lisle Letters*, V, pp.11-13.
3. R. Cook, *The Visitation of the County of Lincoln in 1562-4*, edited by W. C. Metcalfe (1881).
4. K. Hart, *The Mistresses of Henry VIII* (Stroud, 2009).
5. *Lincolnshire Pedigrees vol.I*, edited by A. R. Maddison (1902).
6. W. O. Massingberd, *History of the Parish of Ormsby-cum-Ketsby in the Hundred of Hill and County of Lincoln* (Lincoln, 1893).
7. The National Archives, PROB 11/43: Will of George Fitzwilliam Esquire of Mablethorpe.
8. Mary is given her third husband's surname in the Will of her brother George, which was made on 22 November 1591 (Massingberd, *History of the Parish of Ormsby-cum-Ketsby*, p.262).
9. A. R. Maddison, *Lincolnshire Pedigrees*, Harleian Society, vols 50-52 and 55, four volumes (1902-06).
10. Cook, *The Visitation of the County of Lincoln in 1562-4*.
11. A. R. Maddison, *Lincolnshire Pedigrees*, vol.3 (1904).
12. 'Monumental Inscriptions in the Church of Beakeby [Bigby],

Lincolnshire', *The Topographer*, vol.I, no.III (1789), pp.113-16; *Lincolnshire Church Notes Made by Gervase Holles, AD1634 to AD1642*, edited by R. E. G. Cole, Lincoln Record Society vol.1 (Lincoln, 1911), p.120; Nikolaus Pevsner and John Harris, *The Buildings of England: Lincolnshire*, second edition revised by Nicholas Antram (Harmondsworth, 1989), p.144; listed building description All Saints' Church, Bigby, available on-line at http://list.english-heritage.org.uk/resultsingle.aspx?uid=1063405, accessed December 2013.
13. J. Hooke, *The Life and Times of Sir Peter Carew* edited by J. Maclean (1859), p.15.
14. A. Somerset, *Ladies in Waiting* (1984), p.17.
15. *Letters and Papers, Foreign and Domestic, of the Reign of Henry VIII, Vols I-XXI*, edited by J. S. Brewer, J. Gairdner and R. H. Brodie (1862-1932), (hereafter *L&P*), vol.XIII pt I, 795 (Sir Thomas Hennege to Cromwell, 17 April 1538).
16. *Lisle Letters*, V no.1394.
17. *Lisle Letters*, V no.1414.
18. *Lisle Letters*, V, p.12.
19. M. Newton, *South Kyme: The History of a Fenland Village* (South Kyme, 1995), p.17; Alan Rogers, 'Parliamentary electors in Lincolnshire in the fifteenth century (part 2)', *LHA*, 5 (1970), pp.47-58, esp. pp.54-56.
20. W. C. Richardson, 'The surveyor of the King's prerogative', *English Historical Review*, 56 (1941), pp.52-75, esp. p.60.
21. The National Archives, C142/31/41.
22. *L&P*, vol.I, 2979.
23. E. Norton, *Bessie Blount* (Stroud, 2011).
24. *L&P*, vol.IV pt I, 390 (Commission of the peace in May 1524), *L&P*, vol.IV pt I, 2002 (Commission of the peace in February 1526), *L&P*, vol.IV pt II, 5083 (Commission of the peace in three areas of Lincolnshire in December 1528).
25. *L&P*, vol.III pt II, 3282 and 3504.
26. *L&P*, vol.III pt II, 3583 (Sheriff Roll, November 1523) *L&P*, vol.IV pt I, 819 (Sheriff Roll, 10 November 1524), *L&P*, vol.IV pt I, 1795 (Sheriff Roll, November 1525).
27. *L&P*, vol.IV pt III, 6042.
28. *L&P*, vol.III pt II, 2356.
29. *The Statutes of the Realm ... From Original Records and Authentic Manuscripts*, vol.III (1817).
30. S. T. Bindoff, *The House of Commons 1509-1558*, three volumes (1982). vol.III, 419.
31. Elizabeth, Lady Tailbois to Cardinal Wolsey, 11 June 1528 (West Yorkshire Archive Service, WYL 230/3788) and Elizabeth, Lady Tailbois to Mr Thomas Heneage, 1 April 1529 in *Letters of Royal and Illustrious Ladies of Great Britain, from the Commencement of the Twelfth Century to the Close of the Reign of Queen Mary*, edited by Mary Anne Everett Green (née Wood), three volumes (1846), vol.II, pp.43-45.
32. *L&P*, vol.IV pt III, 5750.
33. Elizabeth, Lady Carew, to Lord Cromwell, 1539 in *Letters of Royal and Illustrious Ladies*, vol.III, pp.110-11.
34. R. Mitchell, *The Carews of Beddington* (1981). p.27.
35. Quoted from J. Maclean, 'Remarks on the Barony of Tailboys' *Proceedings of the Society of Antiquaries of London*, 3 (1856), pp.244-46.
36. In the late eighteenth century it was commented that the roads to the village were good in summer but likely to be very bad in winter, something which must have made South Kyme feel isolated for much of the year, John Byng Torrington, *The Torrington Diaries: Containing the Tours through England and Wales of the Hon. John Byng (later fifth Viscount Torrington) between the years 1781 and 1794* edited by C. B. Andrews, four volumes (1970), vol.2, p.357.
37. *L&P*, vol.XVI, 1489.
38. Elizabeth Blount received a gift in 1529, see M. Hayward, 'Gift giving in the court of Henry VIII: the 1539 New Year's gift roll in context', *The Antiquaries Journal*, 85 (2005), pp.126-75. Elizabeth's gift is known from the reward given to her

servant by the king on New Year's Day 1529 for bringing her gift (*L&P*, vol.V, 307). In 1532, Elizabeth received the heaviest present of plate given to any lady below royal rank (The National Archives, E101 420/15 f.3). Mary Boleyn also received a gift in 1532.

39. *L&P*, vol.XVIII pt I, 802(52).
40. *L&P*, vol.XIX, 312.
41. The National Archives, SP1/70, f.56, Lord Leonard Grey to Thomas Cromwell.
42. The National Archives, SP/70, f.144, Lord Leonard Grey to Thomas Cromwell.
43. *The Life and Times of Sir Peter Carew*, p.46.
44. *The Life and Times of Sir Peter Carew*, p.44.
45. *Lisle Letters*, V no.1513a.
46. *L&P*, vol.XIV, 572.

Archaeological Investigations along the Route of the A1073, Spalding-Eye Improvement Scheme

Andy Failes and Mark Peachey
with contributions by Sarah Percival, Anne Irving,
Alex Beeby and Gary Taylor

Introduction

A programme of archaeological investigation was carried out by Archaeological Project Services in advance of construction of the A1073 Spalding-Eye Improvement Scheme (Fig.1) (Peachey, *et al.*, 2011). Investigations took the form of strip, map and sample excavation of areas identified during earlier evaluations (Fig.1; Fig.2), (Hall, 2002; Cope-Faulkner, 2003; Kenney, 2004; Trimble, 2002), and a watching brief conducted during the excavation of road side ditches throughout the scheme. Small excavations were also carried out where the new road crossed the Car Dyke Roman watercourse and the site of Green Bank near Crowland.

Archaeological Project Services was commissioned by Jacobs Engineering UK Limited (Jacobs) on behalf of Lincolnshire County Council to undertake the investigations, which were carried out between 21 April 2008 and 14 October 2009.

For much of its twenty-two kilometre length the A1073 follows a completely new alignment through the Fens, linking the A16 south of Spalding to the A47 west of Eye, Cambridgeshire. Between these points the new road crosses four major soil types, each deposited in distinct environments which have greatly influenced the history of occupation in the Fens. To the north the road cuts through silts deposited during a post-Roman marine transgression, probably between the fifth and seventh centuries AD (Rackham, forthcoming). These silts lie above a sequence of similar deposits also laid down during a marine incursion, but this time much earlier, probably at around the end of the second millennium BC during the late Bronze Age (Hayes and Lane, 1992).

Further south, towards Crowland, the clays and sinuous silty extinct creek beds were formed during the Bronze Age and early Iron Age when the area was an active salt marsh. Further south, the road extends across the peaty soils around Crowland and Borough Fen, before rising onto gravels between Peterborough and Eye,

Cambridgeshire. The peat formed from the Neolithic (4500BC to 2300BC) period onwards when this area was freshwater fen.

Results of the excavations

Results are presented chronologically and by site number.

Prehistoric

Site 11

Just south of Thorney Road, Newborough, the road crossed a small gravel island protruding through the surrounding peats, silts and clays. Previous work nearby had identified material of Mesolithic and Neolithic date (French and Pryor, 1993) and it was thought that the island would be a likely location for prehistoric occupation. The gravel outcrop, of which a one hundred metre long and thirty metre wide area was impacted on by the road, is a westward extension of an approximately 400m by 200m island plotted immediately to the east during the Fenland Survey (Hall, 1987).

Ten unstratified flint flakes of late Mesolithic to Neolithic date were recovered from across the area of investigation during topsoil stripping and hand cleaning. Cut features were recorded only at the southern end of the investigated area and comprised a single pit and three post holes. The pit was trapezoidal in plan and tapered from just over one metre to a half a metre wide from north-west to south-east. Similarly, in the same direction, the pit deepened from six centimetres to forty centimetres. Artefacts were absent from the silty sand primary fill, although the charcoal-rich silt which formed the secondary fill contained a single sherd of late Neolithic/early Bronze Age pottery and two flint flakes.

Two of the post holes were spaced just over one metre apart, located two metres from the north-west end of the pit, with the third lying fifteen metres to the north-west. The south-west to north-east alignment of the three post holes matches that of the pit and it is tempting to associate this group of features. From the two post holes closest to the pit a Bronze Age end scraper and a residual Mesolithic flint flake were recovered.

As the sherd of probable late Neolithic\early Bronze Age pottery is unlikely to be residual, the pit can be dated to this period with a reasonable level of confidence. This being the case, it is possible that the three post holes are of similar date. Also, occupation would not have been possible much after this time due to the encroaching salt marsh and subsequently, the development of full fen conditions which persisted until the post medieval period.

The pit, post holes, flints and pottery indicate activity of late Neolithic/early Bronze Age date on the edge of an island of higher ground within a developing salt marsh. No other Neolithic finds are known from Borough Fen although this island, at least, was occupied, however briefly, during this period.

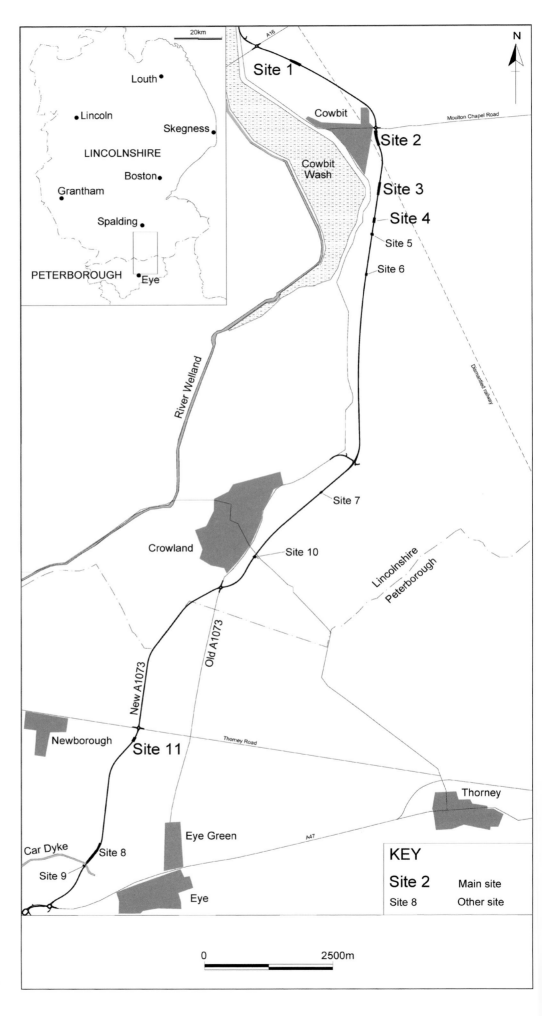

Fig.1. Site locations.

Watching Brief

Cleaning of one of the roadside ditches along White Post Road just north of Site 8, at the southern end of the route, revealed the silts of an extinct creek (roddon) over a distance of around 175m. These silts were overlain by greyish brown silty sand to the south and purple grey organic silt to the north. Two Bronze Age worked flints were recovered from the latter layer and both deposits probably represent buried soils or palaeosols which developed on the banks of the extinct creek. These buried soils were sealed by peat overlain by alluvial clay and finally a second, upper peat. The extinct creek has been previously recorded during Hall's survey of the area undertaken as part of the Fenland project and is thought to have functioned as a major palaeochannel within a dendritic creek system during the Neolithic period (Hall 1987, Fig.9). The presence of buried soil on the infilled creek and the recovery of worked flints suggests a dry phase of sufficient duration for development of soil on the raised silts of the extinct creek prior to development of freshwater fen during the Bronze Age.

A further undated buried soil overlying sand and gravel was revealed in a section of new dyke just west of the new Thorney Road roundabout. This sand and gravel probably represents the edge of the former small island recorded at Site 11.

Late Iron Age and Early Roman

Site 2 (Fig.3)
Located immediately to the south of Moulton Chapel Road, Cowbit, Site 2 measured 260m long by 30m wide and was situated on a large silt roddon elevated slightly above the surrounding land. Late Iron Age to early Roman features were recorded only at the north end of this site, within Area A.

In the north-east corner of this area was a narrow, eighty centimetre wide and almost vertical sided, L-shaped linear feature (Fig.3, G309) (Fig.4, Sections 38, 48). The shorter side to the north-east measured three and a half metres long but was truncated to the west by a post medieval ditch. The north-west to south-east aligned side measured six metres long but extended beyond the eastern limit of excavation. The steep sides and sharp, ninety degree corner of this feature are characteristic of structures of sill-beam construction and it is possible that the foundations of two sides of a small building are represented. Perhaps the remaining sides were formed by wattle screens or similar, traces of which had not survived. This would suggest some kind of outbuilding rather than living quarters. However, the presence of hearth waste within environmental samples retrieved from the feature indicate the proximity of domestic settlement.

Immediately to the north-east of the possible building, was a rectangular pit containing second-century pottery, burnt bone fragments as well as domestic hearth waste recovered from an environmental sample (Fig.3, [131]). Two nearby ditches did not contain dateable ceramics but their alignments suggest an association with the possible building, perhaps as a surrounding enclosure (Fig.3 [G310] and (014)).

Pottery of second-century AD date was recovered from sections excavated on the west side of the sill-beam structure, with earlier, first-century ceramics being retrieved from two sections excavated along the north-west to south-east aligned portion. Overall, the feature contained pottery from twenty-nine vessels, including an elaborate cordoned bowl in a particularly fine shell-tempered fabric, probably produced near the Thames estuary or possibly imported across the Channel from *Gallia Belgica*. Also among the pottery was a piece of South Gaulish Samian and sherds of possible *Terra Nigra*. This group of pottery indicates a relatively high standard of living for the occupants of the site (Beeby, below).

Site no.	Parish	Area(m²)	NGR	Height O.D.
1	Cowbit	5792	TF 2530 1935	1.4m-1.95m
2	Cowbit	7860	TF 2686 1787	2.15m-2.8m
3	Cowbit	5210	TF 2692 1683	0.25m-1.6m
4	Cowbit	3805	TF 2682 1619	1.68m-2.04m
5	Cowbit	1002	TF 2678 1591	1.15m-1.3m
6	Cowbit	1790	TF 2666 1510	0.9m-1.2m
7	Crowland	1262	TF 2560 1072	1.5m-1.7m
8	Newborough	20600	TF 2140 0350	0.65m-1.5m
9	Peterborough	744	TF 2115 0320	8m
10	Crowland	120	TF 2480 0940	1m-1.5m
11	Newborough	2722	TF 2215 0580	0.55m-1.8m

Fig.2. Table showing location, area and OD heights of sites.

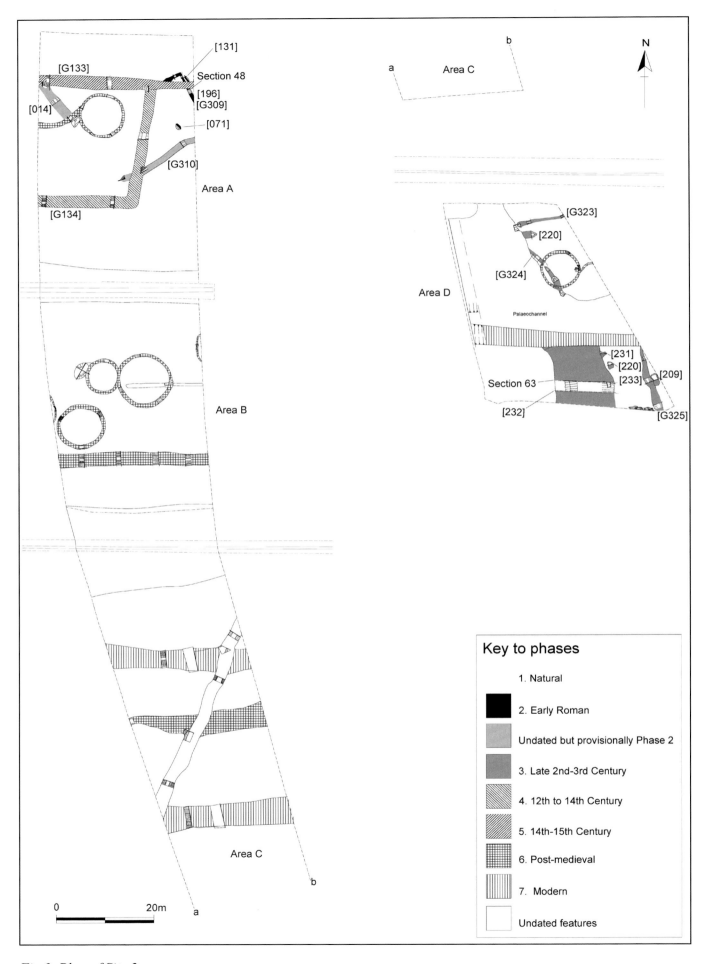

Fig.3. Plan of Site 2.

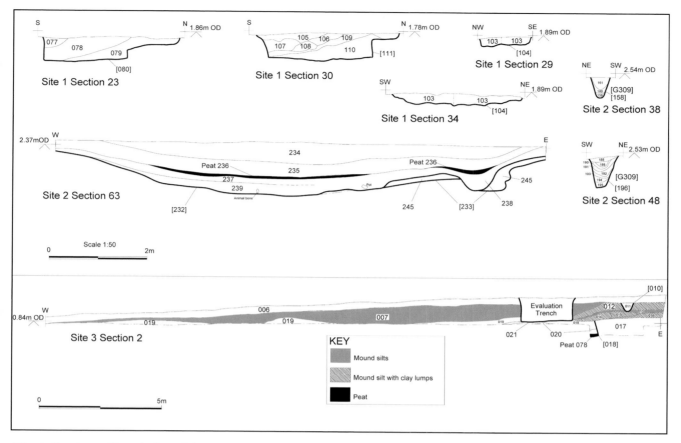

Fig.4. Sections, Sites 1, 2 and 3.

Site 4

This site, a late Iron Age to early Roman saltern with two phases of salt production, lay in a wide, silt-filled natural hollow on the eastern edge of Peak Hill, approximately two kilometres south-east of Cowbit. An area measuring 104m long and 35m wide was investigated with features relating to the saltern being located at the north end.

The defining feature of the first phase of salt production was a sub-circular enclosure ditch with a one metre wide eastern entrance (Fig.5 and Fig.6 [G411]/(137)). Although heavily truncated by later features to the north, enough of the ditch survived to estimate its size and shape. The proposed extent of the enclosure ditch is plotted on figure 6. The internal dimensions were just over seventeen metres from east to west and nearly thirteen metres from north to south. The ditch was up to two metres wide and nearly a half a metre deep.

The base of the ditch contained a possible clay lining overlain by layers of silty clay and silt. A dumped layer of silt and ash was deposited over the clays followed by a deposit of red silt containing crushed briquetage. After these episodes of dumping there is evidence for significant flooding at the site in the form of layers of laminated clays and silts. The entire enclosure ditch was filled with flood silts although the effects of the flooding were more severe to the west where fifty centimetres of clean laminated silts filled and extended beyond the ditch, creating a new land surface.

Subsequent to the flooding of the site, extensive dumping of deposits containing briquetage took place in the eastern area of the enclosure ditch (Fig.7). Contents ranged from 'red earth' deposits, composed largely of tiny briquetage fragments and charcoal flecks, to deposits yielding large container fragments and supports as well as complete pedestals and large pieces of structural debris. Overlying the demolition deposits were silty clays, clays containing briquetage and clean flood silts, the latter representing marine flooding which overwhelmed the saltern.

A second phase of saltmaking was defined by two rectangular pits and the ephemeral shallow traces of a second enclosure ditch (Fig.6 [306], [302]; [066]/[172]/[188]/[251]). These features were cut into the flood silts which buried the majority of the first saltern. The eastern section of this enclosure ditch measured just under two metres wide and nearly a half a metre deep, while the western terminus measured over one and a half metres wide by thirty centimetres deep. The projected shape of the ditch is shown on figure 6. The rectangular pits are thought to represent tanks used to contain salt water and settle out impurities in advance of a heating process to produce crystalline salt. Deposits filling the settling tanks ranged from silts and clays containing briquetage fragments to reddish silts containing crushed briquetage.

Enclosures of the type recorded at Site 4 surrounding salt making hearths and settling tanks are a typical feature of salterns of late Iron Age\early Roman date, including

Fig.5. Plan of Site 4.

the two examples recorded at Wygate Park near Spalding (Trimble and Wood, forthcoming; Lane, 2005a, Fig.4). Their function is not fully understood but it is possible that they acted as reservoirs for capturing salt water or as a drain for the enclosed area.

Roman

Site 4
Evidence of Romano-British activity at Site 4, other than the saltern, occurred exclusively at the southern end of the site and comprised a number of ditches, pits and a spread of dark soil, most of which contained fills from which ceramics of Roman date were recovered.

Although heavily truncated by a post medieval ditch, a roughly east to west oriented ditch which contained two fragments of Roman pottery represents the most substantial of the Roman features (Fig.5, (043)). A shallow, north-west to south-east aligned feature located towards the eastern limit of excavation was also truncated by the post medieval ditch but did contain a total of seventy-six sherds of Roman pottery, representing thirty-nine separate vessels and six fragments of briquetage (Fig.5, [G402]). Near to the northern terminus of the Roman ditch was an irregularly shaped feature filled with a dark deposit containing a further fifteen sherds of Roman pottery and a single intrusive sherd of medieval pottery (Fig.5, [176]). A short north to south aligned ditch located on the west side of the excavated area contained Roman pottery from at least six separate vessels and was also truncated by the post medieval ditch (Fig.5, [G401]). Although the variety of alignments among these Roman features indicates the possibility of more than one phase of occupation, any stratigraphic relationships to illustrate this have been truncated by the west-east post medieval ditch.

Two ditches in the south-eastern corner of the site merged together and shared some of the same fills, with both features containing Roman pottery fragments belonging to the same vessels (Fig.5 [G409] and [G410]). The southernmost produced a fragment of Roman triple vase, an unusual find for rural Lincolnshire. They were cut through a firm, thirteen centimetre thick black silty spread which containing a significant amount of Roman pottery (ninety-one fragments representing seventy-five different vessels) (Fig.5 (213)). This deposit was disturbed by later activity and contained a small amount of medieval and early modern pottery.

A north-west to south-east oriented ditch in the south-western corner of the site contained twenty-one sherds of Roman pottery from fifteen different vessels and also three sherds of medieval pottery which were probably intrusive (Fig.5, [G400]). This ditch was truncated by a west to east aligned ditch, phased as Roman or later, which contained a single sherd of pottery and an undated amber bead (Fig.5, G404). A single pit recorded in the south-western corner of the site contained four sherds

of Roman pottery, including a fragment of *patera* pan handle, a rare item often associated with the army (Fig.5, [089]).

Site 2
During the second and third centuries occupation became focussed at the south end of Site 2 where a number of ditches and pits located adjacent to a palaeochannel were revealed (Fig.3). At the south end of Area D the palaeochannel was aligned approximately north to south and measured ten metres wide by just over one metre deep. North of a west to east aligned post medieval ditch, the channel intersected, or branched into west to east aligned creeks which were probably part of the same system.

Grey silt formed the lower fill of the palaeochannel and contained sherds from sixty-three vessels of mid second- to late third-century date (Fig.4, Section 63). This pottery was in noticeably fresh condition with some sherds joining to form near complete profiles, suggesting primary deposition, probably the dumping of refuse, including a number of freshly broken pots. Although not active, the channel was open during this phase of occupation and formed a significant topographic feature. A linear ditch is aligned transverse to the channel and terminates very close to its eastern edge (Fig.3. [G325]). A sandy silt fill of this ditch contained second- to third-century pottery and in addition no Roman features cut the top fill of the palaeochannel.

A linear feature at the north end of the Area D roughly followed the alignment of the channel at the north end of Area D but also seemed to be truncated by the creek at its northern limit (Fig.3, [G324]). However, continuing erosion of the sides of the channel may be responsible for this. To the north the section excavated across the ditch was filled with brownish grey silt which contained mid second- to third-century pottery. To the south the central section contained early to mid second-century ceramics while the upper fill of the southernmost section contained single sherds from twenty-nine vessels of first- to early third-century date. An environmental sample from this fill contained probable burnt roofing or flooring materials (rushes and sedge). It seems likely that these ditches formed small enclosures or drains aligned onto the palaeochannel.

At the south end of Area D a similar arrangement was recorded with a ditch running six metres to the east of, and parallel to the channel (Fig.3, [G325]). This ditch was filled with clayey silt from which second- to early third-century pottery, mid second- to third-century pottery and animal bone were recovered. Roman remains at the south end of Area D also include four pits, one of which truncates the upper fill of the ditch, suggesting a degree of structural phasing within the remains of this period (Fig.3, [209]). This ovoid pit contained a clayey silt fill which produced mid second- to third-century pottery,

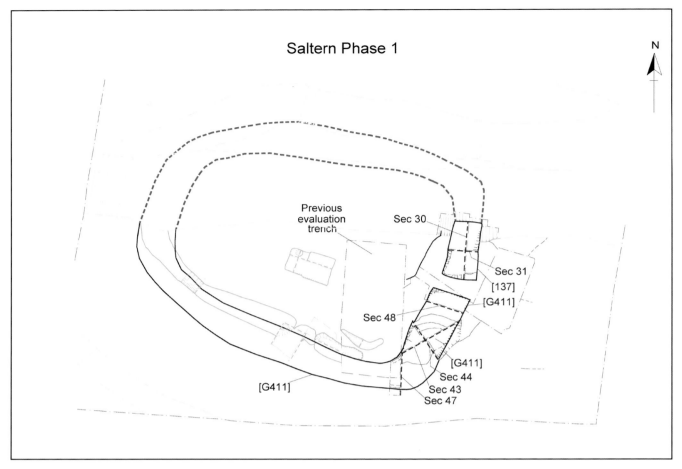

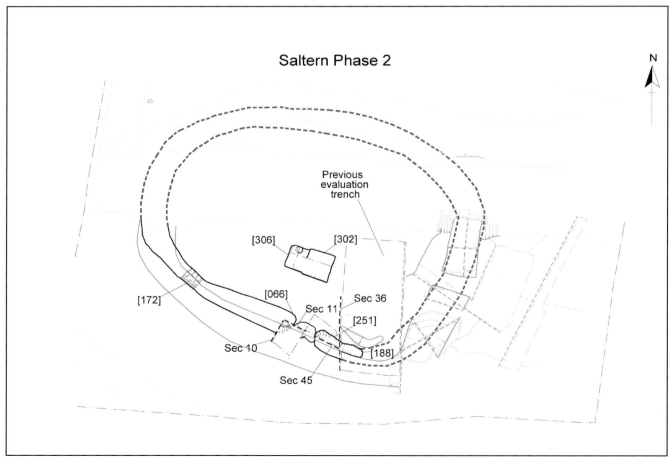

Fig.6. Saltern phases 1 and 2.

Fig.7. Site 4, section 43 (eastern half).

a bone hairpin (Fig.11.1) and environmental evidence for probable hearth waste. Nearby, a sub-rectangular pit filled with sandy silt contained mid second-century pottery while at the south end of the site a copper alloy brooch (Fig.11.2) was recovered from a layer of subsoil (Fig.3, [220], (256)). The remaining pits were much more irregular in character and include one example which cut into the fills of the open palaeochannel, more or less at the same level as the dumped pottery (Fig.3, [233]). Two more pits were located close the edge of the palaeochannel, one truncated by the eroded edge of the creek, the other just over two metres to the south (Fig.3, [231], [220]).

Nearby domestic occupation is indicated by the presence of pottery, animal bone, the copper alloy brooch, and environmental evidence for roofing and flooring materials and hearth waste. The character of this occupation is difficult to determine from the limited evidence but a small farmstead located mainly to the east of the roadline is most likely.

A radiocarbon date of Cal. AD 350 to 420 at 1 Sigma was obtained from a peat overlying the layer containing the freshly dumped pottery in the palaeochannel. This indicates a rising water table in the late Roman period and the development of reed swamp in the channel. Pollen evidence from the layers, likely to be contemporary with the settlement, indicates that cereals were grown but that pasture predominated (Rackham, forthcoming). Within the peat layers the presence of pollen from plants tolerant of saline conditions towards the top of the sequence attests to a growing marine influence.

Site 9 The Car Dyke

This site was targeted to investigate the area immediately south of the Roman Car Dyke in Eye, Peterborough. Topsoil stripping of the area measuring approximately forty metres by twenty metres revealed a light grey clay at the north end of the site adjacent to the steep slope of the Car Dyke channel. The clay was also slightly higher than the natural clays and it was thought that this might represent the remnants of a bank or upcast from the initial excavation of the channel. A section excavated through the clay did not reveal a buried land surface or buried soil and it remains unclear whether this fifteen centimetre layer represents upcast or a change in natural deposits.

Within the scheduled area two, five metre square trenches excavated on the site of temporary bridge supports on the north bank of the Car Dyke revealed only post medieval material, most likely a product of periodic cleaning of the channel, overlying probable original bank material.

Watching Brief

On the Lincolnshire section of the watching brief, some 200m to 300m north of Site 2 at Cowbit, a cluster of features containing Roman pottery and briquetage was recorded during roadside drainage works. Towards the north end of this area were two probable pits, one of which contained late Iron Age/early Roman pottery, the other first- to second-century sherds and two fragments of briquetage. Fifty metres south a steep sided ditch contained an ashy upper fill which contained twenty-eight sherds of second- to third-century Roman pottery, two fragments of briquetage and a fired clay loomweight. Briquetage was also found in a second probable pit near the ditch.

Medieval and post medieval

Site 1

Site 1 lies approximately one and a half kilometres north-west of Cowbit, and comprised a 260m long and twenty-two metre wide area located immediately west and east of Drain Bank. Recorded remains at the site comprised various pits and ditches of medieval and post medieval date. Two phases of medieval activity were recognised, the earliest almost certainly representing salt making, the second land boundaries associated with an agricultural landscape.

The saltern

In the central part of Site 1, an ovoid shallow pit and two closely spaced, rectangular steep sided pits were located just over six metres apart (Fig.8, [104]; [080], [111]). The north ends of the rectangular pits were both positioned immediately adjacent to an east to west aligned ditch which extended for thirty metres from the western limit of excavation to where it was truncated by a post medieval ditch (Fig.8, [G208]). The upper fills of the ditch closely resembled those in the pits, supporting the suggestions that these features were contemporary and deliberately positioned together.

The rectangular pit to the east (Fig.8, [080], Fig.4, Section 23) measured just under three metres long, two metres wide and a half a metre deep with vertical sides, except to the north, which was stepped, and a flat base. The three fills in the pit showed evidence of dumping from the north or ditch side, with the earliest, a silty clay (Fig.4, Section 23 (079)), containing a single sherd of thirteenth-century pottery, fired clay fragments and charcoal flecks. This primary fill was overlain by a clayey silt which contained thirteenth-century pottery and many fired clay fragments, some salt bleached, along with charcoal flecks. A silty clay formed the latest fill and contained more pieces of fired clay, some also salt bleached, and occasional charcoal flecks (Fig.4, Section 23, (079)).

To the west the adjacent pit (Fig.8, [111]) was similar in size and shape and also contained fills which showed signs of tipping from the north or ditch end (Fig.9). The primary fill was clayey silt with occasional flecks of fired clay from which late twelfth- to thirteenth-century pottery was recovered (Fig.4; Section 31 (110)). This was overlain by a probable flood silt, an indicator of a marine environment. The later fills all contained fired clay and charcoal flecks with a single sherd of twelfth- to thirteenth-century pottery from a second flood silt which formed the latest deposit in the pit. The lower fill of the adjacent ditch comprised a black silt containing salt bleached fired clay (Fig.8, [G208]). The silty clay upper fill of a recut of the ditch contained thirteenth- to early fourteenth-century pottery and sixty-two pieces of fired clay. An environmental sample from this fill contained burnt straw or cereal processing waste.

The spatial arrangement of the pits and the adjacent ditch would indicate that the latter acted as a source of salt water for the two pits which served as reservoirs or tanks for the settling of sediments prior to the heating stage of the salt making process. Similar arrangements have been recorded on Romano-British sites and also at the medieval saltern at Parson Drove in Cambridgeshire (Pollard *et al.*, 2001). The charcoal and fragments of fired clay are likely to comprise debris from the direct heating phase of the salt making process.

Located six metres to the north of the rectangular pits an ovoid pit (Fig.8, [G104]) measured nearly three metres long by one metre wide and twenty centimetres deep with a flat but slightly uneven base. This shallow pit was filled by clayey silt which contained a single sherd of thirteen-century pottery and frequent fired clay pieces, some of which were salt bleached (Fig.4, Sections 29, 34). Although no remnants of a superstructure were identified it is possible that the pit represents the basal remnants of a hearth over which brine was heated to produce crystalline salt. The surrounding clay, however, showed few signs of heating and this interpretation is based on the morphology and position of the features. Immediately north of the possible hearth was a west to north-east aligned curvilinear gully (Fig.8, [G207]) which contained several silty clay fills all containing late twelfth- to thirteenth-century pottery.

Medieval land divisions

A series of linear ditches recorded over the central area of the site are also of medieval date but relate to later medieval land divisions associated with fields and paddocks of an agricultural landscape.

Immediately east of Drain Bank a four and a half metre wide north to south aligned ditch was dated through the recovery of later thirteenth-century pottery from a primary fill, and a recut containing a single sherd of thirteenth-century pottery (Fig.8, [G203]). Further east, a ditch on a similar alignment truncated the salt making ditch, providing stratigraphic evidence for the change in landscape use represented by the medieval phase. At the east end of the site two more ditches on a different, predominantly south-west to north-east alignment, also contained dateable pottery of thirteenth- to early fourteenth-century date (Fig.8, [G210] and [G211]). Of these two, the ditch with a sharp corner leading to a ten metres long south-east to north-west aligned section, possibly formed part of an enclosure.

Site 2

None of the post Roman features on this site was particularly well dated with pottery generally being highly abraded. However, in Area A, an L-shaped ditch contained only twelfth- to fourteenth-century material and may have formed part of a stock enclosure in conjunction with the east to west ditch at the north end of

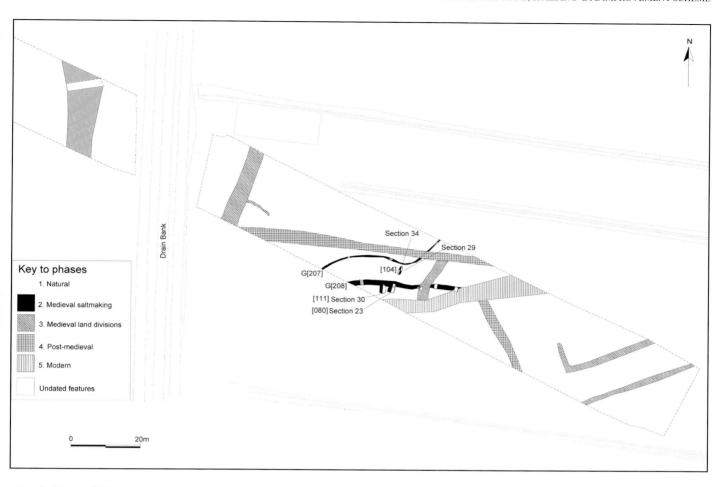

Fig.8. Plan of Site 1.

the area (Fig.3, [G134], [G133]). Environmental evidence showed the ditches from this period were usually water-filled and located in a landscape of damp, short-turfed grassland, supporting the stock enclosure interpretation. It also indicated that they were regularly maintained and well removed from habitation.

Up to nine roughly circular ditches, or parts thereof, were excavated on Site 2 along with a further example on Site 7 which had a noticeably topsoil-like fill. A similar, undated, example was excavated at Morton Canal, Lincolnshire (Crowson *et al.*, 2000, p.133). Wilson (1978) suggests that these represent drainage ditches dug around haystacks predominantly during the medieval period, although they are commonly undated. Post middle Anglo-Saxon examples are known from Gosberton, near Spalding (Crowson *et al.*, 2005, p.97).

Site 3 Goll Grange
Two low silt mounds were excavated near Goll Grange, Cowbit, the origin and purpose of which remained uncertain, despite prior evaluation.

The southern mound was sub-oval in shape and just over eighty-seven metres long and twenty-two metres wide within the stripped area. A thirty-nine metre length of a single roughly north to south aligned curvilinear ditch was revealed beneath the mound, in a two metre

wide machine slot extending north to south from the centre to the perimeter of the mound (Fig.10). This had been encountered previously in the south end of an evaluation trench dug in 2003 (Cope-Faulkner, 2003). The ditch, up to just over one and a half metres wide and sixty-five centimetres deep, contained late twelfth- to fourteenth-century pottery. The mound was formed of a sequence of deposits sealing this ditch (Fig.4, Section 2). In the central area, small dumps of silt contained lenses of redeposited clay. Sealing these, and forming the vast majority of the mound, was a mottled pale/light brown mix of silts and soft clay up to sixty-five centimetres thick (Fig.4; Section 2 (007)). In contrast, the northern mound was formed solely of up to seventy centimetres of mid yellow, sandy silt. This mound was sixty-two metres long and extended six and a half metres into the stripped area. Both mounds were located on a natural high spot, probably the raised bank of a silted creek.

The mixed nature of the deposits forming both mounds indicated that they were the result of deliberate dumping, which must have taken place between the probable fourteenth-century backfilling of the ditch, which the south mound sealed, and the excavation, in the top of this mound, of small, sub-rectangular, flat-bottomed pit containing fifteenth- to sixteenth-century brick and tile. Several probable boundary ditches were recorded at the

31

south end of the stripped area, all of which were dated to the fifteenth to sixteenth centuries by associated pottery.

Around the east side of the north mound was an area of dark greyish brown silty clay just over a half a metre deep which contained a moderate amount (well spread out) of fifteenth- to sixteenth-century pottery and brick. This was interpreted as a former marshy area or pond into which bricks, made nearby, had been discarded.

Site 4
Medieval remains at Site 4 were sparse and the dating of them is not wholly secure. A curvilinear ditch located towards the centre of the site produced a small heavily abraded sherd of late Iron Age to Roman pottery (probably residual), two fragments of briquetage and a large sherd of medieval pottery (Fig.5, [G408]).

A second possible medieval ditch was recorded to the north of the saltern area (Fig.5), extending across the width of the site and truncated by post medieval ditch (Fig.5, [295]/[286]). The possible medieval ditch produced three sherds of medieval pottery and twelve fragments of residual briquetage.

Two sherds of medieval pottery were recovered from an east to west aligned ditch (Fig.5, [070]), one of a series on this orientation recorded across the site and probably used for drainage. Towards the south end of the site a east to west aligned ditch extended across the site with a smaller ditch branching off from it in a north-westerly direction (Fig.5, [G406], (G407)). No stratigraphic relationship between these two features was observed in either plan or section suggesting that they may have been open at the same time. Towards the southern end of the site another east-west ditch was recorded, but had been almost completely obliterated by a later, post medieval ditch (Fig.5, (130)). Although no finds were retrieved from this feature, its truncation by the post medieval ditch may indicate a possible medieval date.

A series of east to west aligned ditches ran across the width of the site and were dated by pottery to the post medieval period and are also likely to have acted as drains and field boundaries. One of these recorded in the northern half of the site truncated the saltern features and contained fragments of seventeenth- to early nineteenth-century clay pipe (Fig.5, [270]/[084]). A ditch recorded in the southern half of the site (Fig.5) was also oriented east to west but was noticeably wider than the other ditches from this period (Fig.5, [031]). At the southern end of the site an east to west aligned ditch truncated several features of Roman date and also the ditch of possible medieval date (Fig.5, [G405]).

Sites 5-8 and Site 10
Sites 5 to 8 revealed only late post medieval, modern and undated features while results from Site 10, located to investigate the poorly understood late Anglo-Saxon 'Green Bank' (Hayes and Lane, 1992, p.202) proved

inconclusive, with no trace of earthworks or a channel associated with the watercourse depicted on early maps and thought to date to the late Anglo-Saxon period. However, Crowland had once been surrounded by substantial expanses of deep peat which, by the mid nineteenth century, had 'vanished from considerable tracts in the neighbourhood of Bourne, Spalding and Crowland' (Skertchly, 1877, p.134). Watercourses such as Green Bank had been dug when peat growth flourished and its channel may well have been originally excavated entirely within the peat. With the substantial loss of peat following drainage it may be that the channel in the peat was just eroded away. A similar example is the Roman Bourne-Morton canal, about ten kilometres to the north, where a line of silt from the base of the canal is the only trace of its existence through the former peatland, although its channel remains extant through the higher, seaward, silts to the east (Crowson *et al.*, 2000, p.131).

The Finds

The Briquetage

Sarah Percival

Site 4
A moderately large assemblage of briquetage totalling 4,272 pieces weighing 183.65kg was recovered from Site 4, associated with two phases of salt production separated by an episode of flooding and of clearance or demolition. The briquetage could not be dated by associated pottery and no material suitable for absolute dating was available, however, the assemblage dates typologically to the second century AD (Morris, 2001).

The condition of the briquetage varied and the assemblage included examples of pedestals alongside many fragmentary supports of various forms, sherds of container and numerous pieces of oven structure (Percival, 2011).

The spread of briquetage within the main salt making phases shows high percentages of container pieces, as does the flooding phase. The demolition phase assemblage is composed mainly of structural debris, indicating that any oven or hearth structures associated with the first salt making phase had been levelled and dumped (Percival, 2011). No diagnostic briquetage was present to distinguish the duration or individual chronology of the two salt production phases (*ibid.*).

Recent work has produced a typology that can be used to refine the dating sequence for briquetage (Lane and Morris, 2001; Morris, 2008). The assemblage at Site 4 dates from at least Morris' Briquetage phase 2, beginning some time after the second century BC (Morris 2007, p.435). This phase is characterised by organic-tempered containers with both cut and rounded rims which are heavily whitened by exposure to salt (Morris 2008, p.97), increased use of hand squeezed pedestals and

Fig.9. Site 1, probable settling tank [111], Section 30, looking north-west.

the introduction of indirect heating structures or ovens, producing greater quantities of structural debris in the archaeological record. Other chronological indicators from the Site 4 assemblage, such as bars, tapering bricks and removable slabs or platforms suggest that salt production continued into the early Roman period encompassed by Morris's Briquetage phase 3 (Morris, 2007, p.435).

The Pottery

Site 1

The Medieval Pottery

Anne Irving and Alex Beeby

Site 1 produced pottery from 159 vessels dating largely from the thirteenth to fifteenth centuries. The material is quite fragmentary with a high proportion of abraded pieces and soot and carbonised matter residues perhaps indicating that the pottery may have been used as part of a production process. This is not a typical domestic group and there are an unusually large number of bowls and jars; these types accounting for 71% of the total. In addition, there are at least four but quite possibly more, curfews (vessels for covering burning embers on a hearth) and/or fish smokers present. Although such vessels could conceivably have been used as measuring pans during

the salt making process (Blinkhorn, forthcoming), they can be abundant in coastal assemblages where they are most likely related to domestic fish smoking.

The saltern settling tank produced fragmentary pieces of Bourne, Baston and Ely-type wares with a likely early to mid thirteenth-century date, whilst the ditch features, active in the medieval phase following the salt making, produced a similar range of wares, as well as medieval Bourne and Toynton types suggesting continued activity on the site as a whole, into the fourteenth century.

It remains speculative as to whether any of the pottery was deposited at a time when the saltern at Site 1 was in still use. There is little material directly associated with the feature and it is interesting that there are no vessels with salt residues or bleached fabric.

Site 2

The Roman Pottery

Alex Beeby

Pottery from a maximum of 269 vessels was recovered from Site 2. The material dates from the early Roman period to the later third century and also includes shell-tempered examples in the late Iron Age tradition. Much of the 'native' type pottery is likely to be associated with domestic activities which occurred in the vicinity of the

Fig.10. Site 3, section 18 through south mound looking north-east.

probable building in Area A at some time before the late first century AD, possibly even immediately post-conquest.

A bowl from the possible sill-beam slot is of particular note. This vessel, the fabric of which has very fine shell-tempering, has a series of horizontal body cordons and a sharply in-turned rim, with the upper most cordon being placed so as to create a groove or lid seat along the top of the rim. The abundant shell temper in this piece is densely packed and very fine; notably different to that seen in locally produced items. The form cannot be directly paralleled in the published literature and although a continental origin cannot be ruled out this vessel should most likely be placed into the native tradition of in-turned rim grog-tempered ware bowls found in south-eastern England and the south-east Midlands (Steve Willis, pers. comm.). Cordoned vessels with a similar rim formation are known from Essex, Hertfordshire and Bedfordshire, where they are usually dated to the early to mid first century AD (Thompson, 1982, pp.342-45). The source of the shell within the fabric seems to be estuarine in origin (Alan Vince, pers. comm.) and so a source on the northern side of the Thames estuary seems plausible.

The ceramic evidence suggests that the focus of settlement shifted south over the course of the Roman period, with material of later date being concentrated near the palaeochannel or creek in Area D. In particular context (238) produced sherds from sixty vessels including many pieces in noticeably fresh condition with some sherds joining to form near complete profiles, suggesting primary deposition, probably the dumping of refuse. This context included a number of examples of smashed vessels. This small group is dominated by products of the Lower Nene Valley industries including grey wares and colour-coated vessels none of which are likely to postdate AD300.

The Medieval Pottery

Anne Irving

Site 2 yielded material from a maximum of sixty-four vessels dating from the medieval to the early modern period. This probably represents a background scatter of material and its highly fragmented condition suggests most of this pottery is residual.

Site 4

The Roman Pottery

Alex Beeby

This site produced pottery from a maximum of 216 vessels dating from the first to the third centuries AD. Unlike

Site 2 there are no vessels in the Iron Age tradition. Most of the pottery came from the southern end of Site 4 with just a few fragments recovered from the saltern area. The character of the assemblage is generally utilitarian, although there is a notable number of vessels connected with drinking, eighteen percent of the assemblage falling into this category. This seems to suggest a different focus to that of a 'typical' low status domestic group.

It is unclear why there should be such a bias towards drinking utensils, but the recovery of two further sherds of special note, a *patera* pan handle from pit fill (088) and a triple vase fragment from ditch fill (154) do seem to suggest the occurrence of ritual activity nearby. These items are usually associated with the army, or Romanised urban contexts and to find either of these in a rural location such as this is a surprise. Triple vases are elaborate items, with an assumed ritual function, intended to hold oils or some other liquid substance. *Paterae* may have also been used ritually, possibly including during funeral ceremonies (Woodfield, 2005, pp.209-11). Good regional parallels for similar pan handle types are known from Longthorpe (Dannell and Wild, 1987, Fig.35.119), and Ancaster (Darling, 2006, fig.1). Both of these forms are relatively early, neither likely to postdate the second century AD.

Whether the deposition of this assemblage is connected to the use of the saltern or domestic habitation is not clear, although some of the material is contemporary with pottery recovered from the nearby salterns at Morton (Trimble, 2001) and Spalding Wygate (Trimble and Wood, forthcoming). A military connection, possibly related to the production of salt, cannot be ruled out.

Other Artefacts

Gary Taylor

Site 2
Domestic artefacts are limited and represented by a bone hairpin, from pit fill (210), and a brooch from layer (256) both of which are of Romano-British date. The pin (Fig.11.1) has a rather crude flattened terminal and is closely comparable to pins from the Roman settlement of Baldock, Hertfordshire, where they were dated from about AD180 into the fourth century (Stead, 1986, pp.163-65).

The brooch (Fig.11.2) has a narrow bow and a foot plate at right angles to the bow. This is a knee brooch and closely similar examples have been recovered at Piercebridge (Butcher, 2008, pp.187, 195; fig.D11.72, no.15) and from Pannonia (modern western Hungary and adjacent areas) and dates to the second century AD (Hattatt, 2007, p.335, no.472). Although the type was produced on the continent, chemical analyses suggest the possibility that some examples were made in Britain (Butcher, 2008, p.187). This brooch type is common on the German *limes* where they date to about AD150-200 and are regarded as

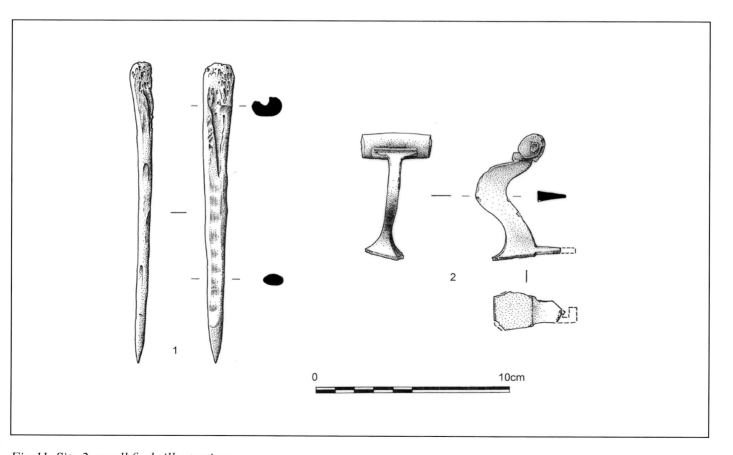

Fig.11. Site 2, small finds illustrations.

'soldiers' brooches'. In Britain they have been found on military sites and, in addition to Piercebridge, examples have been recovered from the northern military zone of Roman Britain including Nether Denton, Chesters, Old Penrith and Newstead, and in the south-east at Dover and Richborough (Butcher, 2008, p.195), although more than forty have been recorded by the Portable Antiquities Scheme from Lincolnshire.

Discussion

Prehistoric

A number of unstratified flint flakes of late Mesolithic to Neolithic date retrieved from Site 11 probably represent a small-scale knapping episode on the edge of higher ground surrounded by salt marsh conditions. A sub-rectangular pit and a post hole of late Neolithic/early Bronze Age were also revealed on Site 11.

A buried soil containing two Bronze Age worked flints overlay a roddon at White Post Road on Borough Fen indicating an early demise for this particular channel. The buried soil was similar to that found during the South-West Fen Dyke Survey Project of the 1980s on the sand and gravel peninsula at Crowtree Farm on Thorney Road, 500m north-west of Site 11. This soil overlay a narrow peninsula of sand and gravel extending north-eastwards from the early prehistoric fen edge. The high density of flint artefacts suggested the peninsula was a 'site' utilised for at least part of the year (French and Pryor, 1993, p.36). This seasonal use may also have been repeated at the White Post Road roddon. The buried soils at both locations were overlain by the Lower Peat, that at Crowtree Farm yielding a radiocarbon date of 2460-1890 cal. BC (*ibid.*).

Late Iron Age and Early Roman

In the north-east corner of Site 2, on Area A, was a small rectangular structure, a probable early Roman ancillary domestic building, within an enclosure which, although undated, was on the same alignment.

Smashed vessels indicated settlement on, or very close to, the Area A site. The pottery assemblage indicated limited early first-century occupation of the site with the main activity occurring in the late first to early second centuries. The assemblage included imported wares, namely early Samian, possible *Terra Nigra* and a Gallo-Belgic vessel of a form also found at Spalding Wygate (Trimble and Wood, forthcoming), suggesting some affluence.

The probable building may have been part of an adjacent settlement or an outlier from the feature-rich area of the watching brief 200m to 300m to the north. Some of the Site 2 features also contained briquetage suggesting proximity to a saltern. The Fenland Project (Hayes and Lane, 1992, figs 107 and 108) recorded two salterns in the general vicinity.

Evidence for salt making during this period was also revealed in the northern half of Site 4. Dating of the saltern was problematic as the charcoal recovered was too fine and ashy to obtain a radiometric date and only four abraded sherds of Roman pottery were found associated with the production site. However, analysis of the briquetage suggested a late Iron Age to early Roman date for the saltern.

Two phases of salt making and a number of other phases of activity were identified. The first phase of salt production was defined by an ovoid enclosure (Fig.6). The enclosure ditch appeared to have a clay lining at its base, which suggests that it was used for water management. As with the ditches surrounding the salterns at Middleton, Norfolk (Crowson, 2001), the Site 4 ditch may have served a water entrapment function, collecting and holding brine prior to its transfer to settling tanks (or the ditch may have acted as a settling tank itself). Clay lined pits or settling tanks are found consistently at Roman salt making sites and are thought to have been used to enable sediments and impurities to settle out of the water and further concentrate the brine prior to evaporation (Fawn *et al.*, 1990; Lane, 2005b).

Truncation seems to have removed any traces of oven or hearth structures at the site. Ovens provided the heat source needed to evaporate the brine once it had been transferred from settling tanks to briquetage containers. The presence of an oven associated with the first phase of salt production is, however, clearly demonstrated by structural remains within the briquetage assemblage.
The first phase of salt production appears to have been cut short by significant flooding of the site which saw the majority of the enclosure ditch fill with flood silts. The flooding was severe to the west, leaving silts overflowing the enclosure ditch to a significant depth and creating a new land surface. Subsequent to this (probably disastrous) phase of flooding, extensive dumping of briquetage occurred in the still partially open eastern area of the enclosure ditch. Much of the briquetage retrieved during the investigation came from this first phase and was composed of structural debris, including whole pedestals and large fragments of hearth structure, though quantities of containers and supports were also high. The size of the briquetage fragments and unbroken condition of many of the pedestals suggests that the site was deliberately dismantled and abandoned soon after the flooding. A second phase of salt making probably occurred relatively soon after the flooding event as there was no distinction between the briquetage of either phase.

Features from the second phase include two settling tanks and the ephemeral traces of a second enclosure ditch from which a significant amount of briquetage was retrieved (Fig.6).

Roman

Aside from the saltern, evidence for Romano-British occupation at Site 4 occurred exclusively at the southern end of the site (Fig.5). Remains consisted mainly of ditches, along with a spread of dark soil containing occupation debris, a pit and an irregular shaped feature.

The south-eastern corner of the site appeared to be a focus for artefact deposition. A shallow ditch in this area produced a significant amount of Roman pottery, as did a spread of dark soil to the south (probably the result of dumping). A fragment of a Roman triple vase, an unusual item in a rural Fenland context, was retrieved from a ditch which cut into the dark soil. Vessels of this type are probably of relatively early date, no later than the second century and are usually assumed to have a ritual function, intended to hold oils or some other liquid substance.

The south-western corner of the site contained features with significantly smaller amounts of pottery. Of particular note was a pit from which a fragment of *patera* pan handle was recovered. Such rare items are often associated with the army and possibly linked to funerary rituals.

There is a clear bias towards drinking vessels in the Roman deposits at Site 4. The presence of the *patera* and triple vase suggest that those at the site had adopted or brought with them some very 'Romanised' habits, probably including elements of religious practice. These rare and unusual items, taken with the bias towards drinking, suggest that some sort of religious/ritual activity may have been taking place in the area. The density of finds in the south-eastern corner of the site suggests the possibility of further Roman activity to the east of the road line and given the unusual finds, it is tempting to suggest that this may have had a religious/ritual component to it.

Site 2 occupation shifted to the south end of the site during the second and third centuries, focussing on the banks of an open, but not active palaeochannel. This creek contained the freshly broken pottery of a primary refuse deposit sealed by late third-century peat. The pottery assemblage from Area D is similar to, although slightly later than, that from the nearby Backgate site (Precious, 2003) and both contain a high proportion of Nene Valley wares with much evidence for cooking in the form of external sooting. Residual briquetage within the creek probably dates to the late Iron Age or early Roman period when the channel was active.

An environmental sample from an adjacent ditch contained probable burnt roofing or flooring materials (rushes and sedge) while a pit produced a bone hairpin and environmental evidence of hearth waste. Wide trade links are indicated by a lava quern from western Germany and gritstone querns from the North Derbyshire/Sheffield area. It seems likely that settlement continued to the east of the road line. Analysis of pollen from a sample from the palaeochannel indicates cereals were grown in the region but that pasture was predominant. A radiocarbon date from the peats demonstrates that water levels were

rising by the late Roman period and towards the top of the sequence the presence of pollen from salt tolerant plants shows a growing marine influence. A similar picture of an open landscape with mainly pasture and some arable during the Roman period on the silt fen during the Roman period was also drawn from the pollen analysis of samples from Wygate Park, Spalding (Alison *et al.*, forthcoming). A full marine transgression dating to between fifth to seventh centuries was also identified at this site (Rackham, forthcoming).

In contrast to the hints of ritual, ceremony and possible links to the Roman army at Site 4, the second- to third-century Roman ditches and pits revealed on Area D, at the south end of Site 2, are indicative of the edge of a settlement on the banks of an extinct palaeochannel and present a more prosaic picture of a small farmstead engaged in arable and pastoral farming, but with a material culture indicating integration within a wide trade network.

The Roman sites revealed on the A1073 support the results of the Fenland Survey which found that much pottery was imported from the Nene Valley along with millstone grit from the Pennines while exports would have included salt, reeds, rushes, fowl and fish. There was evidence for a decline in the third and fourth centuries with the freshwater fen extending across the area in Anglo-Saxon times (Hayes and Lane, 1992, pp.210-15). This was largely corroborated by the evidence from Site 2.

Medieval

A possible thirteenth-century medieval saltern was the earliest and most notable feature of Site 1, comprising a hearth and two rectangular pits, probably settling tanks. The settling tanks were located adjacent to a ditch which also contained salt making debris. Water would have been evaporated in pans (probably of lead) placed over a nearby hearth. The pottery from this phase was mostly utilitarian, possibly reflecting use in the salt making process. This saltern activity was replaced by a later thirteenth-century field system.

The saltern does not resemble the known coastal examples of medieval date such as the as those excavated at Wainfleet (McAvoy, 1994). Instead, its layout resembles those of Iron Age and Roman date. For example, a Roman saltern at Holbeach St Johns consisted of a water channel with two rectangular pits close to one side (Gurney, 1999). A saltern of fourteenth-century date excavated at Parson Drove in north Cambridgeshire, however, is of similar layout to that on Site 1. Environmental evidence indicated that conditions of brackish water flooding, probably during the high spring tides, were exploited for salt production at Parson Drove. Several rectangular pits served as settling tanks for saltwater collected in an adjacent ditch. These allowed the muddy brackish water to clear before further processing. The water would have been collected from the tanks in large ceramic vessels, unlike the briquetage used in Roman times, and evaporated over a hearth until only the salt remained. There was no definite hearth found at Parson Drove although there was a concentration of hearth material around a shallow pit (Pollard *et al.*, 2001).

A similar saltern of late Anglo-Saxon, tenth-century date was excavated on the Marshchapel 2 site, in the coastal marshes of north-east Lincolnshire. Two rectangular pits, again of similar dimensions to those on Site 1, were situated adjacent to a channel bringing water from a nearby creek. This saltern's similarities to the later medieval Parson Drove and Site 1 examples suggests they reflect an older tradition and style of salt production techniques, one that may have continued in some areas for at least four centuries (Fenwick, 2001). They probably represent a local salting tradition removed from the more industrialised coastal saltworks.

Among the Site 1 pottery assemblage were several probable curfews or fish smokers. The latter suggests the possibility of fish smoking as an alternative (or additional) industrial process taking place on site. None of the pottery was bleached or coated with salt residues, unlike the fired clay (which may have come from a deliberately broken up hearth lining). However, the range of pottery at Site 1 and at the Parson Drove saltern was similar, with larger vessels than would be expected from a domestic assemblage, some with holes for hanging the vessel over a fire, and often a coating of soot or carbonised deposits.

Environmental evidence from Site 1 indicates that the immediate area was largely pasture by the thirteenth to fourteenth centuries, while retaining some wild fen with undisturbed muddy creeks, to one of which the saltern ditch was probably connected.

Site 3
The main features of Site 3 were two low mounds of silt, the larger of which sealed a probable fourteenth-century ditch. This could be part of the rectilinear field system of the late thirteenth-century Goll Grange visible on the east side of the Wheatmere Drain on an aerial photograph (Hallam, 1953). The ditch appeared to fit this system well although it does post date the Wheatmere Drain, which is referred to in a mid thirteenth-century document (Hallam, 1953, 9).

The mound was cut by a fifteenth- to sixteenth-century pit and was respected, to the south, by a number of ditches of similar date. Other post medieval pits had been revealed cutting the mound on the evaluation. The mounds were the result of deliberate dumping of large quantities of silt, the reasons for which remain unclear.

A large number of misfired or mis-shaped examples among the brick retrieved from the large possible pond or marsh feature, to the north of the larger mound, suggest brick production in the immediate vicinity. A fifteenth- to sixteenth-century date was indicated by the bricks' size and associated pottery, relatively early for Lincolnshire brick production. The bricks were of poor quality and showed evidence of grass or straw used as temper or bedding material.

At the south end of the site the pond, and a similar, but undated, feature could have been former clay extraction pits used for adjacent brick making. A few of the bricks had traces of mortar adhering, although no structure was revealed. An alternative theory for the mounds is that they represent upcast cleared from the areas of clay extraction. There was a wide scatter of post medieval brick making sites in the silt fens, especially in villages and on the western fen edge (Robinson, 1999).

Conclusions
The new road passes through a varied landscape and has revealed a number of archaeological sites, many of which proved typical of those already known in from the work of the Fenland Survey (Hall, 1987; Hayes and Lane, 1992; Hall and Coles, 1994).

As with many road schemes, the sites encountered on the route of the A1073 were not unique or rich, but were the homes and workplaces of the ordinary people who have occupied this area throughout the ages. The excavations have enabled us to catch a glimpse of the lives of ordinary rural people over a period of at least four thousand years. Whether they be Neolithic farmers on gravel islands at the south end of the route, medieval or late Iron Age or Roman salt makers at Sites 1 and 4 at Drove Bank and Peak Hill, or Roman period rural settlers as at Site 2 in Cowbit, the new road has revealed facets of their ordinary lives in this extraordinary landscape.

Acknowledgements
Archaeological Project Services wishes to acknowledge the assistance of Lincolnshire County Council, who commissioned this investigation, and Rob McNaught of Jacobs who acted as consultant to Lincolnshire County Council. The work was co-ordinated by Dale Trimble who edited this report with Tom Lane. The sites were supervised by Mike Wood, Mark Peachey, Andy Failes, Thomas Bradley-Lovekin, Mary Nugent, Fiona Walker and Ross Kendall. Other site staff were Maria Gale, Bob Garlant, Lavinia Green, Ellen Kendall, Maria Leroi, Jeff Nicholls, Jim Robertson, Karon Rosser, Jonathon Smith, Gary Crawford-Coupe and Mats Nelson. Surveying was undertaken by Mary Nugent and the finds were processed by Denise Buckley. Finds illustrations are by the late David Hopkins. The pottery was recorded by Barbara Precious, Alex Beeby, and Anne Irving. Special thanks are due to Barbara Precious for all her help in preparing the data for the client report and to Steve Willis, Gwladys Monteil and the late Alan Vince for providing helpful thoughts on the cordoned bowl from Site 2.

Bibliography
Alison, E., Gale, R., Giorgi, J., Kitch, J., Kreiser, A., Locker, A., Martin, G., Rackham, J., Scaife, R. and Langdon, C., forthcoming, 'Environmental archaeology' in D. Trimble and M. Wood, *Archaeological Excavation of a Roman Saltern and Settlement at Wygate Park, Spalding (SWP05)*, Archaeological Project Services.

Blinkhorn, P., forthcoming, 'The pottery' in P. Cope-Faulkner, *A medieval salt-making complex in King's Lynn – Investigations at the former Queen Mary's Nurses Home, 2002-2003* (Site 37404 KLY).

Butcher, S., 2008, 'Part II: The Romano-British brooches and enamelled objects' in H. E. M. Cool, *Roman Piercebridge*, Barbican Research Associates, pp.186-207.

Cope-Faulkner, P., 2003, 'Archaeological Evaluation on land at Goll Grange, Cowbit, Lincolnshire (CGG 02)', unpublished Archaeological Project Services Report No.6/03.

Crowson, A., Lane, T. and Reeve, J., 2000, *Fenland Management Project Excavations 1991-1995*, Lincolnshire Archaeology and Heritage Reports Series, no.3.

Crowson, A., 2001, 'Excavation of a late Roman saltern at Blackborough End, Middleton, Norfolk' in *A Millennium of Saltmaking: Prehistoric and Romano-British Salt Production in the Fenland*, Lincolnshire Archaeology and Heritage Reports Series, no.4, edited by Tom Lane and Elaine L. Morris, pp.162-249.

Crowson, A., Lane, T., Penn, K. and Trimble, D., 2005, *Anglo-Saxon Settlement on the Siltland of Eastern England*, Lincolnshire Archaeology and Heritage Reports Series, no.7.

Dannell, G. B. and Wild, J. P., 1987, *Longthorpe II – The Military Works-Depot: an Episode in Landscape History*, Britannia Monograph Series, no.8.

Darling, M. J., 2004, 'Guidelines for the archiving of Roman pottery', *Journal of Roman Pottery Studies*, 11, pp.67-74.

Darling, M. J., 2006, 'Roman pottery' in N. Hall, 'Archaeological Evaluation on land at Baird's Mill, Ermine Street, Ancaster, Lincolnshire (ABM06)', unpublished Archaeological Project Services Report No.45/06.

Fawn, A. J., Evans, K. A., McMaster, I. and Davies, G. M. R., 1990, *The Red Hills of Essex, Salt-Making in Antiquity*, Colchester Archaeology Group.

Fenwick, H., with a contribution by Lillie, M., 2001, 'Medieval salt-production and landscape development in the Lincolnshire Marsh' in *Wetland Heritage of the Lincolnshire Marsh*, edited by Stephen Ellis, Helen Fenwick, Malcolm Lillie and Robert Van de Noort, Humber Wetlands Project, University of Hull, pp.231-41.

French, C. A. I. and Pryor, F. M. M., 1993, *The South-West Fen Dyke Survey Project 1982-86*, East Anglian Archaeology, no.59.

Gurney, D., 1999, 'A Romano-British salt-making site at Shell Bridge, Holbeach St Johns: excavations by Ernest Greenfield, 1961' in Antony Bell, David Gurney and Hilary Healey, *Lincolnshire Salterns: Excavations at Helpringham, Holbeach St Johns and Bicker Haven*, East Anglian Archaeology, no.89, pp.21-69.

Hall, D., 1987, *The Fenland Project, Number 2: Cambridgeshire Survey, Peterborough to March*, East Anglian Archaeology, no.35.

Hall, D. N. and Coles J. M., 1994, *Fenland Survey: An Essay in Landscape and Persistence*, English Heritage Archaeological Report, no.1.

Hall, R. V., 2002, 'Archaeological Evaluation of the Peterborough Section of the Spalding-Eye Road Scheme (SER 02)', unpublished Archaeological Project Services Report No.218/02.

Hallam, H. E., 1953, 'Goll Grange, a grange of Spalding Priory', *Lincolnshire Architectural and Archaeological Society Reports and Papers*, vol.5, part 1 (new series), pp.1-18.

Hattatt, R., 2007, *A Visual Catalogue of Richard Hattatt's Ancient Brooches*, Oxbow Books.

Hayes, P. P. and Lane, T. W., 1992, *The Fenland Project No.5: Lincolnshire Survey, the South-West Fens*, East Anglian Archaeology, no.55.

Kenney, S., 2004, 'Iron Age, Roman and Medieval Archaeology along the Proposed Route of the A1073 Relief Road between Eye, Peterborough and Spalding, Lincolnshire: An Archaeological Evaluation', Cambridgeshire County Council, unpublished report no.701.

Lane, T., 2005a, 'The wider context of the Cheshire salt industry: Iron Age and Roman salt production around the Wash' in *Brine in Britannia. Recent Archaeological Work on the Roman Salt Industry in Cheshire*, edited by Michael Nevell and Andrew P. Fielding, Archaeology North West, vol.7, issue 17, CBA North West, The Lion Salt Works Trust, The University of Manchester Archaeology Unit, pp.47-54.

Lane, T., 2005b, 'Roman and Pre-Roman salt-making in the Fenland of England' in *Salt Works and Salinas: The Archaeology, Conservation and Recovery of Salt Making Sites and their Processes*, edited by Annelise M. Fielding and Andrew P. Fielding, Lion Salt Works Trust Monograph Series, research report No.2, pp.19-26.

Lane, T. and Morris, E. (editors), 2001, *A Millennium of Saltmaking: Prehistoric and Romano-British Salt Production in the Fenland*, Lincolnshire Archaeology and Heritage Reports Series, no.4.

McAvoy, F., 1994, 'Marine salt extraction: the excavation of salterns at Wainfleet St Mary, Lincolnshire', *Medieval Archaeology*, vol.38, pp.148-52.

Morris, E., 2001, 'Briquetage' in Tom Lane, 'An Iron Age saltern in Cowbit Wash, Lincolnshire' in *A Millennium of Saltmaking: Prehistoric and Romano-British Salt Production in the Fenland*, Lincolnshire Archaeology and Heritage Reports Series, no.4, edited by Tom Lane and Elaine L. Morris, pp.33-63.

Morris, E., 2007, 'Making magic: later Prehistoric and early Roman salt production in the Lincolnshire Fenland', in *The Later Iron Age in Britain and Beyond*, edited by Colin Haselgrove, and T. Moore, Oxbow Books, pp.430-44.

Morris, E., 2008, 'Briquetage' in Tom Lane, Elaine L. Morris and Mark Peachey, 'Excavations on a Roman saltmaking site at Cedar Close, March, Cambridgeshire', *Proceedings of the Cambridge Antiquarian Society*, vol.XCVII, pp.89-109.

Peachey, M., Failes, A. and Bradley-Lovekin, T., 2011, 'Archaeological Investigations along the Route of the A1073, Archaeological Strip and Record and Watching Brief Lincolnshire and Peterborough (SPEY08)', unpublished Archaeological Project Services Report No.29/11.

Percival, S., 2001, 'Briquetage' in Andy Crowson, 'Excavation of a late Roman saltern at Blackborough End, Middleton, Norfolk' in *A Millennium of Saltmaking: Prehistoric and Romano-British Salt Production in the Fenland*, Lincolnshire Archaeology and Heritage Reports Series, no.4, edited by Tom Lane and Elaine L. Morris, pp.182-202.

Percival, S., 2011, 'Briquetage from sites 2 and 4, A1073 Spalding to Eye improvement scheme' in Mark Peachey, Andrew Failes and Thomas Bradley-Lovekin, 'Archaeological Investigations along the Route of the A1073, Archaeological Strip and Record and Watching Brief Lincolnshire and Peterborough (SPEY 08)', unpublished Archaeological Project Services Report No.29/11, Appendix 6.

Pollard, J., Hall, D. and Lucas G., 2001, 'Excavation of a medieval saltern at Parson Drove, Cambridgeshire' in *A Millennium of Saltmaking: Prehistoric and Romano-British Salt Production in the Fenland*, Lincolnshire Archaeology and Heritage Reports Series, no.4, edited by Tom Lane and Elaine L. Morris, pp.426-55.

Precious, B., 2003, 'Roman pottery' in T. Rayner, 'Archaeological Excavation and Watching Brief at Backgate, Cowbit, Lincolnshire (CBG00, CBG01)', unpublished Archaeological Project Services Report No.78/03.

Rackham, J., forthcoming, 'The environmental evidence' in D. Trimble and M. Wood, *Archaeological Excavation of a Roman*

Saltern and Settlement at Wygate Park, Spalding (SWP05), Archaeological Project Services.

Robinson, D. N., 1999, *Lincolnshire Bricks: History and Gazetteer*, Heritage Lincolnshire.

Skertchly, S. B. J., 1877, *Geology of the Fenland*, Memoirs of the Geological Survey of Great Britain.

Stead, I. M., 1986, 'Jet and bone objects', in I. M. Stead and Valery Rigby, *Baldock: The Excavation of a Roman and Pre-Roman Settlement, 1968-72*, Britannia Monograph Series, no.7, pp.163-67.

Thompson, I., 1982, *Grog-tempered 'Belgic' Pottery of South-Eastern England*, British Archaeological Reports, British Series, no.108.

Trimble, D., 2001, 'Excavations of an early Roman saltern in Morton Fen, Lincolnshire' in *A Millennium of Saltmaking: Prehistoric and Romano-British Salt Production in the Fenland*, Lincolnshire Archaeology and Heritage Reports Series, no.4, edited by Tom Lane and Elaine L. Morris, pp.99-161.

Trimble, D., 2002, 'Archaeological Watching Brief of Test Pits Excavated on Spalding, Lincolnshire to Eye Green, Peterborough Road Realignment (SER00)', unpublished Archaeological Project Services Report No.160/02.

Trimble, D. and Wood, M., forthcoming, *Archaeological Excavation of a Roman Saltern and Settlement at Wygate Park, Spalding (SWP05)*, Archaeological Project Services.

Wilson, D. R., 1978, 'Groups of circles in the silt fens', *Proceedings of the Cambridge Antiquarian Society*, vol.LXVIII, pp.43-46.

Woodfield, C., 2005, 'Rare *tazze, paterae* and a broad hint at a *lararium* from *Lactodorum* (Towcester)', *Journal of Roman Pottery Studies*, vol.12, pp.209-12.

Diary of an Epidemic: Scotter 1890

Moira Eminson

Thirteen people died in Scotter during the epidemic of 1890, and a further eight in the nearby villages of Scotton and Messingham: a frighteningly high number in this small rural community, but hardly warranting a government-level enquiry. And yet, because of a serious difference of opinion between the two doctors most closely involved with this episode, the authorities in London were asked to instigate a 'local medical inquiry'.

The two men concerned, Henry Wright, Medical Officer of the Gainsborough Rural Sanitary Authority, and Franklin Eminson, physician and surgeon of Scotter, clashed over the question of how the disease was being transmitted. In Henry Wright's opinion, 'inclement and variable weather' had spread the disease, but a month later, considered that 'direct infection from person to person' was a more likely explanation.[1] Franklin Eminson, the only doctor to have attended epidemic victims and survived, was convinced Scotter's south sewer was the primary cause. In a process he described as indirect infection,[2] he explained how 'sewer air ... would carry the specific germ into the outside atmosphere'.[3] The chief purpose of the inquiry was to resolve this question of infection, and work began on 9 July, three months after the first victim died in Scotter.

James Barker, a bricklayer, had died on 10 April. An active eighty-two year old, living on his own in a thatched cottage on The Green, he was not at church on Easter Sunday, although he had been seen working in his garden the day before. Found collapsed on his bedroom floor, he died four days later. Robert Eminson, registrar of births and deaths (and father of Franklin) gave the cause of death as old age[4] – his usual diagnosis for any patient dying over the age of eighty, and naturally assumed to be worn out.[5]

Three weeks and six deaths later, the two doctors were still no nearer to identifying the fatal disease. Although rales (rattles) in some victims' lungs indicated a form of pneumonia, the epidemic presented in different forms, as can be seen from some of the given causes of death: old age, diarrhoea, cerebral congestion, apoplexy and influenza pleuro-pneumonia.[6] For this reason the doctors did not immediately recognise they were dealing with the same infection, and Franklin Eminson was to remember the many anxious conversations with his father: Robert Eminson had said that in all his fifty-five years of medical practice in Scotter, 'he had never seen anything resembling this epidemic'.[7]

Unlike a classic pneumonia, the incubation period was too short, twenty-four to forty-eight hours,[8] and death too sudden and unexpected. There was also no clear pattern of infection. The early cases had occurred singly, and mostly in the houses nearest to the south sewer – yet despite the closest of contacts between patient and nurse – eating the victim's leftover food, for example, and sharing the same bed, sometimes for the entire illness,[9] there were no multiple cases in these households. Without evidence of contagion, and the identity of the disease itself still uncertain, the doctors did not report the outbreak, but as a precaution in early May, disinfected some of the more suspect sewer inlets with carbolic acid, and perchloride of mercury.[10]

Only with the death of the tenth victim, Henry Chantry, did the Eminsons consider they had a case of direct infection. He had been at the bedside of his sick mother in Scotter for three nights, after walking from Susworth every evening after work, and home again next morning.[11] Mrs Harriet Chantry died on 30 April, and five days later, her son too was dead. That day, 5 May,[12] Franklin Eminson informed the Medical Officer by letter, of a disease with an 'undoubted infectious nature', and asked for assistance.[13] Robert Eminson reported the death to the Board of Guardians in Gainsborough – this time as typhoid pneumonia.

On 8 May, the 'owd' doctor himself was suddenly stricken, and blamed the contaminated air in Henry Chantry's wretchedly fetid sickroom for his illness.[14]

> The only case whose history lends any support to the belief that the disease may be contracted through breathing air with solid particles derived from the bowels, is that of my father. The condition ... existing at the house where he believed he contracted pneumonia was simply terrible. A room no larger than a closet, and incapable of efficient ventilation; a patient helpless and afflicted with uncontrollable diarrhoea; the bed saturated and skilled nursing entirely absent ... he was nauseated and believed that it was the polluted atmosphere which caused his illness.[15]

Yet even in this case, Franklin Eminson thought the sewer a more likely source of his father's sickness. Robert Eminson had told him 'he had long known the south sewer was not safe',[16] and going about the village on his medical rounds, could not avoid the harmful stench. Even in his garden at Mount House, he could not escape the foul smells from the outfall, which was some distance away.

Almost as Robert Eminson fell ill, heavy rain began to flush the stinking filth from the sewer. Early on the morning of 11 May, Franklin Eminson stood above the outfall on the banks of the River Eau and watched the rising water turn black with nauseous effluent pouring from the pipes.[17] In the evening, and back at the river, he found the water-level had risen by two feet.

About the same time, the deadly infection was unexpectedly identified in *The British Medical Journal* of 10 May 1890. This carried the synopsis of a local medical inquiry into the three hundred and sixty-nine epidemic deaths in Middlesbrough in 1888. The Inspector, Dr Edward Ballard, had invited the pioneering bacteriologist, Dr Edward Emanuel Kline, to examine the organs of some Middlesbrough victims, and he had successfully isolated a small bacillus, 'hitherto undescribed', in their lungs and in samples of fresh sputum.[19] As a result, Dr Ballard had declared the outbreak 'A new specific fever: pleuro-pneumonic fever',[19] and the symptoms described were immediately familiar to Franklin Eminson: he had already seen them in his patients.

With his father ill, and the epidemic claiming a second victim in the nearby village of Scotton on 9 May, it must have seemed to him that north Lincolnshire was on the verge of an epidemic of Middlesbrough proportions. On 15 May, and increasingly alarmed by the lack of response from the Sanitary Authority, Franklin Eminson took matters into his own hands. He wrote to the Local Government Board in London, and informed the Principal Medical Officer, Dr George Buchanan, of a very serious epidemic in Scotter – an epidemic with many of the characteristics of pleuro-pneumonic fever.

The day his letter arrived in London, 16 May, the Local Government Board acted. An immediate letter was sent to the Authority in Gainsborough, and minuted at their monthly meeting on 20 May:[20]

> ... they [the Local Government Board] had received information that exceptional mortality from inflammatory disease of the lungs has recently been observed in the Parish of Scotter, and requesting the authority to obtain from the Medical Officer of Health a report on the extent and fatality of the disease in the District ... and of the circumstances in which it has prevailed.

The minutes also record the Medical Officer's *Special Report*, his opinion that the onset of cold, wet weather was responsible for the epidemic deaths. The Committee agreed his report should be sent to London, but there is no record in the minutes of Franklin Eminson's letter of 5 May, notifying Henry Wright of a deadly, infectious disease at Scotter.

On 22 May, Dr Ballard wrote to Franklin Eminson. He needed evidence to prove the Scotter epidemic was the same pleuro-pneumonic fever found in Middlesbrough, and asked the doctor to conduct a very simple experiment on white mice.[21] He was to feed them with bread soaked in the sputa of the sick and the dying. As the mice died, so their bodies were to be posted immediately to Dr Klein, at the Brown Animal Institute in Wandsworth.

Franklin Eminson took three weeks to find suitably tame mice, preoccupied as he was with the dying of his brother, and father, the further spread of the disease to Messingham, and in writing Robert Eminson's obituary for *The British Medical Journal*:[22]

> In less than three weeks, he devotedly attended about ten cases of this terrible disease, most of them being fatal, several dying within a few hours, and hardly one extending over a week. His own case has been the most protracted observed, beginning suddenly early on the morning of May 8th and terminating in death on June 8th ... . His end was hastened by the news of the death of his third son of the same disease.

Robert Astley Cooper Eminson, aged forty-one, was buried on 31 May, followed by Robert Eminson, aged eighty-one, on 11 June. On 13 June, Franklin Eminson settled to his experiments with the mice,[23] and to answering Henry Wright's *Special Report* of 20 May.

At this time, when pneumonia was known as 'a disease of chill',[24] unsettled cool weather was a valid medical reason for lung infections. Unfortunately for the Medical Officer, Scotter had been experiencing unseasonably dry and warm conditions when the first ten epidemic victims died – conditions that had been in place since early February 1890. With less than half the usual rainfall,[25] the sewer had remained unflushed, and sewage from eighty-six houses, four or five farm yards, two slaughter houses, the school urinal and solid excreta from the one W.C. in the village (the Rector's),[26] had fermented in the pipes and became, in Franklin Eminson's words, 'the breeding grounds of the disease germ'.[27]

Like many other doctors in the late nineteenth century, Franklin Eminson's concern about drain effluvia[28] was driven by a growing understanding of the connection between dirt and disease: 'that filth and sewer air are capable of causing pneumonia'.[29] Scotter folk, however, were not to be persuaded. They believed in the maxim, a 'wholesome stench will hurt no one',[30] and regarded noxious smells from the sewer as an unavoidable evil.[31] 'Gross surface filth' around the village was a fact of life, as was the persistent stink from the sewer.[32]

Unlike the villagers, Franklin Eminson knew the history of the south sewer. It had been built, fourteen years earlier, to carry water, not sewage. Consequently it had none of the necessary safeguards, like traps and ventilation shafts, in place. Essentially a storm drain, and constructed with loose joints, it was designed to divert contaminated surface water away from the village wells, and into the Eau, so putting an end to the frequent outbreaks of typhoid that had made Scotter notorious.[33]

In 1868, when the village was suffering a worse than usual summer of typhoid,[34] Robert Eminson had realised that the wells were the source of the fever. Many were shallow, only six to twelve feet deep in some parts of the village, and in hot weather their water levels dropped. He had noted how often typhoid broke out after thunderstorms when heavy rain had filled the wells with water that had washed through the human, and animal, waste stored close to the cottages. As this was a valuable source of income to many village families, and sold to local farmers and gardeners as manure,[35] the only solution was to drain the foul water away from the yards and streets, and into the Eau.

By 1874, when Robert Eminson was appointed the first Medical Officer of Health to the newly constituted Gainsborough Rural Sanitary Authority,[36] a drainage system for Scotter was already being planned. The following year, and under his direction, nine-inch diameter pipes were laid along the main street, eighteen inches deep, with connecting branches into the cottage yards. Completed in 1876, at a cost to the Scotter ratepayers of £356, the results were dramatic. During the ten years from 1882, when Franklin Eminson first joined his father in the Scotter practice, only five cases of typhoid fever were recorded, and all exceptionally mild.[37]

Almost as dramatic was the rise in cases of pneumonia – and the increasing quantities of sewage in a system built for flash floods. A new sewer was recommended to the Sanitary Authority, at the meeting on 25 March 1890, and the Surveyor, William Eyre,[38] ordered to take levels, but the question of buying a new spirit level was adjourned. On 22 April the Surveyor was authorised to find, and buy, a second-hand level, but had no success, as Gravenor Roadley of Scotter Manor informed the meeting on 20 May. At this point, with the Local Government Board demanding a report on the Authority's response to the Scotter epidemic, there were few options left: the Surveyor was given permission to buy a new level at a cost of £14 10 shillings.[39]

No doubt Franklin Eminson learnt at this same meeting that his letter of 5 May had not been brought to the attention of the Sanitary Authority, for after the funerals of his brother and father he wrote a second letter, again emphasising the dangers of indirect infection from the Scotter sewer. This was briefly minuted at the 17 June meeting as, 'read a letter from Mr T. B. F. Eminson as to this epidemic'.[40] Henry Wright's report, his reconsidered

opinion that direct infection was responsible for the spread of the epidemic, was minuted equally crisply, 'also read the Medical Officer's Report on the subject'.

In view of the conflicting professional opinions, the Sanitary Authority had no alternative. A unanimous resolution was passed, referring the matter to London:[41]

... a letter be written to the Local Government Board asking them to cause a local inquiry to be held with a view of ascertaining the origin and cause of the outbreak and suggesting any necessary steps to prevent any similar outbreak in any part of the District.

With their letter went Mr Gravenor Roadley's plan of Scotter parish, showing the sewer and the houses affected, together with an extract from the Medical Officer's Report giving his newly-formed opinion on direct infection.[42]

Meanwhile, at Gonerby House, centre of the practice, and home to Franklin and Clara Eminson and their three small boys, experiments with the mice continued. On 26 June, the doctor was surprised by the death of two mice within thirty hours of eating infected bread, instead of the usual four to seven days.[43]

In London, Dr Klein found their lungs 'intensely congested, dark-purple in colour, and ... red-hepatized' (like liver)[44] – very similar to the lungs of the victims of the Middlesbrough epidemic. Significantly, he also succeeded in isolating the same 'short bacillus ... in the juice expressed from the inflamed lung' – confirmation that the Scotter and Middlesbrough epidemics were indeed caused by the same bacilli.[45]

The sputum that killed the two mice had come from a Scotton farmer, John Clark. The onset of his disease had been signalled by a rigor in the early hours of 19 June, after a visit to Scotter, and a long, wet day working his fields and garden. The course of his illness followed much the same pattern as other victims: the same high temperature when he first took to his bed complaining of a headache, and the same pain over the liver region, yet by 26 June, he appeared to be recovering. Five days later, when his temperature was almost normal, he unexpectedly died 'early on the morning of July 1st, having sat up in bed to sing a hymn with his children shortly before'.[46] The death toll for Scotter and district had now reached fifteen.

John Clark's death coincided with an extra meeting called by the Sanitary Authority for 1 July. On the agenda were two letters about Scotter's infected sewer. One, from Franklin Eminson, enclosed a sketch map of the village with each epidemic case marked.[47] This showed that twelve of the sixteen cases were in houses closest to the south sewer, evidence that the drain was the primary source of the fatal pneumonia.[48]

The other, dated 30 June, from William Eyre, Surveyor and Inspector of Nuisances, reported the first repairs to the Scotter sewer: the replacement of the four decaying mason's traps[49] in the main street with earthenware gullies.[50] He had also opened one section of the pipes and found it 'perfectly clean', with no signs of leakage from the joints. 'This, I think proves' he wrote 'that there can have been no smell arise from the course of the sewer',[51] but he made three recommendations: flushing in dry weather, manholes to facilitate regular inspections and ventilation shafts. The Committee ordered the Surveyor of Highways to proceed with the work, and confirmed William Eyre's annual retainer of £22 10 shillings.

In London, on 2 July, the Local Government Board instructed Dr Henry Franklin Parsons to undertake a local medical inquiry at Scotter, into a 'very serious and fatal epidemic of a disease described as pleuro-pneumonia',[52] establish the origin and cause of the outbreak and suggest how it could be contained. A week later, on 9 July, he arrived in Scotter, and immediately began investigations into the most likely sources of infection: the sewer, the water supply and the home-cured bacon.

He examined the main sewer in two places and found it clean, but defective and untrapped.[53] Cause for concern was the condition of the pipes closest to the houses on The Green, the centre of the outbreak. These were still choked with black sediment.[54] The wells, he was told, were kept reasonably unpolluted by a constant supply of underground water from Scotton Common, but saw for himself that many were unhealthily close to household privies and drains, and warned of the risk of contamination.[55]

The bacon proved safe. A sample from John Clarke's house at Scotton, had been sent to Dr Klein on 11 July and fed to laboratory mice. They survived the Lincolnshire bacon unscathed.[56] In contrast, the mice fed on Middlesbrough bacon in 1888, had died: their lungs had been found 'congested, and cultivations made from the organs yielded the bacillus *pneumoniae*'.[57] Franklin Eminson explained the reason. Scotter bacon was home-cured, and thoroughly cooked. Middlesbrough bacon was cured in sheds and yards, exposed to contaminated air and eaten raw, or occasionally warmed through on a fork.[58]

By 18 July, Dr Parsons had concluded his initial inquiry, and a long meeting with the members of the Sanitary Authority, the body responsible for financing the local inquiry. Eight days later, on 26 July, his written report was complete, although he later added a postscript dated 2 September 1890. This recorded information received of the death of a second doctor, Mr Arthur Wellesley Wales. A young Irishman from Belfast, he had died on 16 August at Burringham, leaving a heavily pregnant widow. His patient, Thomas Wakefield of Messingham, had died three days earlier.

Two reasons account for the speed of the Parsons' inquiry. Firstly, it was too late. By 9 July, the epidemic in Scotter was almost over, flooded out of the sewer by the rains of 9 to 11 May, or so Franklin Eminson came to believe. There were no emanations[59] from untrapped drain inlets to be investigated, and no sudden onsets of pleuro-pneumonic cases to examine – only three convalescent patients, and the relatives and friends of the dead to interview. The only professionally qualified witness of the events of April and May 1890 was Franklin Eminson himself, and Henry Parsons acknowledged his help: 'most of the circumstances mentioned in this report had already been ascertained, and put on record by him'.[60]

And this, 'putting on record' was the second reason for the completion of the inquiry, and report, within seventeen days. Franklin Eminson not only supplied most of the essential information, but also wrote seven of the report's twenty-one pages – a measure of the close working relationship between the two men. They had much in common. Both had trained at St Mary's Hospital, London, and both were district medical officers of health, Franklin Eminson for Scotter and District, and Henry Parsons for Selby and Goole.

Franklin Eminson's contribution to their joint publication was twofold. A full account of the malignant sewer, and seven clinical histories, each one selected to illustrate the varied symptoms of pleuro-pneumonic fever. There was a record of Astley Eminson's last ten days, his temperature, pulse and respiration rates. The others were medical notes, still echoing with the Lincolnshire voices of Dr Franklin's patients.[61]

> Case 1: G. H. J. aged 37 farm labourer [Scotton][62] [George H. Jackson]
> Present Illness: He began to be ailing about April 24th, but did not lay by entirely, and on Saturday, April 26th, he came down to Scotter, a distance of a mile or more, but felt done up on his return, and wrote a letter to me to ask for a little medicine as he was 'sick and bilious' and had a 'bad cough'. The following day April 27th I was sent for ...

George Jackson died, delirious, four days later, with Dr Franklin, as he was known in the village, at his bedside, where he had been since the previous night.

On 2 December 1890, the Parsons' Report was laid on the table at the meeting of the Authority,[63] 'and, a long letter was read by the Chairman from Mr T. B. F. Eminson addressed to Mr Osborne, afterwards destroyed when the Medical Officer explained his opinion.' The minutes leave no clue to the reason for this extraordinary action, but the report itself appears a possible cause.

Henry Parsons had steered a magisterial course between the two warring doctors but, despite an evident sympathy for Franklin Eminson, exhibited some reservations about indirect infection.[64]

> I admit that infected sewer and drain air may probably have been at Scotter one of the channels by which the contagion of the disease was conveyed ... but I do not think that this view alone explains all the facts of the case, and some other agency ... perhaps unsuspected, seems to be required for the propagation of the disease in outlying places ... I think it likely that direct infection played a larger part than Mr Franklin Eminson is willing to allow.

This statement, with its implicit endorsement of Henry Wright's views on direct infection, probably stung, but the inclusion of William Eyre's letter with the Parsons' *Report* seems a more likely explanation for the doctor's strong letter. The Surveyor's claim that 'there can have been no smell arise from the course of the sewer', not only raised questions about Franklin Eminson's professional judgement, but neatly absolved the Sanitary Authority of any responsibility for the epidemic deaths.

The doctor did not let matters rest with an explosive letter. With all the confidence of a man who had won the Pharmaceutical Society's Botany and Materia Medica Medal in 1875, and 'carried off both the two gold medals offered by the Society of Apothecaries' in 1878,[65] he went into print.

Epidemic Pneumonia at Scotter and Neighbourhood: its History Causes and Future Prevention was published in 1892. Written for the information of the inhabitants of the district,[66] the underlying message was stark: if the sewers were not rebuilt, and the heaps of rotting filth not cleared from the cottage yards, and streets, then further and more dreadful epidemics were inevitable. The most terrible of them all, Franklin Eminson reminded his readers, was the Black Death of 1348-50, and the Scotter tradition that skeletons found on the east side of The Green could have been its victims.[67]

Could it be that his destroyed letter to the Sanitary Authority had raised the possibility that the Scotter epidemic of 1890 was, in reality, plague? In 1892 conservative medical opinion believed that such manifestations had been extinct in England since the Great Plague of 1665,[68] but as knowledge of bacteriology increased, so interest in the subject had grown, both in Europe and in England.[69] Franklin Eminson had perhaps hoped that his patients' symptoms, carefully detailed in the Parsons' *Report*, would have attracted informed debate; details like the large abscess on the elbow of George Jackson's young daughter a week before her father fell ill, or the round, punched out ulcers on the swollen leg of the Scotter horse-breaker.[70] Were these recorded because he thought he had found examples

of buboes, the tell-tale swellings in the armpit, neck or groin that announced bubonic plague? There is no evidence of any response to these descriptions.

His speculations about how the disease had reached beyond the Scotter sewer were also inconclusive, but hint at remembered stories of how pestilence came to Eyam in Derbyshire – on a length of cloth infested with plague fleas. Franklin Eminson suggested that soiled bedding, inherited from a Scotter epidemic victim, had carried the infection to the two nearby villages, but could find no corroborative evidence.[71] At Scotton, the epidemic had broken out before the blankets reached the village, and at Messingham, the pneumonia case was at some distance from the home of the recipients.

Plague fleas could also account for indirect infection – the lack of multiple cases among the ten neighbours who had cared for James Barker during his last four days. Only three had fallen ill. Rebecca Vickers had sat with him for one night, and helped lay him out after death. Harriet Chantry had also watched at his bedside and, later, been involved with clearing his cottage. Edwin Fieldstone had been a pallbearer, the only time he had been inside the old man's house.

Franklin Eminson noted that the two women were not sick until the day after they had washed James Barker's effects (on different days), and that they had both emptied their dirty soapsuds into the untrapped sewer inlet, beneath James Barker's pump.[72] The doctor reasoned their water must have forced out an equal volume of germ-laden gases, although fleas, trapped in the dirty bedding or clothes, could be an equally convincing explanation, as could water droplets. Mrs Vickers was up again after only a few days in bed; Mrs Chantry died six days after her close contact with the inlet.

Edwin Fieldstone recovered within six weeks, but his mother-in-law, Mrs Julie Ann Foster died on 26 April, after only four visits to her sick son-in-law. Her neighbour, eighty-two year old Mrs Francis Hutson laid her out, and washed her clothes using one of the untrapped inlets close to her own back door.[73] Fanny Hutson died on 17 May, the first death in Scotter to be recorded as pleuro-pneumonic fever.[74]

Franklin Eminson was to change his mind about pleuro-pneumonic fever. One of his conclusions to *Epidemic Pneumonia* was that the 1890 outbreak was not, after all, a new disease but a more virulent strain of a pneumonia endemic to Scotter.[75] He never wavered, however, in his absolute certainty that the infection came from the sewer – a conviction driven, perhaps, by an unspoken fear that the 1890 outbreak could be the harbinger of an even deadlier epidemic,

> ... the disease may, in a few cases, have been caused secondarily apart from sewer and filth emanations.

That it may be thus caused is all but proved by the infection of the mice through eating sputa in their food. The danger from such secondary causes, however was slight compared with the original sewer danger.[76]

Postscript

In 1980, a Middlesbrough surgeon, G. Stout, took another look at Dr Klein's description of the *bacillus pneumoniae* discovered during the 1888 epidemic.[77] He realised there were marked similarities with the *bacillus pestis,* first described in 1894 during a pandemic of bubonic plague in Hong Kong. In 1896, Dr Klein himself isolated a strain of *bacillus pestis* in a case from the London docks, but does not appear to have revisited either the Middlesbrough or Scotter epidemics. By 1902 plague was being reported from the great ports of Hull, Liverpool, Bristol, Glasgow and London.[78]

In the early 1900s, Franklin Eminson's *Epidemic Pneumonia,* briefly, became a quoted reference work in the *British Medical Journal,* but only on questions of the incubation period of this pneumonia.

Notes

1. Dr Parsons, *Report to the Local Government Board on an Epidemic of Pneumonia at Scotter, Lincolnshire, and in the Neighbouring Places* (1890), p.9.
2. T. B. Franklin Eminson, *Epidemic Pneumonia at Scotter and Neighbourhood: Its History, Causes and Future Prevention* (1892), p.27.
3. T. B. Franklin Eminson, 'Pleuro-pneumonic fever at Scotter in 1890: the supposed method of extension of the disease to neighbouring places', *The Lancet,* 137, issue 3526 (28 March 1891), p.716.
4. Dr Parsons, *Report to the Local Government Board,* p.3.
5. Eminson, *Epidemic Pneumonia at Scotter,* p.26.
6. Dr Parsons, *Report to the Local Government Board,* p.15.
7. Eminson, *Epidemic Pneumonia at Scotter,* p.26.
8. *Ibid.,* p.43.
9. *Ibid.,* p.45.
10. *Ibid.*
11. *Ibid.*
12. *Ibid.,* p.27.
13. *Ibid.,* p.26.
14. *Ibid.,* p.39.
15. *Ibid.,* p.40.
16. *Ibid.,* p.26.
17. *Ibid.,* p.35.
18. Edward Ballard, 'A new specific fever: pleuro-pneumonic fever', *The British Medical Journal* (hereafter *BrMedJ*), (20 April 1889), pp.899-900.
19. *Ibid.*
20. Lincolnshire Archives, PL/4/804/1, 3 September 1872-July 1890.
21. Eminson, *Epidemic Pneumonia at Scotter,* p.25.
22. T. B. Franklin Eminson, 'Robert Eminson, obituary', *BrMedJ* (21 June 1890), p.1466.
23. Eminson, *Epidemic Pneumonia at Scotter,* p.25.
24. Octavius Sturges, letter, 'Special correspondence – Pneumonic fever, old and new', *BrMedJ* (4 May 1889), pp.1030-31, esp. p.1031.
25. Eminson, *Epidemic Pneumonia at Scotter,* p.33.
26. *Ibid.,* p.10. Note that WCs with poor drainage were blamed for contributing to enteric fever in Dublin in the 1870s, see the summary report on the 'Dublin Royal Sanitary Commission' in *BrMedJ* (18 October 1879), pp.632-34, esp. p.634.
27. Eminson, *Epidemic Pneumonia at Scotter,* p.65.
28. Dr Parsons, *Report to the Local Government Board,* p.9.
29. Eminson, *Epidemic Pneumonia at Scotter,* p.26.
30. *Ibid.,* p.65.
31. *Ibid.,* p.11.
32. *Ibid.*
33. *Ibid.,* p.6.
34. *Ibid.,* p.5.
35. E. Gillett and J. D. Hughes, 'Public health in Lincolnshire in the nineteenth century, part 2', *Public Health,* 69 (3), (1955), pp.55-60.
36. Lincolnshire Archives, PL/4/804/1 3 September 1872-July 1890.
37. Eminson, *Epidemic Pneumonia at Scotter,* p.10.
38. William Eyre is listed in W. White, *Directory of Lincolnshire* (1892), p.347 as 'architect, surveyor & surveyor and inspector to Rural Sanitary Authority', with his home being 158 Trinity Street, Gainsborough.
39. Lincolnshire Archives, PL/4/804/1 3 September 1872-July 1890, pp.430-34.
40. *Ibid.*
41. *Ibid.,* 3 September 1872-July 1890, 17 June 1890.
42. *Ibid.*
43. Eminson, *Epidemic Pneumonia at Scotter,* p.25.
44. Dr Parsons, *Report to the Local Government Board,* p.4, footnote.
45. Dr Henry Franklin Parsons, 'Pleuro-pneumonic fever', *BrMedJ* (15 November 1890), pp.1133-34.
46. Dr Parsons, *Report to the Local Government Board,* p.1.
47. Lincolnshire Archives, PL/4/804/2 5 July 1890-14 January 1896, 15 July 1890.
48. Eminson, *Epidemic Pneumonia at Scotter,* p.15.
49. *Ibid.,* p.10.
50. *Ibid.,* p.10.
51. Dr Parsons, *Report to the Local Government Board,* p.20.
52. *Ibid.,* p.2.
53. *Twentieth Annual Report of the Local Government Board 1890-91* (1891), p.47.
54. Dr Parsons, *Report to the Local Government Board,* p.2.
55. *Twentieth Annual Report of the Local Government Board 1890-91* (1891), p.47.
56. Dr Parsons, *Report to the Local Government Board,* p.9.
57. Eminson, *Epidemic Pneumonia at Scotter,* p.38.
58. *Ibid.,* p.39.
59. *Ibid.,* p.56.
60. Dr Parsons, *Report to the Local Government Board,* p.14.
61. *Ibid.,* p.16
62. In the original document the farm labourer's domicile is given as 'Scotter'. This is a printing error for 'Scotton'.
63. Lincolnshire Archives, PU 4/804/2 5 July 1890 -14 January 1896.
64. Dr Parsons, *Report to the Local Government Board,* p.109, Supplement.
65. 'The opening of the session at the Medical Schools', *BrMedJ* (5 October 1878), pp.535-37, see under St Mary's Hospital, p.536.
66. Eminson, *Epidemic Pneumonia at Scotter,* Preface.
67. *Ibid.,* p.3; notes in the Lincolnshire Historic Environment Record (Scotter parish file) by R. G. Smith citing John Cragg, 'Topographical Notes of Lincolnshire' (c.1824-31), p.174, MS Lincolnshire Archives, [Cragg/1/1].
68. Charles Creighton, *A History of Epidemics in Great Britain: AD 664-1893, vol.1 From AD 664 to the Extinction of the Plague, vol.2 From the Extinction of the Plague to the Present Time* (Cambridge, 1891 and 1894), vol.1, p.692.

69. See for example Augustus Jessopp's review of volume one of Charles Creighton, *A History of Epidemics in Great Britain* and Francis Aidan Gasquet, *The Great Pestilence (1348-9), now commonly known as the Black Death* (1893), in *English Historical Review*, 9, no.34 (July 1894), pp.567-70.

70. Dr Parsons, *Report to the Local Government Board*, pp.16 and 17.

71. Eminson, *Epidemic Pneumonia at Scotter*, p.48.

72. *Ibid.*, p.43.

73. *Ibid.*, p.35.

74. Dr Parsons, *Report to the Local Government Board*, pp.16 and 17.

75. Eminson, *Epidemic Pneumonia at Scotter*, p.55.

76. *Ibid.*, p.56.

77. G. Stout, 'The 1888 pneumonia in Middlesbrough', *Journal of the Royal Society of Medicine*, 73 (1980), pp.664-68.

78. R[obert] Bruce Low, *Reports and Papers on Bubonic Plague*, issued by the Local Government Board (1902).

Industrial Archaeology Notes

Compiled by Ken Redmore

Donington-on-Bain Station – The Second Platform

Stewart Squires

The railway line between Louth and Bardney opened for goods in 1874 and passengers in 1876. It was a single line and so two stations were provided with loops where trains travelling in opposite directions could pass. These were at Wragby and Donington-on-Bain. Wragby station was provided with two platforms and has been said to have been the only branch station so provided, but recent research has shown that for a period there was a second platform at Donington-on-Bain also.

The two platforms at Donington-on-Bain are shown on a Great Northern Railway map of 1895 held at Lincolnshire Archives (Fig.1). They also both appear on the Ordnance Survey County Series twenty-five inch (1:2500) Ordnance Survey map of 1888, but by the time of the second edition County Series map of 1905 the platform had gone. It is, therefore, likely that it was provided when the station was built but was removed in the period 1895 to 1905.

The platforms at Wragby were of the conventional form, that is directly opposite each other. At Donington-on-Bain they were staggered, end to end on each side of the line. This was a less common arrangement, although not unusual. Other examples in the County were at Aby and Authorpe stations between Louth and Grimsby on the East Lincolnshire Line.

This raises the question of why the platform was built in the first place and why was it removed after around twenty years. The loss of a platform at a rural station was a very rare event indeed.

If trains have to cross on a single line railway, a loop, that is a section of double track, has to be provided. If two passenger trains are crossing then each needs to draw up to a platform. By contrast, if a goods train needs to cross with a passenger train then the latter needs to be at a platform but the goods does not. Passenger trains must run to a strict timetable. This is especially important when they cross, as a delay to one will also cause a delay to the train waiting at the loop. A goods train also runs to a timetable but, on a rural branch like this, where the level of traffic ebbed and flowed depending on occasional and seasonal needs, some flexibility was built into the timings. Hence, dependent upon the progress of passenger trains, a goods train was held back or sent forward to the next passing place, providing some flexibility for shunting to attach and detach wagons from the train at intermediate stations.

The need for two platforms and crossing places at Wragby and Donington-on-Bain can be determined from a study of timetables for passenger trains from 1876 to 1951.[1] This shows that that the pattern of passenger service in 1879 and in the 1880s was four trains each way a day. Of these, two crossed at Wragby every day. In 1897 there were four each way plus a late evening Saturday only train from Louth to Donington-on-Bain and return, and one additional down train, Fridays only, from Bardney to Louth. The latter crossed with another train at Wragby. In 1904, 1910 and 1922 there was no late Saturday evening train but the pattern of four each way with the additional Friday only train continued. In 1935 and 1938 the service increased to five trains each way, none crossing at Wragby. Between 1941 and 1949 the service fell to three each way, none crossing.

This shows that Wragby needed its second platform as, up until the 1880s, one train a day crossed here. Between 1897 and 1922 at least, one train a week crossed at Wragby. At no time did passenger trains cross at Donington-on-Bain.

So why was the second platform at Donington-on-Bain provided when, in practice, it was not needed? The Louth and Lincoln Railway, incorporated in 1866, was in financial trouble from the start.[2] Eight years elapsed before any traffic was carried. The line opened in 1874 for goods traffic only between Bardney and South Willingham. Although the Great Northern Railway (GNR) agreed to work it, they would not invest any money in it. Receipts were poor; a receiver was appointed and made efforts to sell the line to the GNR. This they were reluctant to take on but eventually did so in 1881, paying less than half of the cost of construction.

Herein lies the probable cause. Unfounded optimism by the original company led to financial difficulties. Indeed, between 1876 and 1881 income was never enough to pay the bank interest.[3] Fewer trains were needed and because the second platform at Donington-on-Bain was not required for the traffic, it was removed. The location is shown in figure 2.

Figure 1 is very interesting. This was for a proposal in 1895 to extend the railway bridge and acquire additional land to extend the station site. So far no contemporary documents have been found to add information to this but the form of what was proposed does give evidence for a reasoned speculation of what the intention may have been.

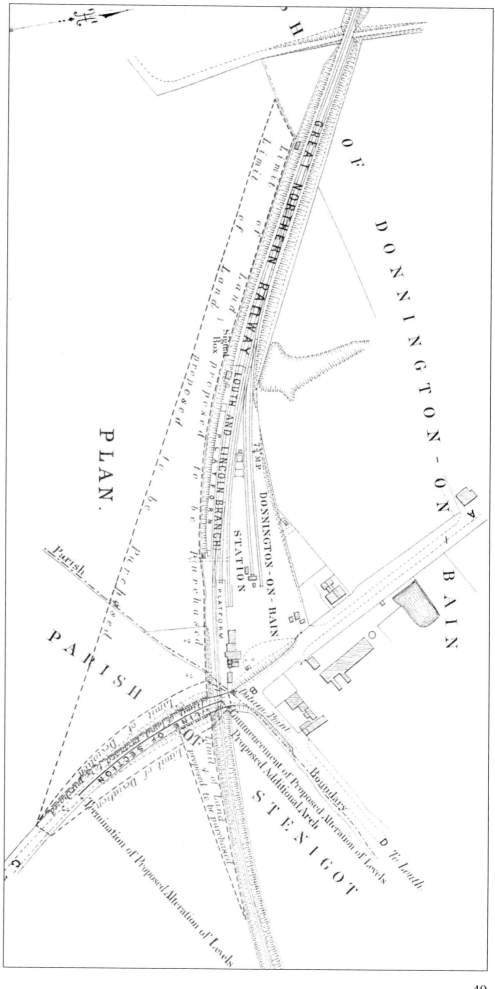

Fig. 1. Extract from a Great Northern Railway plan dated 1895 for a proposed extension of the overbridge and the purchase of additional lands. This shows the second platform, immediately below the words 'AND LINCOLN BRANCH'. (Note the spelling of the station name. This was the original station name spelling, which was altered from 1 January 1877. Why the GNR persisted with the former spelling is not known.) (Extract from document held by Lincolnshire Archives and reproduced with their permission).

Fig.2. Donington-on-Bain station in 1951. The second platform occupied the space in the background, to the left of the line where the passing loop can be seen. It extended from the lineside hut almost to the signal box. (Stewart Squires collection).

The purchase of the small triangle of land to the east of the road bridge and the widening of the bridge, that is widening the access through it for trains and extending the embanked road approach, can only have been to facilitate a second line of rails. The triangle of land to the south of the line and west of the bridge is more extensive. It is likely to have been for a fan of sidings with a head-shunt to the west, very similar to the existing goods yard to the north. The road access to the new yard would be from the south-eastern corner, at the south end of the road embankment where the ground levels coincided.

This proposal may have included a second platform in the conventional position opposite the station buildings. However, the timetable interpretation makes clear that there was to be no need for it. So the additional land is more likely to have been to provide for additional sidings with a repositioned passing loop. The loop would be used to enable goods trains to pass with passenger trains.

This can lead to further speculation. Why was the second platform removed? It could simply have been left and not used. There would be a cost for removal. One reason may be that it was unstable. We do not know its construction but it was built on the top of a shallow embankment. The sandy soil here may not have been able to support a brick platform, hence its removal. An alternative reason may relate to the 1895 proposals. It may have hindered the new passing loop and the

additional sidings and hence was removed to facilitate development which did not subsequently take place.

Notes
1. Passenger trains ran from 1876 to 1951 and timetables from 1879, the 1880s, 1897, 1904, 1910, 1922, 1935, 1938, 1941, 1947, 1948 and 1949 have been examined.
2. John Wrottesley, *The Great Northern Railway, volume 2, Expansion and Competition* (1979), pp.27-28.
3. A. J. Ludlam and W. B. Herbert, *The Louth to Bardney Branch*, second edition (1987), p14.

Sutton Bridge Dock

Ken Redmore

Sutton Bridge dock, a few hundred metres north of the eponymous bridge, was built for small ocean-going vessels sailing the adjacent river Nene which outfalls in The Wash about six kilometres to the north. The purpose of the dock was to export coal from the Midlands and to import timber and general cargoes. Railway sidings were brought to the dock side from the Midland and Great Northern Joint Railway line to Spalding.

The dock was extremely short lived; it opened in May 1881 but was forced to close within a few weeks when sections of the dock wall collapsed. The underlying soil – running silt – was unsuitable for the type of construction employed; all attempts to repair the dock

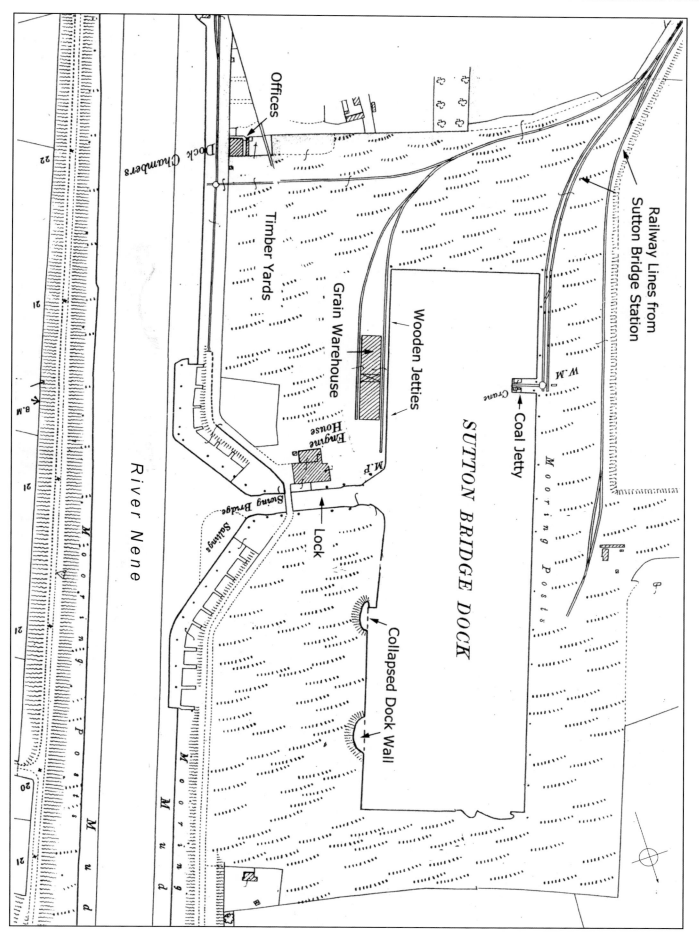

Fig.1. Sutton Bridge dock. Extract from the Ordnance Survey County Series map, 25 inch (1:2500), second edition (1904), with annotations.

Fig.2. Dock wall, near the north-east corner of Sutton Bridge dock (photograph March 2012, Ken Redmore).

and make it watertight proved unsuccessful. Fortunately, a large portion of the dock site has been under the benign occupation of a golf club for most of the period since its closure, and several original features have survived. The SLHA Industrial Archaeology team undertook a brief survey of the dock in March 2012.

The dock is rectangular in shape, about 430m long by 120m wide, enclosing an area of 5.2ha (Fig.1). Most of the perimeter wall is in the form of a sloping earth bank faced with concrete. Parts of the wall were undermined and collapsed when the dock was first filled with water, but, after closure and drainage of the dock, considerable

Fig.3. Plate girder of the former swing bridge, east of the lock (photograph March 2012, Ken Redmore).

Fig.4. Timber jetty on the south-east side of Sutton Bridge dock (photograph March 2012, Ken Redmore).

lengths of original wall on the south, east and west sides of the dock have survived with little deterioration. Today, the concrete facing is heavily pitted and partially covered in light vegetation (Fig.2). The angle of sloping wall is approximately 40° to the horizontal.

The lock between the dock and the river, constructed in concrete and brick on timber foundations, was 60m long and 15m wide. Following the closure of the dock, the lock was filled in. A section of wall forming part of the apron at the west entrance to the lock can still be examined; this is faced in blue engineering brick laid in English bond and is in sound condition.

A swing bridge was built over the east end of the lock for road access along the west bank of the Nene while allowing tall vessels to enter the dock. After the dock's closure, the bridge was secured in a fixed position but was partially removed later when the area was redeveloped. The plate girder which supported the western side of the bridge deck remains in position, and, on the southern side, there are surviving shafts and gears which suggest the bridge had the option of manual operation (Fig.3).

A timber jetty, about 150m long, extends along the east side of the dock to the south of the lock entrance, and has survived (Fig.4). This carried a railway siding and was adjacent to a large warehouse. No evidence was found of fixed cranes adjacent to the jetty. Details of the pine structure of the jetty comprising uprights (300mm by 300mm) with diagonal braces (300mm by 150mm) are shown in figure 5. Parallel longitudinal timbers (300mm by 300mm) on top of the jetty structure correspond to standard railway gauge (1435mm).

The depth of water in the dock was planned to range between 5.5m and 7.5m, depending on tidal conditions. Today, the height of the timber jetty above ground level is about 3.5m. On the supposition that the highest water level in the dock was one metre below the top of the quay, the original dock floor is at least 5m below current ground level.

On the west side of the dock, served by a railway siding, is a projecting jetty encased in mass concrete (Fig.6). This supported a fixed crane or hoist for the transhipment of coal from railway truck to ship. The jetty projects 20m

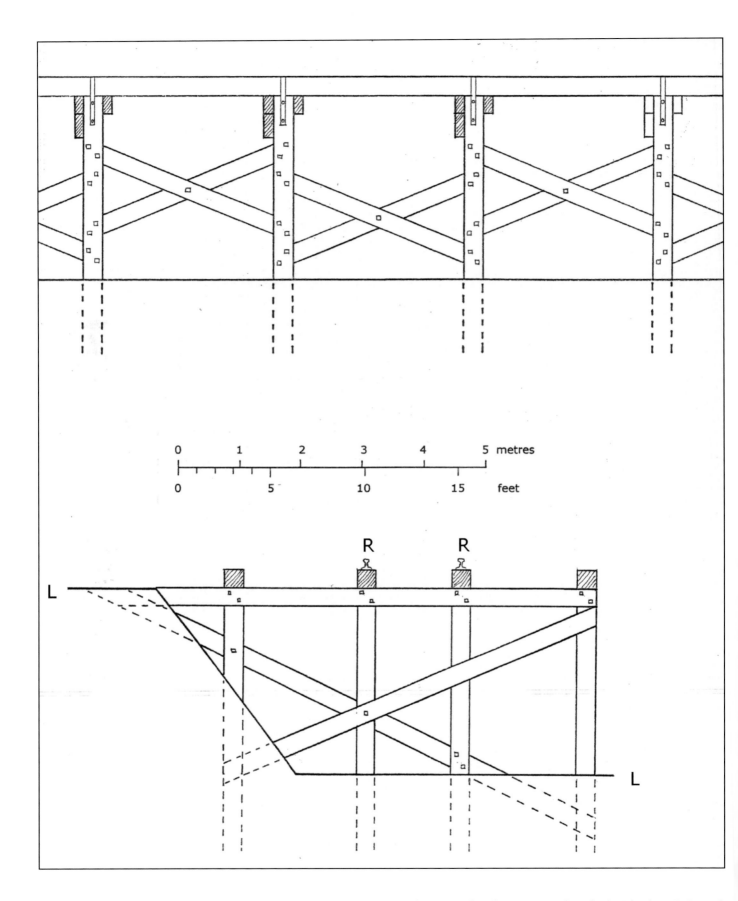

Fig.5. East elevation and section of the timber jetty, on the south-east side of Sutton Bridge dock. The line L-L is the current profile of the dock wall and ground level; the level inside the dock was initially at least 5m lower. R = position of railway siding. (Ken Redmore).

Fig.6. Coal hoist jetty, Sutton Bridge dock (photograph March 2012, Ken Redmore).

into the dock and is 12m wide; it is now about 4m in height. A small, bolted steel-plate and a group of six, sawn-off steel-rods, embedded in the concrete surface, are all that remain of anchor points for the hoist. There is a small section of railway line of standard gauge about 100m beyond the south-west corner of the dock. This is part of the siding which served the coal jetty.

Note: A detailed account of the construction of Sutton Bridge Dock and its short history is given in Neil R Wright, *Sutton Bridge – An Industrial History* (Lincoln, 2009), pp.35-42

An oath of allegiance to King George III, 1781–1804

Albert J. Schmidt

This document, transcribed opposite, is the subject of discussion in the next paper in this Journal (pp.59–69).

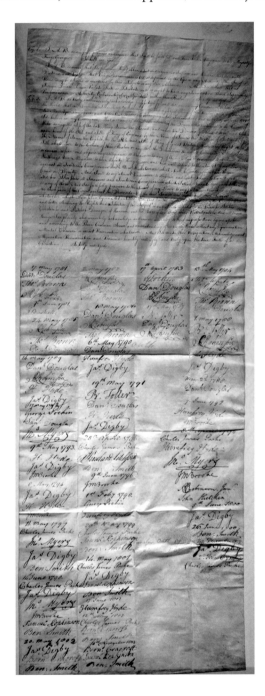

Fig.1. The oath of allegiance to King George III (Photograph Emilio Pabón).

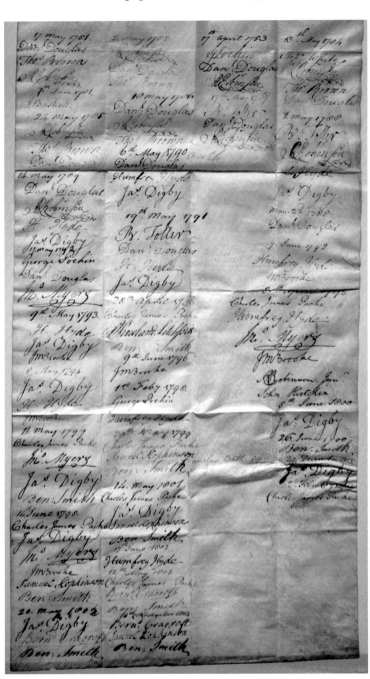

Fig.2. Lower section of the oath of allegiance to King George III, showing the signatories, 1781–1804 (Photograph Emilio Pabón).

The following is a complete transcript of the oath and its signatories:

I A.B. do sincerely promise and swear That I will be faithful and bear true Allegiance to his Majesty / King George. So help me God.

I A.B. do swear that I do from my Heart abhor detest and abjure as Impious and Heretical that damnable / Doctrine and Position that Princes excommunicated or deprived by the Pope or any Authority of the See of / Rome may be deposed or murdered by their Subjects or any other whatsoever. And I do declare That no / Foreign Prince Person Prelate State or Potentate hath or ought to have any Jurisdiction Power Superiority / Pre eminence or Authority Ecclesiastical or Spiritual within this Realm. So help me God.

I A.B. do truly and sincerely acknowledge profess testify and declare in my Conscience before God and / the World That our Sovereign Lord King George as lawful and rightful King of this Realm and all other / His Majestys Dominions and Countries thereunto belonging. And I do solemnly and sincerely declare that / I do believe in my Conscience, That not any of the Descendants of the Person who pretended to be Prince of / Wales during the Life of the late King James the Second, and since his Decease pretended to be and took / upon himself the Stile and Title of King of England by the Name of James the Third, or of Scotland, by / the Name of James the Eighth, or the Stile and Title of King of Great Britain, hath any Right or / Title whatsoever to the Crown of this Realm or any other the Dominions thereunto belonging. And I do / renounce, refuse, and abjure any Allegiance or Obedience to any of them. And I do swear That I will bear / Faith and true Allegiance to his Majesty King George, and him will defend to the utmost of my Power / against all Traiterous Conspiracies and Attempts whatsoever which shall be made against his Person / Crown or Dignity. And I will do my utmost Endeavour to disclose and make known to his Majesty / and his Successors all Treasons and Traiterous Conspiracies which I shall know to be against him / or any of them And I do faithfully promise to the utmost of my Power to support maintain and defend / the Succession of the Crown against the Descendants of the said James and against all other Persons / whatsoever which Succession by an Act intitled "An Act for the further limitation of the Crown and better Securing the Rights and Liberties of the Subject"[1] is and stands limited to the Princess Sophia / Electoress and Dutchess Dowager of Hanover[2] and the Heirs of her Body being Protestants And all these / things I do plainly and sincerely acknowledge and swear according to these express Words by me spoken / and according to the Plain Common Sense and understanding of the same Words without any Equivocation / Mental Evasion or Secret Reservation whatsoever. And I do make this Recognition, Acknowledgement / Abjuration Renunciation and Promise heartily willingly and truly upon the true Faith of a / Christian. So help me God.

Signatories with dates of initial signing and renewal:[3]

17 May 1781
Dan'l Douglas[4]
Thos Brown[7]
R. Robinson[8]

7 June 1781
J. Bashell[9]

24 May 1785
R. Robinson
Thos Brown
Dan'l Douglas

14 May 1789
Dan'l Douglas
R. Robinson
H. Hyde
Jas Digby

17 May 1792
George Pochin
Dan'l Douglas
Jno Myers[14]

9th May 1793
H. Hyde
Jas Digby
J M Brooke

8 May 1794
Jas Digby

2 May 1782
R. Robinson
Dan'l Douglas
Thos Brown

18 May 1786
Dan'l Douglas
R. Robinson
Thos Brown

6th May 1790
Dan'l Douglas
Humfrey Hyde
Jas Digby

19th May 1791
B. Toller
Danl Douglas
H. Hyde
Jas Digby

28th April 1796
[Land tax meeting]
Charles James Packe
J. Rowland Litchford[16]
Ben: Smith[17]

9th June 1796
J M Brooke

1st Feby 1798

17th April 1783
G. Pochin[5]
Dan'l Douglas
R. Robinson

17th May 1787
B. Toller[10]
Dan'l Douglas
R. Robinson

13th May 1784
Steph'n White[6]
R. Robinson
Thos Brown
Dan'l Douglas

1 May 1788
B. Toller
R. Robinson
H. Hyde[11]
Jas Digby[12]

May. 22d 1788
Dan'l Douglas

7 June 1792
Humfrey Hyde
J M Brooke[13]

30th April 1795
[Land tax meeting]
Charles James Packe[15]
Humfrey Hyde
Jno Myers
J M Brooke
R. Robinson Junr[18]
John Hutchin[19]

H. Hyde
J M Brooke

[Appeal day]
George Pochin
Humfrey Hyde

5th June 1800
Jas Digby

11. May 1797
Charles James Packe
Jno Myers
Jas Digby
Ben: Smith

29th May 1799
Charles James Packe
Samuel Hopkinson[20]
Ben: Smith

26 June 1800
Ben: Smith

29 December 1803
Jas Digby

14 May 1801
Charles James Packe
Jas Digby
Samuel Hopkinson
Ben: Smith

2d February 1804
Charles James Packe

14th June 1798
[Stow horse fair]
Charles James Packe
Jas Digby
Jno Myers
J M Brooke
Samuel Hopkinson
Ben: Smith

17th June 1802
Humfrey Hyde

12th May 1803
Charles James Packe
Bern'd Cracroft
Ben: Smith

20 May 1802
Jas Digby
Bern'd Cracroft[21]
Ben: Smith

10th November 1803
Bern'd Cracroft
Samuel Hopkinson
Ben: Smith

Notes

1. Commonly known as the Act of Settlement, 1701 (12 & 13 Will.3, c.2), which secured the Hanoverian succession.

2. Sophia, Electress of Hanover, was a granddaughter of James I and VI of England and Scotland and heiress to the throne of England after Queen Anne. Sophia died shortly before the latter.

3. Besides Daniel Douglas (who signed twelve times) and Benjamin Smith Sr (eight), there were sixteen others: those who signed more than twice included five laymen – James Digby (eleven times), Charles James Packe (nine), Robert Michael Robinson Sr (nine), Thomas Brown (five), George Pochin (three) – and five clerics, of whom the Rev. Humphrey Hyde was the most frequent signatory (nine), followed by Brooke (six), Hopkinson and Myers (four times each) and Cracroft (three). Five laymen (Litchford, Hutchin, Bashell, White and Robinson Jr) signed twice or a single time. Robinson Jr may have been merely a stand-in for his father. Many were clients/social acquaintances – the Tollers and Douglases, Brown, Digby, Brooke, Cracroft, Hopkinson, Robinson Sr, and Myers, Pochin and Hyde – whom Smith variously entertained or by whom he was entertained.

4. Daniel Douglas (1735-93), who was probably the chief organizer of the oath of allegiance, was prominent as an enclosure commissioner and Sheriff of Lincolnshire. Douglas is discussed in detail in the paper which follows in this journal.

5. George Pochin (1732-98), who served as a colonel in the Leicestershire Militia and was Deputy Lieutenant of the counties of Leicestershire and Lincolnshire, was also involved with local turnpike matters.

6. Stephen White, mentioned once as a signer – identity uncertain.

7. Thomas Brown was no doubt of the affluent and politically connected Brown family of Horbling, although a Thomas Brown with feasible dates does not fit credibly any known genealogy. He was, nonetheless, the Thomas Brown who collaborated with Daniel Douglas and Edward Brown both on turnpike matters and enclosures. Further, Horbling Enclosure Act and the *Proceedings of the Commissioners for Enclosing Horbling* (LA, DIOC/ LDAP/2/5) cite a Thomas Brown (again, very likely this one) as 'Gentleman and Lord of the said manor and proprietor of a considerable part of the said fields and meadows, etc', leaving little doubt that Brown the oath-taker was, indeed, the turnpike venturer and Horbling encloser.

8. Robert Michael Robinson Sr of Hawthorpe was signer of the oath, sheriff of the county of Lincolnshire in 1791 and identified with the local land tax and turnpike commissions.

9. John Bashell, although an initial oath-taker, signed only once. His name appears as a tenant in the Horbling Act: *Proceedings of the Commissioners for Enclosing Horbling, 1764-71.* Nothing more is known of him.

10. Rev. Brownlow Toller of Billingborough (near Horbling) signed three times before his death at sixty-one in 1791. The Tollers and

Benjamin Smiths were close friends, as evidenced by the care for and comforting of Widow (Anne) Toller by the Smiths. Anne died in 1803 at age sixty-eight. Toller was listed as a proprietor in the enclosure proceedings for Horbling in 1764.

11. Rev. Humfrey Hyde (*c*.1737-1807), rector of Dowsby and vicar of Bourne, 1763-1807. His daughter Catherine married oath-taker James Digby of Bourne in 1796.

12. James Digby (d.1811) of Red Hall, Bourne signed the oath of allegiance nine times. Digby served on the turnpike commission and was Deputy Lieutenant of the county. He married Catherine (d.1836), sole daughter and heiress of the Rev. Humfrey Hyde, vicar of the parish of Bourne and himself a frequent signer of the oath. Digby, mentioned frequently in the Smith diary as a family friend, was also a Smith client.

13. The Rev. John Moore Brooke (1757-98), the son of the novelist Frances Brooke neé Moore (1724-89) and the Rev. John Brooke D.D. (1709-89), was rector of Folkingham, a member of the Folkingham Association for the Prosecution of Felons and a familiar attendee at land tax meetings. He emerges in young Benjamin Smith Jr's diary as a family friend (LA, Smith 15/3/1: mentions on 5 Feb, 13 & 30 Apr, 7, 12 and 19 May 1795). The modern spelling of Folkingham rather than the eighteenth-century version, Falkingham, is used here.

14. Rev. John Myers of Folkingham, a frequenter at land tax and turnpike commission meetings, was most likely the Rev. John Myers who married Alice Thorold in 1778.

15. Charles James Packe (1758-1837) of Claythorpe was descended from the Husseys who had been at Caythorpe since the mid sixteenth century. His father was Charles James Packe (1726-1816) and his mother Charlotte was a Pochin.

16. Rowland Litchford, who signed twice, is mentioned with some frequency in Ben Smith Jr's diary. He attended land tax meetings and was a friend of Frank (1778-1844) and Edward Smith (1788-1813), second and third sons of Benjamin Smith Sr. In *Lincolnshire Pedigrees* A. R. Maddison notes, but does not explain why, Thomas Rowland after his marrying Mary Welby in 1726 called himself Litchford. His descendants, as evidenced by Rowland Litchford, followed suit.

17. Benjamin Smith Sr (1732-1807), born St Peter's Eastgate, Lincoln, practised as an attorney in and around Horbling from the 1760s until retirement in 1798. For more, see the text of the main article which follows in this journal.

18. R. Robinson Jr is the son of Robert Michael Robinson, and he signed but once.

19. John Hutchin, a 'single' signatory, attended Folkingham land tax meetings.

20. Rev. Samuel Hopkinson (1754-1841), vicar of Morton and Bourne.

21. The Rev. Bernard Cracroft (1752-1821), fifth son of Robert Cracroft of Hackthorn and rector of Rippingale. Three times a signer of the oath, he also served as a turnpike commissioner.

Allegiance to King George III: loyalism, property and taxes in the lives of south Lincolnshire countrymen, 1781-1804*

Albert J. Schmidt

Images and a transcript of the document relating to this article can be found on pages 56–58 of this journal.

This article proposes delineating an eighteenth-century document, an oath of allegiance to King George III, which languished for more than two centuries among bundles of papers in the attic of the solicitors' firm of B. Smith & Co in Horbling, Lincolnshire.[1]

A third of this document (the whole measuring ten inches by twenty-nine inches) comprises the oath itself, and with it a vilification of the king's Jacobite and papist enemies. The remaining two-thirds consists of the oath-takers' signatures beneath the dates of the original signing and subsequent renewals. The south Lincolnshire countrymen who performed this ritual did so between 1781 and 1804.

That this oath is more than one of mere praise of the king and castigation of his enemies makes it of particular interest. Its uniqueness lies in the consequences of identifying each signatory and determining his individual purpose or as member of a group. Ascertaining such motivation, the theme central to this article, begins by exploring possible meanings of the document that relate to this group. These include allegiance doctrine, the *mentalité* of rural conservatism, an apotheosis of George III, reactions to the American War of Independence (1775-82), the crowd, 'politeness', 'reformation of manners' and other themes current in the late eighteenth century. Finally, the relationship of allegiance to landed property is explored, especially the anomaly of the eighteenth-century Lincolnshire land market. Such property in Lincolnshire leads to a consideration of three south

Lincolnshire power brokers, two of whom were leaders in the oath-swearing. They galvanized the oath-signatories, while at the same time profiting mightily from the fluid land market. The various signatories come alive as their respective natures and those of the power brokers emerge from diary passages. When it becomes evident that this 'middling sort'[2] often used land tax meetings as a venue for both business and socializing – even swearing an oath to King George – it is feasible to conclude that this oath, when viewed through the lens of land tax meetings, while still opaque is more consequential than meets the eye.

Layers of meaning

On the face of it, this document reflects those contentious political and religious issues which smouldered and occasionally ignited during England's 'long eighteenth century'.[3] It appears, moreover, to epitomize Herbert Butterfield's long-ago classic, *The Whig Interpretation of History*.[4] The present essay, however, suggests that developments more nuanced than Jacobitism and anti-popery were at play here and deserve particular scrutiny. These once-energizing ideologies had largely become a spent force by century's end; moreover, nice distinctions between late seventeenth-century allegiance and contract theories of governance had also flagged.[5]

An exception is Jonathan Clark's brand of conservatism.[6] His view that 'allegiance and sovereignty, not representation and reform' prevailed in English political life has found acceptance; further, his citing Roger North's[7] 'few rational principles' concerning civil power, besides being insightful to his own thinking, also meshed with that of the Lincolnshire oath-signatories:[8]

> That no plan can be made sense of, except the doctrine of allegiance against which they have been taught to clamour; and that resistance to civil government, asserted on principle, is nothing but the extravagance and nonsense of designing writers, who want to be resisting everything for their own private ends.

Yet Clark's conservatism alone neither explains nor even shows a linkage with the new popularity of George III and the recurring theme of the crowd engaged variously in protest, reform and loyalism. Linda Colley's 'Apotheosis of George III' in the 1780s – the 'conflation of royal and patriotic with religious terminology' – does at first glance appear to fit the mould of the oath.[9] That the Lincolnshire oath-signatories liked their king better later than they had earlier speaks pointedly to the first decade of their oath-taking. On the other hand, Colley's idea of the forging of a British nation during that 'long eighteenth century' and the monarchy's role in it were alien to their parochial thinking.

---

* This article is dedicated to three direct descendants of Benjamin Smith Sr, a lead player in the present narrative. Residing in the south-west of England, they are Charlotte and her brother Benjamin IV (both Gould-Smiths) and their cousin Sophie Holdway (also Gould-Smith). I especially include in this dedication Shirley Gould-Smith, their grandmother, who has been unfailingly helpful in my researching the firm of B. Smith & Co. My thanks to Dr Wendy Atkin, who succeeded admirably in editing a very complicated manuscript.

Such dissimilar thinking applies to any explanation of the oath in terms of the mob/crowd theory.[10] The Lord Gordon riots, launched in opposition to greater toleration for Catholics, appeared germane because of their nearness in time, place and even bigotry. That said, the Gordon rioters were simply too removed in their activism from the Lincolnshire countrymen: the latter's rhetoric about Jacobitism and popery should not be mistaken as a call to riot.[11]

Regarding the oath-signatories themselves, can they be reasonably identified or defined by such themes as 'politeness' and 'manners'? As alien as both appear in a rural context, they did resonate. Politeness, defined as the 'pursuit of genteel status and the acquisition of polite manners', played vitally in the social life of the middling countrymen and even had political consequences in both Lincolnshire and London. The 'reform of manners movement', which fused reform with morality, seems also to have had a place in countrymen's *mentalité*. In an environment of 1780s gloom and despair, Joanna Innes discerns a moralizing that seems akin, if nothing more, to what might have been mouthed by the oath-signatories.[12] Hers is a pessimistic portrait of England in the doldrums – a country's coping with unwanted isolation (even vulnerable to foreign coalitions) and a demoralized people's moralizing, all within this tumult called 'manners'. Mirroring Innes' 1780s pessimism, Philip Harling moralizes about parliamentary reform and the politics of 'the Old Corruption'.[13] Where Colley heralds a new age of British nationhood, Innes despairs over a country adrift in idleness, vagrancy, crime and intemperance.

When the troubled 1780s unfolded into the revolutionary maelstrom of the nineties, new urgencies are likely to have spurred Lincolnshire oath-signing. The most obvious were concerns of impending French raids or even invasion of coastal England. While such worries no doubt prompted loyalty-swearing to the king and even organizing militias to fend off invaders, the same troops were conveniently positioned to intimidate a sullen underclass suffering the ill effects of weather and landlord oppression.[14] This matter of landlords and property resonates here in explaining the mystery of the oath document. Why is this so?

The notion of allegiance and propertied sorts

Until now, this paper has focused largely on allegiance and the *mentalité* of those swearing it. Although the oath in and of itself made allegiance central, by the end of the eighteenth century the notion of allegiance had ebbed and is, in this paper at least, replaced in centrality by property. Property, newly enclosed and improved, became the unquestioned medium of politics and instrument of power. As Paul Langford exclaimed in his 1990 Ford Lectures at the University of Oxford:[15]

> A world without property was almost inconceivable to eighteenth-century Englishmen. The most diverse thinkers shared the assumption that law and government alike must be based on propertied foundations...It became almost impossible to conceive of rights and liberties except in terms which implied individual proprietorship.

In swearing an oath of allegiance to their king, Lincolnshire countrymen of the 1780s were doubtless exercising their rights and liberties as propertied Englishmen in demonstrating their loyalty. Implications of property notwithstanding, the countrymen still harkened to the ancient mode of proclaiming allegiance to their sovereign. Here, a clash of old (seventeenth-) and new (eighteenth-century) ideologies was at hand. Langford argued (the present author's insertion in *italics*):[16]

> There was a growing tendency in the eighteenth century to view the rights of individuals in terms of their property and public affairs as an expression of propertied interests. Competing with it there was also an older tradition that made relations between the citizen and the community a matter of ideology, even theology, properly regulated by state-imposed oaths and tests *[as against Catholics and Dissenters]*. The theory behind this tradition came to seem increasingly anachronistic...Only the threat of revolution and the prejudices of George III prevented wholesale abolition of the code of legal discrimination.

Could it have been that denouncing Jacobitism and popery, while not alien to their thinking, either masked or inadvertently obscured their 'middling' interests of protecting newly enclosed and enhanced turf?[17] Diverse views of the land market in eighteenth-century England suggest so. The first of these was the widely acclaimed dictum of H. J. Habakkuk, who held that:[18]

> The general drift of property in the sixty years after 1690 was in favour of the large estate and the great lord; and while the movement was probably not so decisive as that which, in the hundred years before 1640 consolidated the squirearchy, it clearly marks one of the great changes in the disposition of English landed property.

Notably, historian B. A. Holderness took exception to this view, at least insofar as it applied to Lincolnshire. He argued that estate lands there were bought up not just by magnates but also by gentry, affluent farmers and graziers.[19] He also cited new kinds of landlords – those who, having accumulated wealth from commerce or banking in the City, bought into the county squirearchy.[20]

Nor was Holderness alone in citing the crucial role played by lesser landowners – some beyond Lincolnshire. Paul Langford also spoke of 'the growing wealth and importance of the middle orders of society'. These were the 'great body of merchants, moneyed men, and farmers [who] had transformed the face both of urban and agrarian society.'[21] Nicholas Rogers, who wrote approvingly of Langford's work, detailed the matter:[22]

> The term 'middling sort', which was used more frequently than 'middle class' in Hanoverian discourse, had a long lineage stretching back into the previous century, and it would be useful to know just how this construction changed over time. Whereas the term initially referred principally to independent small

producers as an interposition between the gentry and the labouring poor, by the eighteenth century it denoted a more diverse (if proportionately smaller) group of entrepreneurs, professionals, farmers and tradesmen who rose to prominence with the expansion of the state, overseas commerce and changing productive relations in industry and agriculture after 1660. The Georgian middle class, in other words, grew out of the complex changes which transformed Britain into an expansive imperial power, and was predicated on a sustained agricultural surplus and an enlarged market for manufactures and services.

This 'middling sort' included, besides wealthy farmers and graziers, a mix of professionals – lawyers, clergy, land agents, surveyors, bankers, auctioneers, enclosure commissioners and others, who were either land-grabbers or such who abetted them.[23] Sir Charles Anderson of Lea had their kind in mind when he observed, 'I have long been of opinion that the Co. of Lincoln is ruled chiefly by Agents and Attorneys, and that in no County have they such dower.'[24]

Like acquisitive farmers and graziers, attorneys satisfied their appetite for land by enclosing, or at least facilitating enclosure of, wastelands, commons and even precariously tenured copyholds.[25] Then they set about 'improving' their own holdings and those of others by building, draining fenlands, laying out turnpikes and securing them by self-help policing to fend off or apprehend transgressors. Their aggrandizement notwithstanding, these 'industrious improvers'[26] won status as good and loyal subjects, which they celebrated by swearing allegiance to their king.

Folkingham power brokers – Douglas, Smith, Heathcote and the rest

The 'middling sort' encloser/improver and professional facilitator are epitomized here by enclosure commissioner Daniel Douglas (1735-93) and attorney Benjamin Smith Sr (1732-1807). The merchant/banker/ City capitalist role was represented by Gilbert Heathcote (1652-1733), 1st Baronet, who bought into the rural magnate crowd.[27] Each family at one time or other took up residence in the market town of Folkingham, indeed Douglas was born there;[28] moreover, like Douglas, Gilbert Heathcote (1773-1851), 4th Baronet, was a client of the Smith attorneys. The aforementioned personages are treated hereafter in some detail, noting especially how loyalty to kingship, as evidenced by the oath, intersected with landlordship.

Daniel Douglas and Benjamin Smith Sr discovered ways of making civic virtue profitable through their work on commissions and other public bodies. Their being of the landed interest made each a rallying point for confirming political loyalties and mobilizing solidarity. The politically ambitious Sir Gilbert Heathcote, 4th Baronet, also figured in this economic equation when Smith and the Heathcote steward, Thomas Forsyth, garnered profits in clothing and victualling Heathcote's militia (positioned to quieten

down a sullen underclass smarting from bad weather and hard times and to guard against smuggling) no less than shield the Lincolnshire coast from the French.

As his obituary tells it, Douglas was a forceful figure in local politics:[29]

> In January last he called a meeting of the town of Folkingham and its vicinity to enter into resolutions in favour of our present constitution ... and, by his arguments, shewed himself a compleat master of the subject, and plainly convinced every one present of the necessity of subordination amongst all mankind; and also evidently proved the impropriety of any innovations, when the fruits our present constitution brought forth were peace, liberty and plenty.

From the 1760s, Douglas became fully engaged with the 'improver' community and in county politics. Having served as enclosure commissioner and been much engaged in turnpike and drainage matters, he was appointed Sheriff of Lincolnshire in 1786. Late in life, in November 1791, he had married Jane Pinkney, of a 'good family in Northamptonshire'.[30] In addition to the power he wielded, he had accumulated a sizeable fortune, upwards of £50,000 by the time of his death. The oath of allegiance was dear to Douglas, who appears to have initiated it and signed off a dozen times between May 1781 and May 1792, the year before his death.

Douglas's business ventures crossed those of attorney Benjamin Smith Sr at least as early as 1764, when the former headed the Horbling enclosure commission, which Smith clerked.[31] Further, they collaborated on the Black Sluice drainage and turnpike commissions.[32] Smith, not incidentally, as accountant/banker to Douglas, received stipends for his work on both commissions from the personal account, which he (Smith) administered.[33] In gratitude for this loyalty and service, Douglas remembered Smith in his will to the sum of £800.[34]

Born in Lincoln in 1732, three years before Douglas, Benjamin Smith Sr took up residence in Walcot village near Folkingham by the late 1750s.[35] There he began lawyering before moving to nearby Horbling by the mid 1760s.[36] Besides Horbling, his catchment area included the towns of Donington, Folkingham, Bourne, Spalding and numerous fenside villages – all these besides his connections in the City. From the outset of his career Smith established a reputation for diligence and loyalty to the propertied class in Kesteven,[37] serving it in conveyancing, drawing up wills, agreements and the like. Smith's lawyering included clerking for numerous commissions and charities; moreover, he performed as banker/money-scrivener, lending moneys through mortgages and notes.[38]

Smith Sr attended client properties as well as buying his own. Working out of a small shed behind his Red Hall mansion in Spring Lane, Horbling, he routinely served 'improver' landlords by facilitating enclosures and managing their holdings – that is, collecting clients' rents, selling wood, keeping accounts, convening copyhold courts, clerking at land tax meetings,[39] and keeping an eye on turnpikes, irrigation, drainage, embankments, timber and waste. Besides, he was very much a law-and-order person, especially in his role as clerk and treasurer of the self-help Folkingham Association for the Prosecution of Felons.[40] In time, Smith became lord of his own copyholds, enjoying immensely the camaraderie at court banquets, holding court and tallying what was a sizeable fortune.[41] Whatever the nature of his enterprise, it invariably involved landed property and the well-being of its owners, his clients.[42]

In retirement in 1798, the elder Smiths moved from Horbling to Folkingham, where Benjamin Sr died in 1807, some thirteen years before his widow. He had signed the oath of allegiance to King George regularly between 1796 and 1803. The signatories of the oath were those of neighbours and clients, the middling, propertied folk of south Lincolnshire. He was, *par excellence,* their indispensable enabler.

The essential Smith client, magnate Sir Gilbert Heathcote, 4th Baronet, remained conspicuously apart both from the oath-signatories and land tax meetings.[43] Although he was not of the 'middling' mould, he did share the Folkingham power base with Douglas and Smith and was in one way or other – property, militia, interpersonal relations – involved with both. It is difficult to imagine the Douglases and Smiths promoting the oath without involving the 4th Baronet.

This said, who were the Heathcotes? When the historian John Brewer observed that 'the greatest wealth was to be made in government finance', Sir Gilbert Heathcote, 1st Baronet and founder of the family dynasty and fortunes, came to mind.[44] He was at once a founder of the Bank of England, director of the East India Company and widely regarded as England's richest commoner, being worth some £700,000.[45]

The Heathcotes had entered onto the Rutland/Lincolnshire stage in earnest by the late 1720s. In 1729 Sir Gilbert, 1st Baronet, purchased what became the family base, Normanton in Rutland. Shortly afterwards he acquired a sizeable Lincolnshire holding, which included the market town of Folkingham.[46] That the Heathcotes acquired this south Lincolnshire property proved crucial to the family's political strategy for the next century. Folkingham, which lies on the main north-south road between Bourne and Sleaford, is to this day graced by Georgian facades lining both the east and west sides of its elongated and sloping main street.[47] Although the Heathcotes spent precious little improving the town's appearance, the handsome Greyhound Inn at its north end proved an exception.[48] While it is tempting to imagine that this power-broker coterie of Douglas, Smith and Heathcote did business there, they apparently preferred the nearby Five Bells, where the Folkingham Association usually met.

The elder Benjamin Smith's ties with the Heathcotes appear to have begun in the mid-1760s with the 3rd Baronet, an earlier Sir Gilbert (c.1723-85). Although he had a brief stint in parliament, this Sir Gilbert Heathcote proved a reluctant player. After turning down a seat offered him in 1756, he sat for Shaftesbury in 1761. Never having spoken in the Commons, he chose not to stand again. In any case, it had been his Lincolnshire property not political ambition that prompted his having engaged the elder Smith early on. This may have occurred in 1765, for the Brownlow Toller account with B. Smith & Co shows a property transaction involving Sir Gilbert Heathcote, among others.[49] In subsequent years, Smith was listed as a steward of several Heathcote copyholds.[50] One could go on.[51]

Apart from routine attorney-client business, both Benjamin Smiths, father and son, entered into undertakings with the 4th Baronet, Sir Gilbert Heathcote, who succeeded his father in 1785.[52] In the early 1790s, for instance, the Smiths and the Heathcote estate steward, Thomas Forsyth, tried turning a profit by clothing and victualling Heathcote's militia.[53] This business nexus tied in with Smith Jr's (1776-1858) exercising his mount with the Heathcote troop and his becoming a political operative for Heathcote. Although Heathcote failed in his pursuit of a parliamentary seat in 1794, the Smith-Heathcote team proved a winner in 1796. Besides accentuating the Folkingham power base, that election marked the beginning of a family alliance which endured for more than half a century.[54]

The oath of allegiance makes sense only when the ties between the lesser-known signatories of the oath and its leaders are understood. Most were farmers, graziers or clergy, usually aligned by business, kinship or friendship; some were of surprising affluence. Because of the need to use banking facilities, make investments, wills, conveyances and the like, these countrymen intersected more often with attorney Smith than with politico Douglas, and almost certainly more than with politico-aspirant Gilbert Heathcote, 4th Baronet. The signatories knew Douglas as an enclosure commissioner and one broadly involved in drainage and turnpike matters; they listened to his harangues at public meetings, where his urgings about allegiance to George III galvanized their 'middling sort' actions. Signatory contacts with Heathcote, on the other hand, were far fewer, relating mainly to property, militia and, of course, his politicking. In any case, the allegiance oath was less likely directed against a discredited Stuart dynasty and its despised popish sponsor than to fortify the signatories for whatever they undertook. Camaraderie among the signatories is evidenced in the pages of Benjamin Smith Jr's first diary (1794-99).[55] Although his diary entries allow little more than a fleeting look at any single player, they do show who socialized with whom, where they met and even evidenced an emergent 'politeness'. Their meeting places varied – private homes, public houses like the Greyhound and Five Bells in Folkingham, the Stow horse and Folkingham fairs, and land tax meetings. They visited or were visited, took tea, dined, gossiped, stayed the night and breakfasted next day. Some visits were brief, others went on for days. Such was rustic society in late eighteenth-century England.

Among the signatories most often singled out by Smith in his diary as guests or hosts were James Digby of Red Hall, Bourne; Rev. John Moore Brooke, rector of Folkingham; and Robert Michael Robinson of Hawthorpe (in the parish of Irnham) and Nottingham Place in London. Others – Rowland Litchford, Rev. Humphrey Hyde, Rev. John Myers, Rev. Samuel Hopkinson and Charles James Packe – followed the same ritual, but less often. Both Frank and Ned Smith, younger sons of Benjamin Smith Sr, counted Rowland Litchford as a friend, and Digby, ever a *confidant* of Benjamin Smith Sr, collaborated with him in clothing Heathcote's militia in 1796.

Even deeper bonds of friendship were revealed between the Smiths and signatory Brownlow Toller's family, the Smiths often entertaining the Toller daughters. When the Widow Toller lost daughter Charlotte in August 1795, the impact on the Smiths was evident: 'Charlotte Toller[56] died this morn between 1 and 2. Mother[57] went there [to Toller's] all day.'[58] And for some days thereafter, Anne Toller often took tea and dined with the Smiths; the Smiths, in turn, were often at Widow Toller's.

Similar endearment existed between the Smiths and Jane Douglas after husband Daniel's death in 1793. Both Smiths, Sr and Jr, dutifully attended to the widow's finances until her own death in 1821.[59] Benjamin Jr and his sister Elizabeth periodically paid social calls on Widow Douglas.[60] Benjamin Jr's exercising his mount with the Heathcote militia also signified neighbourly attachment: '7 July 1795: I went this morn to Folkingham to exercise with the Troop. Sir Gilbert [and] Lady Heathcote were there.' Diary entries for the 1790s also show the Smiths' regard for the Graves family,[61] and, although it had no immediate bearing on the oath, Benjamin Jr married Graves's daughter Fanny in 1821.[62]

Diary references, which bespeak fraternization at land tax meetings between the spring of 1795 and midsummer 1798, offer striking insight into the oaths of allegiance; not infrequently they were same-day happenings. It therefore becomes compelling to view oath-signing through the lens of those who attended land tax meetings. The following diary entries show land tax meetings that match or mismatch with oath-swearing occasions:

> 30 April 1795: Father, Worth, and I went Folkingham land tax meeting. Messrs Packe, Myers, Hutchin, Brooke, Hyde, and Robinson, Jr...were there. [Attendees identical to those signing oath-taking on that date.]

> 28 April 1796: Father and I went Folkingham to Land Tax Meeting. Mr. Packe and Mr. Litchford were there. [Identical to the three who signed the oath on this date.][63]

> 9 June 1796: Father and I went to Folkingham Land Tax Meeting. Myers and Brooke were there. Sir Gilbert Heathcote came from Lincoln. [Only Brooke signed the oath on this date.][64]

> 13 July 1797: Commissioners of Taxes met at Folkingham. Messrs Packe, Hopkinson and Myers were there. [No oath-signing on or near this date.]

> 1 Feb 1798: Appeal Day. Father & I went to Folkingham. Messrs. Pochin, Packe, Myers, Hyde, Digby, Hopkinson were there. [Pochin and Hyde signed the oath on this date.]

> 14 June 1798: Attended Stow Horse Fair. Packe, Brooke, Digby, Myers, & Hopkinson were there. [All of the above signed the oath on this date.]

> 12 July 1798: Father and I went Land Tax Meeting in Folkingham. Packe and Hopkinson were there. [No oath-signing on this date, presumably because of the previous signing after Stow Horse Fair.]

That land tax meetings often occurred in April, June and July suggests that springtime or summer merriment, rites, or at least a mood to socialize, figured in the oath-signing equation. The 30 April 1795 oath-taking coincided with such a tax meeting. Another swearing of allegiance occurred on 28 April 1796, when the Benjamin Smiths, father and son, travelled 'on a fine day' to Folkingham for a land tax meeting. On 14 June 1798 both Smiths spent another 'very fine day', this time at the Stow Horse Fair, before proceeding to Folkingham, where Smith Sr and others signed the oath. Although no land tax meeting was held on that day, there had been an oath-swearing earlier that year on Appeal Day, 1 February 1798.[65]

Whilst matching oath-taking dates with those of land tax meetings may have resolved in some measure when and where the oath of allegiance occurred, it does not explain why the oath was such an important aspect of land tax meetings, but it does suggest that the land tax and the oath were linked.

Taxes and the 'middling sort'

England of the 1780s and 1790s, and until Waterloo, was a country beset by a debt largely incurred from its imperial wars. As Daunton observes, 'Britain in the eighteenth century was a nation at war, locked in a worldwide struggle with the French, which ended with the battle of Waterloo in 1815'; it was in other words a 'fiscal-military state', one in which the government was

> dominated by the needs of the army and, above all, the navy for money to wage war. The outcome was an efficient system of tax collection and public finance which allowed Britain to bear a heavier financial burden than France, yet without a political crisis threatening the state.[66]

A statesman like Edmund Burke[67] sought answers to funding by weeding out Old Corruption, while the younger William Pitt[68] focused on servicing the nation's debt by inventive, economical reforms, which included old and new taxes and a pair of sinking funds.[69]

There were two main forms of taxation in the eighteenth century – direct and indirect. The former was raised in the form of land tax, paid by the more prosperous sections of society, and was designed to lay most heavily on the more affluent, who also felt the brunt of indirect taxation in the form of duty on windows, carriages, houses, domestic servants and riding-horses. Another form of direct taxation – income tax – was enacted just before the century's end, truly one of last resort. Indirect taxes comprised customs, excise duty and stamp duty.[70] Customs were imposed on imported and exported goods, such as clothing, timber and tobacco, whilst excise duty was paid on home-produced consumables – candles, brick, glass, soap, starch, beer, hops and malt, to name a few. Commercial services, such as newspapers, bills of exchange and fire insurance, incurred stamp duty.[71]

Of all these taxes, the two most important, at least for the purposes of this paper, were the excise and the land tax. The former, organized bureaucratically and collected professionally, provided welcome relief for a state strapped for cash. Along with a long-term national debt and the growth of public credit, the excise became a crucial component of fiscal-military state strategy for Britain's wars. Yet the excise duty was suspect to countrymen wedded to the land tax. The latter, imposed from 1692 to 1831, hereupon becomes the focus of this article during the period of oath-taking, 1781-1804. Land tax returns, which list houses, owners and occupiers, were sent to the Clerk of the Peace for the quarter sessions each spring. Although administration of this tax may have been less effective than that of the excise, its collection was consistent with a longstanding practice in English administrative history – 'self-government at the king's command'. As Daunton observed:

> It was more than just a tax, it was the way in which it was collected. It was collected locally by amateur administrators drawn from the county community and any attempt to check their assessments by salaried supervisors raised a thorny constitution issue of executive power.[72]

Then, too, this tax spurred communal relationships, as suggested by Boyd Hilton: 'The free-born Englishman had always preferred the land tax, which by virtue of its county-based mode of assessment and collection helped to cement local communities, whereas excise duties threatened to disrupt them.'[73]

Not surprisingly, the unpaid collectors of the land tax were invariably the same 'middling' commissioner/ clerk types who, like Douglas and Smith, attended land tax meetings, facilitated enclosures, engaged in self-help law enforcement, and played and prayed together. They were also the same who, by swearing allegiance

to King George, made land tax meetings an occasion for expressing loyalist sentiment. Why then were they so pliant in the face of the excise menace?

In fact, tension did occasionally develop between the separate advocates of land tax and excise. Daunton notes this concern:[74]

> The British government avoided any attempt at using the land tax as a more realistic means of taxation, which would have inflamed the 'country' party against the crown and ministry. Under-assessment was tolerated because it was preferable to non-payment, and the tax was administered locally, by the consent of those who were liable; it underlined local social patterns, drawing the localities into the central administration, unlike in France where the local community was set against the central government and the _Intendant_.

Arguably, it was this fear of the state's undercutting of the land tax that lay at the root of the oath charade which Daniel Douglas began in the early 1780s and was continued by Ben Smith Sr for another decade after Douglas's death in 1793. While the oath was intended as a serious undertaking, it was wholly non-provocative. Douglas's chief tactic, it appears, was one of urging his 'middling' neighbours to pledge allegiance to King George, at once winning royal favour and deflecting royal tinkering with the land tax. Attacking Jacobitism and popery was a subterfuge, the main intent being one of rallying propertied/loyalist sentiment. Besides advertising the countrymen's rebuff to an insolent underclass at home and England's enemies abroad,[75] this evident loyalism even called attention to middling support of a militia equipped to interdict smuggling.

With Douglas's death, the elder Benjamin Smith, hitherto a non-participant, took up the cause of the oath in April 1796. He continued until 1804, well into his retirement and three years short of his own demise. Smith, whose knowledge of copyhold law and expertise in facilitating credit and investment through his local and City connections, made him a natural to succeed Douglas. Singularly connected to the Heathcotes and other magnates, to a broad spectrum of 'middling' property clients, and to myriad surveyors, estate agents and bankers, Smith through his various legal undertakings had accumulated a vast business archive.[76] He was, moreover, a living memory of land transactions through which he had bonded with propertied locals over the years. If less eloquent and even less flamboyant than Douglas, he was likely to have been more able in consolidating middling support for the Kesteven land tax.[77] One imagines, however, that ageing Ben Smith Sr, though still in control, was in failing health by 1804. In any case, he ceased campaigning for the oath, as did those around him.

Conclusion
Objects, people and ideas are not always what they appear or are purported to be. Such a mirage applies to the

Lincolnshire oath of allegiance. Its rhetoric, which harkens to the unsettled state of late Stuart England in the half century after the Glorious Revolution, does not jibe with the less heroic occurrences of post-1750 Lincolnshire. For these later Lincolnshire countrymen, the underlying concerns were property and stability, not allegiance to a martyred dynasty and a Church which sustained it. Supposedly less volatile, even benign, property concerns bestowed a deceptive calm on late eighteenth-century parish life, which sharply contrasted with earlier revolutionary episodes. Such was the scenario, even though occasional insurrections spoiled this tranquil image.

What the 'middling' countrymen were thinking, their *mentalité* – not that of the Burkes and Pitts – is largely the point of this essay. The oath ritual provided the setting and even facilitated the fusion of kinship, patronage, camaraderie, self-interest and politics – at, of all places, land tax meetings. Unanswered questions remain: was oath-signing a heralded public event or a quiet, business-like undertaking? Was it a bold advertisement of loyalty and ceremony to mobilize the 'improver' community and even intimidate, not always subtly, landless farmers who were variously victimized? Or could the oath have been essentially a pronouncement of localism and loyalty intended to deflect an unwanted excise duty which tilted England toward war and empire? Or might it have been none of these – but merely a festive, ceremonial remembrance of a century's bigotry and xenophobia with no well-defined purpose other than accentuating parish 'belonging' – an amalgam of reference for social attitudes, local customs, topography and the economy?[78]

The 'middling sort' were conservative through and through, despite their hardy diatribes against Jacobites and popery and their support for change occurring on the land beneath them. That this beneficial change was engineered through acts of parliament made it legal and soothing to their collective and conservative conscience. Styling themselves 'improvers' or even 'reformers', the 'middling sort' never entertained the notion that they were speculators or expropriators. Their loyalty to King George, doubtless genuine, was confirmed by a litany of anachronistic harangues against Jacobites and papists. However outdated, such prejudices and their accompanying verbiage could be counted as crowd-pleasers at land tax meetings in the 1780s and 1790s.[79]

The oath of allegiance to King George with its many signatures was really a mirror of country thinking about country matters – with national implications. It called for solidarity during a worrisome time in England's history when this 'middling sort' was hard pressed to preserve old ways and yet cope with new situations which it did not fully comprehend.

Author's Lincolnshire Biography

Dr Schmidt has been researching in the Lincolnshire Archives – at the Exchequer Gate, the Castle and its present location – since the early 1950s. His studies have focused on Dr Thomas Wilson, sixteenth-century Elizabethan ambassador and Principal Secretary; the Hyrne family, who settled in South Carolina in the late seventeenth century; and the Benjamin Smith law firm of Horbling since its founding in the late eighteenth century. These articles have appeared in such journals as *Huntington Library Quarterly* (California), *Proceedings of the American Philosophical Society* (Philadelphia), *Bulletin of the Institute of the History of Medicine*, *Law & History Review*, *The London Journal* and The History of Parliament Trust's volume on the Tudor parliament biographies. His first article on Wilson and Lincolnshire appeared in *The Lincolnshire Historian* in 1958. Since 1994 he has published a dozen articles on aspects of the Smith law firm in *Lincolnshire History & Archaeology*, *Lincolnshire Past & Present* and *The London Journal* – touching on the history of the Smith firm and its partners, its connections with lawyer Robert Kelham, the Langdale family of bankers of London, the Heathcotes of Lincolnshire, and the Worth partners and the fashion world of Second-Empire France. While working at Lincolnshire Archives in the 1990s, Schmidt facilitated the transfer to the Archives of the Benjamin Smith Jr diaries (1794-1853) from owner and partner in the Smith firm, Harry Bowden.

Since his retirement as a professor in legal history in 1990, Professor Schmidt has been a Visiting Scholar at the Institute for European, Russian, and Eurasian Studies at The George Washington University in Washington, DC.

Notes

1. The document was given to the author by Harry Bowden, Esq., a retired partner in the firm, in gratitude, he said, for having written about aspects of his firm's history. For many years this framed document has hung on this author's living room wall in Washington, DC.

2. 'Middling sort' is defined here as propertied farmers and graziers, often merchants and manufacturers, especially 'tradesmen of the market towns, mercers, tanners, butchers, innkeepers, attorneys, bankers, land stewards, physicians, parsons, and the like', as noted by B. A. Holderness, 'The English land market in the eighteenth century: the case for Lincolnshire', *Economic History Review*, second series (1974), pp.557-76, especially p.565. See also T. W. Beastall, *Agricultural Revolution in Lincolnshire*, History of Lincolnshire, vol.VIII (Lincoln, 1978), pp.85-107 and R. J. Olney, *Rural Society and County Government in Nineteenth-Century Lincolnshire*, History of Lincolnshire, vol.X (Lincoln, 1979), chapter 3: 'The Middling Sort', pp.46-71 for detailing this topic.

3. The 'long eighteenth century' is the label ascribed to the period 1688 (originating with James II's flight to France) to the defeat of Napoleon in 1815.

4. H. Butterfield, *The Whig Interpretation of History* (London: G. Bell, 1931). Two recent and excellent works on eighteenth-century England are Stephen Conway, *War, State, and Society in Mid-Eighteenth-Century Britain and Ireland* (Oxford, 2006) and Stephen Conway, *Britain, Ireland, and Continental Europe in the Eighteenth Century: Similarities, Connections, Identities* (Oxford, 2011). See also Kathleen Wilson's *Sense of the People: Politics, Culture and Imperialism in England, 1715-1785* (1998). Jacobitism, which took its name from James II, posed a particular threat only when a Stuart claimant acted in unison with a foreign power. This combination did occur in 1789 to 1796, as well as 1714 to 1723 and 1745 to 1753. See Paul Kléber Monod, *Jacobitism and the English People, 1688-1788* (Cambridge, 1939). Butterfield doubtless had in mind the Whig apologist Thomas Babington Macaulay, who glorified the Revolution of 1688 in Whig and Protestant terms. Almost forgotten, the Whig point of view has had a recent revival in William Cronon, 'Two cheers for the Whig interpretation of history', *Perspectives on History*, 50:6 (2012), pp.5-6.

5. The Revolutionary Settlement of 1689 had as its primary purpose the exclusion of a Catholic Stuart succession. This

aim 'largely determined the development of the English state in the seventy years after the Revolution, influencing both the adoption of 'libertarian' policies like religious toleration and the enactment of repressive legislation – the Riot Act, the Septennial Act, the Black Act' (Monod, *Jacobitism*, p.11). '[Nonjurors' opposition] to Lockean contractualism drew [them] into the realm of legal and historical scholarship, resulting in some of their finest work, as well as some of their most tiresome. Their object was to prove that an indefeasible hereditary right to the crown was a fundamental doctrine of English law. With this aim, John Kettlewell settled his "duty of allegiance" in 1691 by demonstrating the concurrence of natural, human and divine law in the hereditary right of James II' (Monod, *Jacobitism*, p.21). For a detailed discussion of the doctrine of allegiance, see Mark Goldie, 'The Revolution of 1689 and the structure of political argument', *Bulletin of Research in the Humanities*, 83 (1980), pp.473-564, Jonathan Clark, *English Society 1688-1832: Ideology, Social Structure and Political Practice During the Ancien Régime* (Cambridge, first edition, 1985) and Jonathan Clark, *English Society 1688-1832: Religion, Ideology and Politics During the Ancien Régime* (Cambridge, second edition, 2000). Clark discusses early allegiance theory, citing John Kettlewell's 1691 treatise, *Duty of Allegiance Settled Upon Its True Grounds, According to Scripture, Reason and the Opinion of the Church* (Clark, *English Society* (first edition), p.196) and David Hume's *Treatise on Human Nature* (Clark, *English Society* (second edition), p.143).

6. In his introduction to *English Society 1688-1832* (1985 edition, p.1), Clark describes the work as 'revisionist tract'. 'It ventures to sound a note of dissent from the methodological conventions which I have come to realise are almost universally shared by a cohort of scholars who have worked in this field in recent decades, the heirs of the "Whig interpretation of history"; secondly, it begins the attempt to outline an alternative model of English society under the ancient regime, built now around the subjects which the received methodology has typically excluded from the agenda, or relegate to a minor place: religion and politics, the Church and the social elite of aristocracy and gentry.'

7. Roger North (1651-1734), gifted author and Tory lawyer who lost favour during the Glorious Revolution.

8. As quoted in Clark, *English Society* (second edition, 2000), p.265.

9. Linda Colley, 'The apotheosis of George III: loyalty, royalty and the British nation, 1760-1820', *Past & Present*, 102 (Feb. 1984), pp.94-129, esp. p.121. This positive view of the king coincided with twin assaults on the English psyche – a patriotism spawned in part by Britishness and Protestantism, and goaded, no less, by a xenophobic and historic hatred of France and the papacy. *Cf.* Paul Langford, *Englishness Identified: Manners and Character, 1650-1850* (Oxford, 2000) for oath-signatory traits.

10. The pioneering work on the crowd in eighteenth- and nineteenth-century politics is George Rudé, *The Crowd in History, 1730-1848* (New York, 1964). See also E. P. Thompson's classic, 'The moral economy of the English crowd in the eighteenth century', *Past & Present*, 50 (Feb. 1971), pp.76-136, which takes exception to pejorative characterizations of 'mob' and 'riot'.

11. On the face of it, the Gordon riots of 1780, precipitated by opposition to a Catholic relief bill, seemed a model for Lincolnshire oath-signatories. Certainly, bigotry, if not violence, was present, but if Wilson is to be believed, 'the [Gordon] riots revealed the limitations of the nativist, xenophobic themes embedded in libertarian politics' (Wilson, *Sense of the People*, p.265). See also Nicholas Rogers, 'Crowd and people in the Gordon Riots' in *The Transformation of Political Culture: England and Germany in the Late Eighteenth Century* edited by Eckhart Hellmuth, (German Historical Institute, London, 1990), pp.39-55; and Nicholas Rogers, *Crowds, Culture and Politics in Georgian Britain* (Oxford, 1998), pp.152-75. Colin Haydon, in 'The Gordon Riots in the English provinces', *Historical*

Research, 63 (1990), pp.354-59, detects some mob action in provincial England, although not in Lincolnshire.

12. Joanna Innes, 'Politics and morals: the reformation of manners movement in later eighteenth-century England' in *The Transformation of Political Culture*, edited by E. Hellmuth, pp.57-118 and Paul Langford, *A Polite and Commercial People, England 1727-1783* (Oxford, 1989), pp.59, 128-29. E. P. Thompson's 'Moral economy', which John Archer calls the most influential study regarding eighteenth-century England (*Social Unrest and Popular Protest in England, 1780-1840* (Cambridge, 2000), pp.37-41), figures broadly in the context of morality and reform. Calls for reform came variously after reversals in the American War of Independence: Wilson's chapter on 'Radicalism, loyalism and the American war', in *Sense of the People*, cited above, notes reformation of manners, prison reform, anti-slavery and the Old Corruption of Parliament among them. See also Innes' introduction to *Rethinking the Age of Reform: Britain 1780-1850* edited by Arthur Burns and Innes, (Cambridge, 2003), pp.7-10.

13. Philip Harling, *The Waning of 'Old Corruption': The Politics of Economical Reform in Britain, 1779-1846* (Oxford, 1996). This work has an extensive treatment of Pittite (Pitt the Younger) reform, pp.31-88.

14. For the English response to internal and external threat, see J. R. Western, 'The volunteer movement as an anti-Revolutionary force, 1793-1801', *English Historical Review*, 71 (1956), pp.605-14 and Kevin Linch, 'A geography of loyalism?: the local military forces of the West Riding of Yorkshire, 1794-1814', *War & Society*, 19:1 (May 2001), pp.1-22. Conway touches on the matter of local loyalties and a greater allegiance, notably regarding militias, and sees no necessary contradiction (*War, State, and Society*, pp.194-97). For rural unrest, generally, see Archer, *Social Unrest and Popular Protest*, especially pp.28-41 on food riots. See also *An Atlas of Rural Protest in Britain, 1548-1900* edited by Andrew Charlesworth (Philadelphia, 1983), pp.97-103. For rural protest in Lincolnshire, see T. L. Richardson, 'The agricultural labourers' standard of living in Lincolnshire, 1790-1840: social protest and public order', *Agricultural History Review*, 41 (1993), pp.1-19.

15. Paul Langford, *Public Life and the Propertied Englishman, 1679-1798* (Oxford, 1991), p.1.

16. Langford added, critically: 'With this process went widespread agreement that the use of oaths to enforce the individual's allegiance was inappropriate and imprudent. It was strengthened by concern at the extended use of oaths for purposes of law enforcement and tax collection, and also by genteel reluctance to incur the risks attendant on binding obligation' (Langford, *Public Life*, p.71).

17. Agrarian change in south Lincolnshire was treated a generation ago by David Grigg, *The Agricultural Revolution in South Lincolnshire* (Cambridge, 1966), pp.1-219. See also Dennis R. Mills, 'Enclosure in Kesteven', *Agricultural History Review*, 7 (1959), pp.82-97. The literature on enclosures is vast. A good introduction to its legal process (and therefore the role of attorneys in it) is Frank A. Sharman, 'An introduction to the enclosure acts', *Journal of Legal History*, 10 (1989), pp.45-69. For a discussion of the enhancement of the landlord's capital in agriculture, see B. A. Holderness, 'Landlord's capital formation in East Anglia, 1750-1870', *Economic History Review*, 25 (1972), pp.434-47.

18. The quotation is from H. J. Habakkuk, 'English landownership, 1680-1740', *Economic History Review*, first series, 10.1 (1940), pp.2-17, p.2. See Holderness, 'Land Market, Lincolnshire', p.557. For more on the eighteenth-century English land market see G. E. Mingay, *English Landed Society in the Eighteenth Century* (1963) and C. Clay, 'Marriage, inheritance and the rise of large estates in England, 1600-1815', *Economic History Review*, series xxi (1968), 503-518. For a survey of the landownership argument, see J. V. Beckett, 'The pattern of landownership in

England and Wales, 1660-1880', *Economic History Review*, second series xxxvii, no.1 (1984), pp.1-22.

19. The more substantial market town tradesmen – mercers, tanners, butchers, innkeepers – also engaged in buying and selling land (Holderness, 'English Land Market', p.565).

20. As in the previous note, Holderness distinguishes between the Lincolnshire land market and that modelled by Habakkuk, concluding that 'the lesser gentry did not disappear as a major social force. Rather they were recruited continually and variously' (Holderness, 'English Land Market', p.565).

21. Langford, *A Polite and Commercial People*, p.61.

22. Rogers' review article 'Paul Langford's *Age of Improvement*' in *Past & Present*, 130:1 (Feb. 1991), p.202.

23. Professionals – attorneys, bankers, physicians, and clerics – were consumed by the land mania, either for themselves or their clients. Holderness pointedly cites attorneys, whose role was that of counselling, conveyancing, litigation, money-lending and estate management: 'Many if not all lawyers benefited from opportunities offered by mortgages and money-lending. The evidence of the business papers of attorneys based in Lincolnshire, but widely spaced out in time – David Atkinson of Louth, Benjamin Smith Sr of Horbling, and George Tennyson of Grimsby – suggests that the number of properties under mortgage to lawyers at a particular time which later ended up as their fee simple was not purely fortuitous' (Holderness, 'English land market: Lincolnshire', esp. pp.565-67; Beastall, *Agricultural Revolution in Lincolnshire*; and Olney, *Rural Society and County Government* mention them as well. The Atkinson (Emeris) papers are listed in the LAO *Archivists' Report*, 6 (1954-55); the Tennyson papers in *Archivists' Report* (1950-51), 10 (1958-59) and 16 (1964-65) and the Smiths of Horbling in *Archivists' Report*, 12 (1960-61) and 13 (1961-62).

24. *Lincoln Date Book* with additions by Sir Charles Anderson, 1868: his comment appears opposite the entry for 24 April 1810 on p.276. 'Dower' – the final word of the quotation – is frequently mistranscribed as 'power', but it is clearly written as 'dower' in the original manuscript, possibly used in the sense of 'share of'.

25. Copyhold is a form of estate tenure based on the title as copied by the steward on the court rolls.

26. For a further discussion of 'industriousness' and 'improvement', see two innovative studies: Craig Muldrew, *Food, Energy and the Creation of Industriousness: Work and Material Culture in Agrarian England, 1550-1780* (Cambridge, 2011) and Jan de Vries, *The Industrious Revolution: Consumer Behaviour and the Household Economy, 1650 to the Present* (Cambridge, 2008). A recent work on 'improvement' is Sarah Tarlow's *The Archaeology of Improvement in Britain, 1750-1850* (Cambridge, 2007).

27. The Heathcotes had assimilated with the county hierarchies of both Rutland and south Lincolnshire, notably intersecting with the Douglases in Folkingham. *Cf.* A. J. Schmidt, 'Lawyering and politics in Lincolnshire: the Smith-Heathcote connection, 1760s to 1850s', *Lincolnshire History and Archaeology*, 44 (2009), pp.31-41.

28. Folkingham was spelled *Falkingham* in the eighteenth century.

29. *Gentleman's Magazine*, 63, pt 2 (1793), pp.773-74.

30. *Ibid.*

31. See A. J. Schmidt, 'The country attorney in late eighteenth-century England: Benjamin Smith of Horbling', *Law and History Review*, 8 (1990), pp.237-71; W. H. Hosford, 'Some Lincolnshire enclosure documents', *Economic History Review*, second series, II (1949-50), pp.73-79; and Lincolnshire Archives (hereafter LA), Smith 5, Enclosures, *An Act for Dividing and Inclosing the Open and Common Fields, Meadow, in the County of Lincoln; and for Draining and Improving the said Fen* (n.d., about 1764) and LA, Smith 5 (Horbling), *Proceedings of the Commission Appointed by an Act of Parliament Intitled 'An Act for Dividing and Inclosing...the Parish of Horbling...Improving the said Fen'* LA, Kesteven Award 42. This document bears the signature

of commissioner Douglas and clerk Benjamin Smith, among others. For other aspects of enclosures in Kesteven, see Dennis R. Mills, 'Enclosure in Kesteven,' *Agricultural History Review*, 7 (1959), pp.82-97 and Adrian Hall, 'Fenland worker-peasants: the economy of smallholders at Rippingale, Lincolnshire, 1791-1871', *Agricultural History Review*, supplement series 1, British Agricultural History Society (1992), pp.24-55.

32. Benjamin Smith served as clerk to the Black Sluice commissioners and was clerk and auditor of accounts for the turnpike commission in the 1790s. In 1793 he was even nominated by his good friend Thomas Forsyth to succeed Douglas, but was found to be ineligible because of his holding the clerkship. For details, see Schmidt, 'The country attorney', pp.248-50 and notes 55-67. See *ibid.* for Smith's and Douglas's Black Sluice ventures, pp.250-51 and notes 69-74. For more on the Lincolnshire fens, generally, see Joan Thirsk, *English Peasant Farming: The Agrarian History of Lincolnshire from Tudor to Recent Times* (London, 1957) and W. H. Wheeler, *A History of the Fens of South Lincolnshire, Being a Description of the Rivers Witham and Welland and their Estuary, and an Account of the Reclamation, Drainage and Enclosure of the Fens Adjacent Thereto* (second edition, Boston, Lincs, 1896), an enlarged edition of that published in 1868.

33. LA, Smith/10: Benjamin Smith's Account with Daniel Douglas, Esq. This sizable document covers the period January 1788 to July 1793, when Smith served as Douglas's banker until the latter's death. A second portion shows Smith continuing as banker to the widow Jane Douglas from 12 December 1793 until 23 October 1805. Smith Sr's creative accounting is impressive: as banker for Daniel and Jane Douglas, he did not distinguish between their personal transactions and those of Black Sluice Drainage and the Turnpike Commission.

34. LA, HD 70/3/21, Will of Daniel Douglas, dated 1 April 1793.

35. See Schmidt, 'The country attorney', pp.237-71.

36. See LA, Smith/5, Horbling Enclosure cited above (note no.31), shows that Smith was much involved with this Act. Whether he resided in Horbling and worked from there in 1764, the date of this act, is uncertain.

37. Lincolnshire is divided into three ancient units of local government known as the parts of Kesteven, Holland and Lindsey.

38. As M. J. Daunton notes: 'Mortgages and trusts gave considerable power to attorneys who were in close touch with landowners and with traders and merchants. They collected rents and handled legacies, marriage settlements, and conveyances, which gave them considerable knowledge of finance and large sums of money to invest. Capital markets were essentially local and personal rather than national and institutional up to the early nineteenth century, and attorneys were key figures in matching the funds of trustees to the needs of mortgagors, acting as intermediaries between borrowers and lenders.' (*Progress and Poverty: An Economic and Social History of Britain 1700-1850* (Oxford, 1993), p.245). That Smith Sr invested select clients' moneys in the City is indicative of the trust and respect he engendered. Both Smiths conscientiously attended their clients' affairs: after the deaths of Daniel Douglas, Brownlow Toller and Thomas Forsyth, the Smiths comforted their widows and attended their finances. Both Smiths also showed great deference to the ageing and cantankerous Edward Brown (1748-1841), whose mother was a Toller.

39. According to Ben Smith Jr, his father received a salary clerking for the land tax commission (Benjamin Smith II Diary, hereafter cited as Smith 15/3).

40. See, generally, 'Good men to associate and bad men to conspire: associations for the prosecution of felons in England, 1760-1860' in Douglas Hay and Francis Snyder, *Policing and Prosecution in Britain 1750-1850* (Oxford, 1989), pp.113-70. As the topic pertains to the Smith firm, see LA, Smith/11, Falkingham [Folkingham] Association.

41. Using LA, Smith/4, Manorial: I have listed chronologically Smith's copyhold stewardships and lordships in endnote no.45

in Schmidt, 'Country attorney', p.264. Although Benjamin Sr's monetary worth is difficult to assess, he did leave generous sums to each of his children. See The National Archives, PROB 11/1460/47, Benjamin Smith. His principal heir was Benjamin Smith Jr (1776-1858), recipient of the estate and who succeeded in the firm, which he managed expertly for another half century. His daughter Elizabeth received £7,000 and sons Francis and Edward £2,500 and £8,000 respectively.

42. His allegiance to the landed interests was absolute, as articulated when he once promised Lord Willoughby to use 'my utmost endeavours to prove to your Lordship you have not made an improper choice. I will have an Eye to your Lordship's interest & hope by my *Impartiality* [author's italics] to please not only your Lordship but the rest of the proprietors, too' (LA, Smith/5 Enclosures: Helpringham, Smith to Willoughby, 16 June 1773).

43. Sir Gilbert Heathcote, 4th Baronet, appears to have attended one land tax meeting, that of 9 June 1796 (Smith 15/3/2).

44. John Brewer, *The Sinews of Power: War, Money and the English State, 1688-1788* (Cambridge, MA, 1990), p.209. Brewer continued: 'The typical eighteenth-century loan manager and contractor was a man with good banking and mercantile connections and, like Heathcote, ought be a Bank of England or an East India Company director.' J. V. Beckett also notes that 'Londoners continued to play a surprisingly important role in the eighteenth-century Lincolnshire land market', mentioning, among others, Sir Gilbert Heathcote, who dabbled in it (*The Aristocracy in England, 1660-1914* (Oxford, 1986), p.76).

45. Neil R. Wright, *Lincolnshire Towns and Industry, 1700-1914*, History of Lincolnshire, vol.XI (Lincoln, 1982), p.14.

46. The Wynnes had resided at Folkingham Manor until the early eighteenth century, when they relinquished it to the Heathcotes, to which Alexander Pope railed loudly: 'Heathcote himself and such large acre men / Lords of fat Evesham and of Lincoln Fen' (quoted in H. John Habakkuk, *Marriage, Debt, and the Estates System English Landownership, 1650-1950* (Oxford 1994), p.565).

47. A rare picture postcard (1905) shows these continuous facades. This illustration graces the cover of *Lincolnshire Past & Present*, 17 (Autumn, 1994).

48. This massive structure, built in the mid-sixteenth century and refronted in the waning years of the eighteenth century, served as the magistrates' court. Standing tall today, the inn partially shields old St Andrews Church, where Benjamin Smith Sr and his wife were interred.

49. LA, Smith/11, Firm's Business, Bill & Debt Book, 1761-66, p.47.

50. Along with his attorney routine regarding copyhold courts, tithes, enclosures and the like, Smith increased his own status and property holdings. Particularly notable was in 1769 when he was listed as deputy steward of Baston Manor to Thomas White, steward to the lord of the manor, Sir Gilbert Heathcote; in 1779 the Smith firm lists charges incurred by the same Sir Gilbert for holding court in the manors of Coningsby, Cherry Willingham, Bicker/Kirkby Underwood, Hacconby and Rippingale; in 1791 Smith is listed as steward to the 4th Baronet Heathcote of Thurlby Manor (*cf.* LA, Smith/4, Manorial, *passim*).

51. See LA, Smith/11, Firm's Business, Bills, 1773-81; Bills, 1781-91; Debt Book, 1783-97, *passim*. For more on the Smith-Heathcote relationship, see Schmidt, 'Lawyering and politics in Lincolnshire', pp.31-41.

52. Sir Gilbert Heathcote, 4th Baronet, was the first son of Sir Gilbert Heathcote, 3rd Baronet, and Elizabeth, daughter of Robert Hudson of Teddington, Middlesex.

53. See Smith 15/3/1, 20 November 1794, when the Smiths, father and son, dined with Thomas Forsyth in Folkingham. The diary indicates further meetings with Forsyth in November 1795 and April 1796. These visits to Forsyth, which included both Smiths, often combined business and pleasure over tea or dinner, as signified in Smith 15/3/1, 19-21 and 23-24 April 1796. Their meetings continued even after the Forsyths retired to Wimpole

54. Street, London, and with Smith Jr's occasional visits with the Widow Forsyth after Thomas's death in 1801.

54. Smith Jr guided not only Gilbert Heathcote, 4th Baronet, and his son Gilbert John Heathcote (1795-1867), 1st Baron Aveland, through difficult parliamentary elections, but was always also on hand to offer sage financial and property advice to the family until he was felled by a stroke in 1854. See Schmidt, 'Lawyering and politics in Lincolnshire', pp.31-41.

55. LA, Smith/15/3/1 and 2.

56. Charlotte, age thirty-two, the daughter of late Rev. Brownlow Toller and Anne Hyde Toller.

57. Elizabeth Fryer (1742-1820) of Spanby, Lincolnshire, married Benjamin Smith Sr of Horbling in 1767.

58. LA, Smith/15/3.

59. LA, Smith/10, Benjamin Smith's Account with Daniel Douglas, as cited in note no.33.

60. See LA, Smith/10, Benjamin Smith Jr, Smith 15/3/1, no.1, *passim*.

61. Widow Graves and daughter. '9 October 1798: Father and I went Langtof[t] and Baston Courts. Dined at Bourne and I [had] tea at Mrs. Graves. Miss [Fanny] G[raves] of age today. Ned there.' LA, Smith 15/3.

62. They were married on 3 January 1821 at Horncastle.

63. On 23 November 1795 Digby, Brooke and Robinson, among others, attended the Folkingham fair, but there was no oath-signing.

64. There were no diary entries pertaining to Lincolnshire from 1 November 1796 to early July 1797, for Benjamin Smith Jr was studying law in London during this period.

65. The day set to hear appeals by commissioners for any overcharge in the land tax, as cited in Richard Burn, *The Justice of the Peace and Parish Officer*, twenty-third edition, edited by George Chetwynd, five volumes (London, 1820), III, pp.160-62.

66. Daunton, *Progress and Poverty*, p.506.

67. Edmund Burke (1729-97), author, political theorist and Whig member of the House of Commons, supported the American Revolution and opposed the French Revolution.

68. William Pitt the Younger (1759-1806), Prime Minister 1783-1801 and again in 1804. Although nominally a Tory, he was an expert administrator known for efficiency and reform.

69. For the reforms of Burke and Pitt the Younger, I have relied on Daunton, *Progress and Poverty*, pp.514-20.

70. For British taxation during this period, see Patrick K. O'Brien, 'The political economy of British taxation, 1600-1815', *Economic History Review*, new series, 41:1 (Feb. 1988), p.26; Daunton, *Progress and Poverty*, chapter 19: Taxation and public finance, pp.507-32; and Brewer, *The Sinews of Power* (chapter, 'Money, money, money: the growth in debts and taxes'), pp.88-134, esp. pp.95-101. According to Daunton, 'The British state developed an efficient tax system upon which an edifice of borrowing could be erected. Taxes could not meet the massive and sudden costs of war, but they could offer the security for [long-term] loans... The crucial role of long-term loans in the wars of the eighteenth century does not mean that the tax system was inadequate. On the contrary, long-term loans and the capacity to levy taxes were intimately related, for investors were only willing to subscribe to large loans because they were backed by a highly efficient tax regime which guaranteed the payment of interest' (*Progress and Poverty*, p.511). The classic work on England's reordering its finances for conducting war is P. G. M. Dickson, *The Financial Revolution in England 1688-1756* (Oxford, 1967).

71. Daunton, *Progress and Poverty*, pp.507-32 is an excellent account of both the excise and land tax; Brewer, *The Sinews of Power*, pp.101-14 presents a graphic account of the excise; Colin Brooks treats tax administration in his 'Finances and political stability: the administration of the land tax, 1688-1720', *Historical Journal*, 17:2 (June 1974), pp.281-300; and Peter Mathias examines 'Taxation and industrialization in Britain, 1700-1870' in *The Transformation of England: Essays in the Economic and Social*

History of England in the Eighteenth Century (New York, 1979), pp.116-30. The literature on the land tax is substantial, especially on the much-debated disappearance of the small landowner. See G. E. Mingay, 'The land tax assessments and the small landowner', *Economic History Review*, 17:2 (1964), pp.381-88; and J. M. Martin, 'Land ownership and the land tax returns', *Agricultural History Review*, 14 (1966), pp.96-103.

72. Daunton, *Progress and Poverty*, p.509. See also M. Turner and D. Mills, *Land and Property: The English Land Tax, 1692-1832* (Gloucester, 1986) and D. Ginter, *A Measure of Worth: The English Land Tax in Historical Perspective* (London, 1992).

73. B. Hilton, *A Mad, Bad, and Dangerous people?: England 1783-1846* (Oxford, 2006), chapter, 'A new vision of government', p.120.

74. Daunton, *Progress and Poverty*, pp.528-29. Patrick O'Brien comments on this delicate balance of politics and revenue: 'Given the strength of opposition to reforms of the land tax (and what comes to the same thing, to the introduction of an income tax)...Chancellors of the day turned to the only other form of taxation available to them...From 1688 down to the introduction of the first income tax in 1799 excises became more widespread, onerous and effectively collected because excise duties alone proved capable of paying for imperial expansion and funding Britain's "blue water" defence strategy' ('The political economy of British taxation, 1660-1815', *Economic History Review*, new series, 41:1 (Feb. 1988), p.26). J. V. Beckett, in 'Land tax or excise: the levying of taxation in seventeenth and eighteenth-century England', *English Historical Review*, 100, (1985), pp.285-308 notes that 'country politicians [were] aroused to fight the possibility of a general excise: as late as the 1780s the issue could still be guaranteed to raise backbench hackles' (p.304). Beckett cites Donald Ginter, *Whig Organization in the General Election of 1790* (Los Angeles, 1967), pp.146-50. For another comparison, see P. Mathias and P. K. O'Brien, 'Taxation in England and France, 1715-1810', *Journal of European Economic History*, 7 (1978), pp.601-50.

75. Regarding rural unrest in Lincolnshire, see note no.14 above.

76. Among the latter, he counted especially the banker family of Garfitt of Boston as staunch friends and political allies. See LA, Kirkby Pedigrees, Garfitt Genealogy, xxvi, 46-47; N. Davis, *Banking in Boston* (Boston, 1976); Wright, *Lincolnshire Towns and Industry*, pp.66-68; and Beastall, *Agricultural Revolution in Lincolnshire*, p.91. For more on the Smith-Garfitt connection, see Schmidt, 'Lawyering and politics in Lincolnshire', pp.31-41.

77. While the Smith-Heathcote connection is not evident in the oath to King George, it must have been a factor in the Benjamin Smiths' investment ties with moneyed interests in the City. Likely they began with the senior Smith's long-lasting bond with his Billingborough neighbour and mentor, Robert Kelham, his London agent. The Smiths made contact through Kelham with the brokers Marmaduke Langdale Sr and Jr, who facilitated investing Lincolnshire clients' moneys. See A. J. Schmidt, 'From provincial to professional: attorney Robert Kelham (1717-1808) in eighteenth-century London', *The London Journal*, 25:2 (2000), pp.96-109; and A. J. Schmidt, 'The Smith-Kelham-Langdale nexus: country attorneys, family connections, and London business in the early nineteenth century', *Lincolnshire History and Archaeology*, 29 (1994), pp.17-27. Since Douglas had no heirs and Smith's son Benjamin Jr evidently chose not to become party to continuing the practice, the oath-taking ceased with the father's infirmity.

78. See K. D. M. Snell, *Parish and Belonging: Community, Identity and Welfare in England and Wales, 1700-1950* (Cambridge, 2006), *passim*.

79. These themes define eighteenth-century English historiography. The most obvious here are historians Monod and Haydon on Jacobitism and anti-Catholicism; Conway's and Jonathan Clark's divergent narratives on England's eighteenth century; Goldie on allegiance doctrine; Colley on the apotheosis of George III and loyalism; Harling and Innes on reform; Kathleen Wilson on England's American War; Daunton, Brewer; and O'Brien on finance and taxation; Rudé, Rogers, and E. P. Thompson on the crowd/mob; Langford, Beckett, and Rogers again on property and the 'middling sort'; Habakkuk and Holderness on 'the general drift of property' and 'the Lincolnshire exception'; Muldrew on 'industrious improvers'; and, finally, Snell on localism, notably 'parish belonging'.

Four Whetstones from Roman Fiskerton: a Wealden (Surrey/West Sussex) product in Lincolnshire

J. R. L. Allen

Introduction

The village of Fiskerton lies in the valley of the River Witham some seven kilometres east-south-east of the city of Lincoln. In 1981 the north bank of the river near the village was the site of a twelve-week excavation of a complex wooden causeway of the middle Iron Age, which proved to be of international archaeological significance.[1] The causeway, perhaps begun for purposes of communication, evolved into a site for votive depositions.

The practice of votive deposition continued into Roman times up to and including the third century AD.[2] The substantial assemblage of Roman artefacts recovered from the causeway and nearby amounted to abundant pottery, some tile and brick, and bronze and iron metalwork including bowls, bracelets and rings. Additionally, four whetstones, two complete though used, were found and recorded.[3] As reported and claimed by D. T. Moore in this account, 'the mineralogical composition of the whetstones is limestone with ostracods, containing quartz and glauconite. This is consistent with Kentish ragstone from the Hythe Beds of the Greensand of Kent.' Reference was made to apparently similar whetstones from sites widely distributed across Roman southern Britain, in particular the hoard of about a hundred whetstone blanks from the late second-century forum at Wroxeter, which had also been attributed to Kentish rag.[4]

A recent comprehensive scientific study of the Wroxeter whetstones has shown beyond reasonable doubt that the source was not Kentish rag but a sandstone (or sandstones) in the slightly older Lower Cretaceous Weald Clay Formation at a location somewhere in the north-west Weald of Surrey or West Sussex.[5] The purpose of the present paper is, therefore, to give a scientific reassessment of the Fiskerton whetstones and to consider the national distribution of similar artefacts, humble but so important for the maintenance of all kinds of edge-tools, whether for domestic, industrial or military use. As Atkinson surmised at Wroxeter, a substantial Roman industry can be shown to have been at work.[6]

Typology

The account of the whetstones by Parker Pearson was illustrated by D. Taylor of the University of Nottingham.[7] Figure 1 depicts again some aspects of these stone bars in order to bring out a number of salient features.

Object 227 is a complete whetstone measuring 327mm in length and with a slightly variable but almost square cross-section of about 34mm by 32mm. The ends are broken and irregular with signs of bruising. The main faces are smooth and flat to faintly convex as a result of use. Along each edge of the illustrated face there are shallow, right-angled rebates that are most conspicuous toward one or both ends of the whetstone, tending to fade in the middle as the result of greater wear in that part. These features are lacking on the opposite edges, which are either rounded or bevelled.

Somewhat longer, at 349mm, whetstone 246 is also complete, but with a more markedly rectangular and slightly variable profile measuring about 35mm by 24mm. The ends are broken and irregular but with no sign of the bruising seen on 227. In the aspect depicted, shallow rebates that fade toward the middle are limited to the ends of one edge; the trace of a rebate is seen at one end of the opposite edge. On the concealed side, these rebates are evident at the ends of the bar, fading toward the middle as the result of use. The edges are otherwise rounded. The main faces are flat, as are the

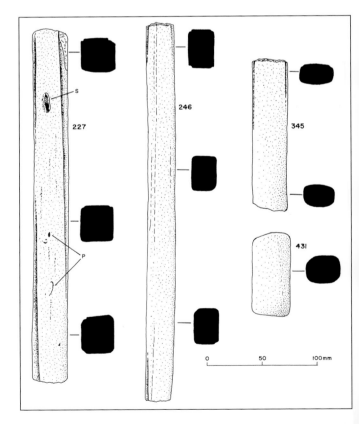

Fig.1. Selected views of the whetstones of Weald Clay Formation sandstone from Roman Fiskerton. P – macroscopic plant material. S – fossil shell.

Fig. 2. Photomicrograph of a whetstone (object 227) of Weald Clay Formation sandstone from Roman Fiskerton. Plane-polarized light.

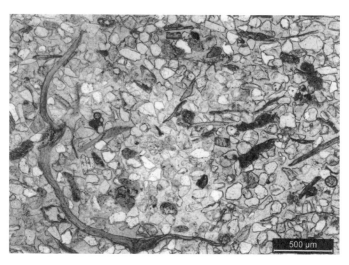

Fig.3. Photomicrograph of a whetstone (object 345) of Weald Clay Formation sandstone from Roman Fiskerton. Plane-polarized light.

subordinate faces, except toward one end where a slight convexity is developed.

Object 345 has a length of 142mm, a rectangular but rounded cross section of about 34mm by 22mm and irregular, broken ends. It could be roughly half of a complete whetstone like 227 or 246. At one end, where the profile is least rounded, there are short but worn traces of rebates similar to those seen on the complete whetstones. There are no traces of these features on the concealed face.

At 76mm, the shortest of the whetstones, object 431, has a squarish, well-rounded profile that measures about 33mm by 28mm. There are no signs of rebates and, in contrast to the other whetstones, the ends are smoothed and rounded with only traces here and there of the originally broken surfaces. This whetstone could also be a fragment broken from a whole specimen.

Material
All four whetstones are of the same rock. In hand-specimen it is a dense, compact, calcareous very fine- to fine-grained sandstone. The colour ranges from light olive grey (Munsell 2.5GY 7/1) in objects 345 and 431 to the slightly darker light greenish grey in 227 (Munsell 2.5-7.5GY 7/1) and 246 (5-10GY 7/1). Traces of delicate, millimetre-scale, parallel laminations are seen longitudinally in all four whetstones. In 246 these are very slightly curved and just perceptibly convergent, giving a noticeably curved overall shape and uneven cross-section to the bar. The rock is slightly micaceous and throughout it are scattered variably abundant black grains taken to be carbonaceous. Locally, they are sufficiently plentiful as to define laminae. Occasionally seen, especially in 227, are macroscopic, carbonaceous, leaf- or stem-like plant fragments (Fig.1). The stem-like ones are circular to oval in cross-section, with an infilling

of sandstone. Fossil shell debris is very occasionally evident. The most conspicuous, again in 227, is part of a bivalve shell ornamented with fine, radial ribs marked by faint growth lines (Fig.1), probably a form of cockle (*Cardium* sp.). The calcareous cement is lustre-mottled on a millimetre scale. It is so firm and complete that the two longest whetstones emit a musical note when suspended from the fingers and lightly struck.

A distinctive character is presented by the rock in thin-section under the petrographic microscope (Figs 2 and 3). The four whetstones are seen to share the same essential components but in different proportions. The rock is a calcareous, very fine (227) to fine-grained (345) quartz sandstone with faintly to boldly marked lamination. Quartz varies from just dominant (345) to predominant (227, 431), in the form of angular to sub-angular grains, exactly what are required in a high-quality whetstone. Grains of coarsely to finely microcrystalline chert are rare. Feldspars are very rare and include orthoclase and microcline. Present in all four thin-sections are scattered grains of muscovite, very occasional green biotite, and occasional bright green grains of glauconite. Clasts of micrite and sandy micrite are occasionally seen (345). Bioclastic material varies from uncommon (227) to abundant (345), chiefly in the form of ostracod and generally subordinate echinoderm debris but including occasional foraminifera. Orange to pale brown fragments of bones and scales are conspicuous but very rare. Varying in abundance from very rare (227, 431) to common (345) are partly pyritized, carbonaceous (?charred) grains, on the whole larger than the associated quartz. They vary considerably in shape, from roughly equant to irregular and markedly elongate, like compressed leaf fragments. Some of these grains display clear anatomical structure and complement the macroscopic plant material seen in hand-specimen (for example, 227). In all cases the cement is calcite lustre-mottled on a millimetre scale.

71

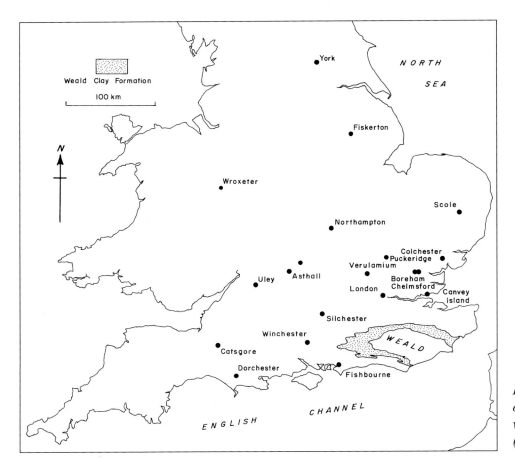

Fig.4. Geographical distribution of Roman sites in southern Britain with whetstones of Wroxeter type (after Allen and Scott, 2013).

Manufacture and use

Compared to Romano-British whetstones generally, those recovered from Fiskerton are of high quality in terms of material, form and method of manufacture. The sandstone used to make them was evidently of the flaggy variety, that is, it could be split along laterally persistent laminae into roughly parallel-sided slabs, which could then be further divided. The process of manufacture was distinctive, and seemingly the same as that of the hoard of whetstone blanks described by Atkinson from Roman Wroxeter.[8] According to him 'A slab of stone having been produced and cut to the approximate width of a Roman foot, parallel grooves were cut about 1 inch apart on each side, sufficiently deep to enable the bars to be successively snapped off by a sharp blow.' The rebates seen along the edges of every blank at Wroxeter, and to an extent reduced by wear at Fiskerton (Fig.1), are the remnants of these grooves. Their roughly right-angled profiles and sharp, straight edges suggests that they could have been cut using a, perhaps slightly convex, saw armoured with wetted sand. They were not fashioned using the cruder mason's point, as Cantrill[9] wrongly supposed for the Wroxeter whetstones but as Manning[10] correctly surmised for the early Roman industry at Usk. In that case the grooves have a V-shaped profile and are irregular along their length.

The whetstones from Fiskerton have all been used, but to different extents and probably in different ways (Fig.1). The short fragment 431 has a well-rounded profile and

well-rounded ends. The latter in particular suggest that it was held stylus-like in the hand and used to burnish metal rather than sharpen edge-tools. The somewhat longer 345, with a rounded profile, may also have been held in the hand, but in order to sharpen tools or weapons rather than burnish metal. The complete whetstones 227 and 246 are most worn by use in the middle but otherwise present mainly broad, flat faces. They could either have been hand-held when applied to a large object, such as a sword or scythe, or placed on a suitable surface and the object to be sharpened moved to-and-fro over them, if the item was a knife or chisel.

Discussion

The Fiskerton whetstones have been directly compared with representative blanks from Wroxeter. Typologically, the Fiskerton bars (Fig.1) are somewhat longer than the Wroxeter blanks, which typically measure from 290mm to 305mm with a few up to 320mm, but are closely similar to a complete specimen seen from a mid-Oxfordshire site at 337mm.[11] In all three cases the long edges carry roughly rectangular rebates. In hand-specimen and microscopic thin-section the materials used at Fiskerton and Wroxeter cannot be distinguished. As described above, the Fiskerton sandstone (Figs 2 and 3) is closely similar in colour, grade, paucity of shelly fossils, and style of cementation to that described from Wroxeter.[12] In thin-section, the Fiskerton rock is a close match for the Wroxeter sandstone: especially notable in both cases is the excellent grain sorting, the very sparse glauconite, the occurrence of ostracods, and

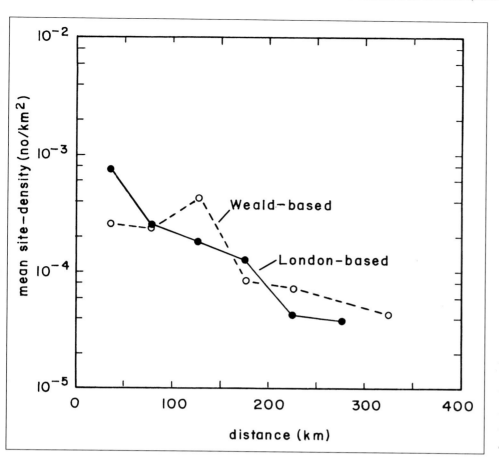

Fig.5. Fall off in the areal density of Roman sites in southern Britain with whetstones of Wroxeter type, based on figure 4 (London counted as a single site). Note the semi-logarithmic scale.

the presence of variable amounts of charred plant material, some displaying anatomical structure.[13] Other points of comparison are the presence in some whetstones of curved laminae and the musical response of the more complete examples to a light tap.

The view widely promoted in the past that the Fiskerton and similar whetstones were made from Kentish rag (Hythe Beds) is now seen to be incorrect. On the grounds of general lithology, microscopic petrography, plant content and detrital heavy-mineralogy, Allen and Scott were able confidently to assign the Wroxeter rock to a sandstone (or sandstones) in the Lower Cretaceous Weald Clay Formation of the north-west Weald. This formation, up to 450m thick and complex lithologically, is of mixed freshwater, brackish and shallow-marine origin. It is predominantly argillaceous, with at outcrop a deep weathering zone, but includes upward of thirty mappable sandstone units, from a few to a few tens of metres thick, which can be traced laterally for distances of hundreds of metres to many kilometres. As summarized by Allen and Scott,[14] the sandstones are typically very fine- to fine-grained, calcareous, lustre-mottled and variably micaceous, many with scattered glauconite and 'coalified' plant fragments. Abundant ostracods are the main shelly fossils, but fossil oysters and cockles are occasionally found. The rocks appear to have been deposited in estuarine-coastal environments where vigorous waves and currents shaped beaches and shoals on which, under Lower Cretaceous conditions,

sand of fluviomarine origin became mixed with charcoal and charred plant material washed in from nearby land by episodic river floods after wildfires, a combination of circumstances now familiar in eastern Australia. The outcrop of the Weald Clay Formation in the north-west Weald is very poorly exposed, however, and today lacks working quarries; the site of the Roman quarries or mines has yet to be found but could lie in a villa-estate.

Fiskerton is far from being the only site at which Wroxeter-type whetstones are recorded (Fig.4). Allen and Scott identified eighteen other locations, including York, Dorchester, Fishbourne, London (several sub-sites) and Colchester, where such tools are found; their details need not be repeated here.[15] At six of these a direct and conclusive comparison with Wroxeter was possible in both hand-specimen and thin section. For the remainder, the published description of the whetstones, typically including petrographic details, was sufficiently comprehensive as to leave little doubt about the geological origin of the sandstone used. There are other, suggestive records, but these sites are not included in the distribution map.

If, as claimed here, the whetstones were manufactured on the outcrop of the Weald Clay Formation in the north-west Weald, the areal density of the mapped sites should fall off with increasing distance away from it. Fiskerton itself lies about 230km as the crow flies from the putative geological source. The available sample is relatively small, and perhaps not without biases, but figure 5 clearly shows the expected overall declining trend. This graph was constructed by first drawing concentric circles an arbitrary 50km apart centred on the putative geological source. The number of sites falling within successive pairs of circles was then related to the approximate land area contained within those pairs to yield the mean site-density (no/km^2). It was thus assumed at this initial stage of analysis that the whetstones were directly traded from the geological production site, but this need not necessarily have been the case. An agent or middleman in operating in London, at the heart of the Roman road system, could alternately have been the effective source. A second analysis based on London makes this highly plausible (Fig.5). Both trends are roughly negatively exponential, as may be expected on the basis of investigations of other artefacts, mainly ceramics and Prehistoric stonework, but that based on London is much the better fit.[16] These trends have a certain predictive quality. Many sites should occur in and around Roman London, as indeed seems to be the case, but few should be expected in the more distant far north and west of the province.

The investigation reported above establishes that the whetstones from Roman Fiskerton belong to a class of stone artefacts with a wide, but not even, distribution in southern Britain from at least the second century AD. These artefacts – whetstones – were neither expensive nor glamorous but, like quernstones, for example, of Old Red Sandstone[17] or Lodsworth rock,[18] also the basis of important stone industries in southern Britain, were vital to everyday life in the Roman world. Atkinson was thus both accurate and prescient when many years ago he wrote of the Wroxeter whetstones that 'we have here a consignment from a quarry which did a large and widespread business',[19] a conclusion later echoed by Peacock,[20] Rhodes[21] and Parker Pearson.[22]

Acknowledgements
I am greatly indebted to Antony Lee (Collections Access Officer, The Collection, Lincoln) for his interest and the generous opportunity to make a scientific examination of the Fiskerton whetstones, to John Jack (University of Reading) for thin-sections, and to Michael Andrews (University of Reading) for photomicrographs.

Notes

1. N. Field and M. Parker Pearson, *Fiskerton. An Iron Age Timber Causeway with Iron Age and Roman Votive Offerings: the* 1981 *Excavations* (Oxford, 2003).
2. N. Field and M. Parker Pearson, *Fiskerton*, pp.115-24.
3. M. Parker Pearson in N. Field and M. Parker Pearson, *Fiskerton*, pp.120-24.
4. F. W. Anderson, F. Macalister and D. Williams, 'Stone implements and other worked stone' in *The Roman Baths and* Macellum *at Wroxeter. Excavations by Graham Webster* 1955-85 edited by P. Ellis (Swindon, 2000), pp.188-90; R. White and P. Barker, *Wroxeter. Life and Death of a Roman City* (Stroud 2002), p.64.
5. J. R. L. Allen and A. C. Scott, 'The whetstones blanks from the forum gutter at Roman Wroxeter: the case for provenance', *Shropshire History and Archaeology*, 87 (2014 [for 2012]), pp.1-12.
6. D. Atkinson, *Report on Excavations at Wroxeter (The Roman City of Viroconium in the County of Salop)* (Birmingham, 1942), p.130.
7. M. Parker Pearson in N. Field and M. Parker Pearson, *Fiskerton*, pp.120-24.
8. D. Atkinson, *Report on Excavations at Wroxeter*, p.120.
9. T. C. Cantrill, 'Report on Uriconium', *Archaeologia Cambrensis*, 86 (1931), pp.87-98.
10. W. H. Manning, *Report on the Excavations at Usk 1965-1976. The Roman Small Finds* (Cardiff, 1995), ch.17.
11. R. Shaffrey (pers. comm, 2012).
12. J. R. L. Allen and A. C. Scott, 'The whetstones blanks from the forum gutter at Roman Wroxeter'.
13. *Ibid.*
14. *Ibid.*
15. *Ibid.*
16. I. Hodder, 'Regression analysis of some trade and marketing patterns', *World Archaeology*, 6 (1974), pp.172-89.
17. R. Shaffrey, *Grinding and Milling. A Study of Romano-British Rotary Querns and Millstones Made from Old Red Sandstone* (Oxford, 2006).
18. R. Shaffrey and F. Roe, 'Widening use of Lodsworth stone: Neolithic to Romano-British quern distribution' in *Bread for the People. The Archaeology of Mills and Milling* edited by D. F. Williams and D. P. S. Peacock (Oxford, 2011), pp.309-24.
19. D. Atkinson, *Report on Excavations at Wroxeter*, p.130.
20. D. P. S. Peacock, 'Whetstones' in B. Cunliffe, *Excavations at Fishbourne, Volume 11: The Finds* (London, 1971), pp.153-55.
21. M. Parker Pearson in N. Field and M. Parker Pearson, *Fiskerton*, pp.122-24.
22. M. Rhodes, 'Stone objects' in L. Miller, J. Schofield and M. Rhodes, *The Roman Quay at St Magnus House, London: Excavations at the New Fresh Wharf* (London, 1986), pp.240-45.

The Historic Environment in Lincolnshire 2012: archaeology and historic buildings

Edited by Mark Bennet

The notes below cover archaeological work and surveys of historic buildings carried out in Lincolnshire largely as a result of development managed by the planning system. The work was carried out between 1 January and 31 December 2012. Most historic environment work carried out in the county is funded by developers and their input is duly acknowledged. Full reports of this work have been deposited with the appropriate Historic Environment Record where they are available for consultation. A summary list of archaeological work for which the results are either entirely, or substantially, negative will be made available on the SLHA website rather than being published in this journal. Assistance in the preparation of these notes was provided by Mike Hemblade of the Environment Team of North Lincolnshire Council and Hugh Winfield of the Development Management Team of North-East Lincolnshire Council. In addition, the society is publishing here a series of notes, compiled by Adam Daubney, on archaeological objects found in Lincolnshire that have been reported to the Portable Antiquities Scheme during 2012.

Abbreviations

AAL	Allen Archaeology Ltd
APS	Archaeological Project Services
CAC	Caroline Atkins Consultants
FAS	Field Archaeology Specialists
FLO	Finds Liaison Officer
HER	Historic Environment Record
LCNCC	The Collection, City and County Museum, Lincoln
LHA	*Lincolnshire History and Archaeology*
MAS	Midland Archaeological Services
NELC	North East Lincolnshire Council
NELM	North East Lincolnshire Museum, Grimsby
NLC	North Lincolnshire Council
NLM	North Lincolnshire Museum, Scunthorpe
OAE	Oxford Archaeology East
PAS	Portable Antiquities Scheme
PCA	Pre-Construct Archaeological Services Ltd
PCG	Pre-Construct Geophysics

Ancaster: electricity cabling, Ermine Street, SK 9841 4389. Report No.R4966 in the HER.

A watching brief was undertaken by AAL along the line of Ermine Street through the Roman small town of Ancaster. Roman and post Roman deposits were recorded. A buried soil and the remains of a limestone wall of likely late Roman date were recorded at Wilsford Lane and included fourth-century Roman material. Further structural remains of likely Roman date were exposed near Paddock Close. A possible ditch or pit, with moderately steep sides, was found at Castle Close although its full extent was not be determined. It contained Roman greyware pottery and animal bone, with further finds of Roman pottery from an underlying buried soil layer. A small quantity of redeposited, late third-century, Roman material was also recovered from opposite St Martin's Church including a single left humerus bone from a pre-natal infant although this could not be confidently dated and is likely to be medieval. To the north of the Roman town, two shallow, north to south aligned graves were exposed. The graves contained the remains of two poorly preserved infant burials. Analysis of the skeletal remains suggests that the individuals were neonatal. Further north of the village by the railway bridge, more fourth-century Roman material was recovered with unstratified late Roman pottery also being recovered from the area. Two large, undated features possibly the remains of former ditches or pits. were also found.

Archive at LCNCC, Accn no.2012.43.

Apley: St Andrew's Church, TF 1092 7504. Report No.R4844 in the HER.

The medieval church of St Andrew deteriorated during the eighteenth century becoming ruinous and by 1816 only the foundations were visible. A resistivity survey and an earthwork survey were undertaken over this scheduled site by APS. The mound where the church stood was surveyed and the resistivity survey identified a linear anomaly that is likely to be one of the buried foundation walls of the church. There were other discrete anomalies which may represent graveyard furniture.

Aubourn and Haddington: Old Church Cottage, Harmston Road, Aubourn, SK 9273 6274. Report No.R4941 in the HER.

A series of pits around this listed cottage were monitored by APS. The investigation revealed a sequence of former topsoils. The date of these topsoils was, in fact, later than the supposed date of the cottage. In addition. limestone blocks used in the foundation of the original cottage were evident in two of the pits, and were embedded into a former topsoil of seventeenth- to eighteenth-century date. This suggests that the sixteenth-century date for the construction of the cottage is an error. Alternatively, it may indicate that the cottage had been rebuilt at its present location, in the eighteenth century, re-using the same material and in its original style. A post medieval pit was also recorded beneath the cottage. Later deposits related to shallow underpinning works and topsoil development of recent date. Finds recovered from the investigation included quantities of medieval and post medieval tile. Archive at LCNCC, Accn no.2012.159.

Belton (by Grantham): Belton Park, SK 9410 3864. Report Nos R4991 and R4992 in the HER.

Archaeological work was undertaken at Belton Park linked to the production of an episode of the Time Team television programme that examined the site of a military training camp during the First World War. A magnetometry survey and a ground penetrating radar survey were undertaken by GSB Prospection. A large number of anomalies were recorded, with several of the former camp buildings and their associated services being identified. Substantial radar responses were recorded in the area of a former camp kitchen block, along with a number of other strong anomalies, thought to indicate the location of stoves for the former barrack blocks. Trial trenching was then conducted by Wessex Archaeology. Eight trial trenches were excavated, and whilst few structural remains of the camp were identified, a substantial number of artefacts was recovered, illustrating many aspects of everyday camp life. Photographs of the site under construction show that the camp was largely comprised of timber-framed buildings, raised above the ground, and built to a standardised design. It is believed that these buildings were dismantled and removed from the site, almost immediately after the camp closed in 1920. The majority of the archaeological features that were recorded related to the provision of services for the camp buildings, and included the remains of a number of drains and water pipes, pathways and road surfaces. A number of construction cuts and postholes were also identified, giving the location of several of the former buildings. A considerable quantity of material relating to the use of the camp was recovered during the evaluation, and included a large assemblage of pottery and glass, mostly comprising various kinds of serving wares and vessels used on a daily basis by the camp inhabitants. In many cases, maker's marks or stamps could be seen on the items, allowing an identification of the manufacturer to be made. It appears that much of the material was not made locally, but rather that the camp was supplied in bulk from centralised, government-appointed suppliers. Other artefacts recovered included a range of military related material including ammunition rounds; badges, buckles and buttons; fragments of army boot soles; and tent pegs and fittings. A small assemblage of animal bone was recovered, including fragments of cattle, sheep and domestic fowl. These almost certainly reflect prepared joints of meat, brought to the camp as provisions for the soldiers.

Bonby: Hall Farm, Middlegate Lane, TA 0158 1696. Report in the HER at NLC.

Trial trenches were excavated by the York Archaeological Trust and three of these investigated the two parallel linear ditches that had been identified in an earlier geophysical survey (see *LHA*, 47 (2012), p.73). Both ditches were major works being between 1.15m and 1.6m deep and between 2.9m and 3.7m wide at the present ground surface. Most of the pottery from these features was shell-gritted, of mid to late Iron Age date, and two sherds, tempered with mineral calcite, may have been traded from East Yorkshire. One environmental sample, from the upper fill of the northern ditch, produced charcoal and cereal grains. The charcoal was from an unusual collection of wood types, including apple/rowan, plum/cherry and oak. This suggests intentional species selection from open scrub woodland. Cereal types included hulled barley, rye and emmer wheat, and possibly spelt wheat. The two ditches were probably too large to be trackside ditches, especially considering the very good natural drainage of the underlying chalk. They were interpreted as land boundaries, adjacent to an access trackway, probably cut in the middle Iron Age with initial silting and backfilling occurring during the late Iron Age. The ditches may have survived as landscape features until as late as the first century AD. Apart from these ditches very few archaeological remains were found in any of the other trial trenches.
Archive at NLM, Accn code BYAN.

Boston: bore columns from the Boston Barrier, TF 3285 4283. Report No.R4791 in the HER.

Palaeoenvironmental examination of the samples and columns taken from boreholes drilled during geotechnical investigations was undertaken by APS. Previous examination of boreholes in the immediate vicinity had revealed prehistoric peat deposits dated to about 3000BC (see *LHA*, 47 (2012)). There was evidence of medieval river silt deposits dating from the thirteenth to the sixteenth centuries, that had probably been laid down after a river wall was installed in the medieval period. In general, the samples showed natural sequences of river silts, coastal marsh, tidal and marine deposits and evidence of freshwater fen. Former ground surfaces, represented by deposits of peat, were recognised. These are likely to be prehistoric in date, however, no evidence of human activity was revealed.
Archive at LCNCC, Accn no.2012.40.

Bottesford: Frederick Gough School, Grange Lane South, SE 9020 0779. Report in the HER at NLC.

A magnetometer survey was undertaken by AAL and one area of possible archaeological interest was detected, a curvilinear positive anomaly in the south-west corner of the survey. Later seven trial trenches were excavated by the same archaeological contractor. Two buried soil horizons were identified one containing a small sherd from an early Bronze Age beaker, decorated with an incised diamond pattern. Both these horizons were thought to be potentially of Bronze Age date. Elsewhere on the site a disc-shaped flint scraper of Neolithic or Bronze Age date was found. Two layers of another former land surface were recorded above these earlier layers. This later land surface was dated by pottery finds to the second and third century AD or later; the pottery was similar to that from the Little London kilns at Torksey. Eleven ditches, orientated east to west, were recorded in one trench. They were all similar in form, with steep sides and largely flat bases and, because of their similarity, they were thought to represent the regular recutting of boundary ditches over a period of time. A single pit or posthole was located to the south of these ditches. In the same trench were the fragmentary remains of five further ditches. A few fragments of Dalesware pottery from one of these dated them to the third century AD. These ditches had been cut by a more substantial ditch on a north-west to south-east orientation. This ditch had been recut twice. Several groups of pottery were found within this ditch including the remains of perhaps six Dalesware jars of the third century AD. Dalesware is thought to have been a local pottery made at Scunthorpe and Messingham. There may have been a production site nearby, or the pottery could have been from a nearby domestic settlement. Two pits were also found and some indication that crop processing took place in the area. An undated north-west to south-east ditch was also found. Archive at NLM, Accn code SCAH.

Bratoft: Bratoft moated manor, TF 4740 6526. Report No.R4867 in the HER.

A programme of survey work in and around the moated site was undertaken by AAL for the National Trust. This included earthwork survey, geophysical survey and augering. The moated site is known to have been the location of Bratoft Hall, a house built by the Markham family, who owned the site between 1409 and 1538. The house subsequently passed through marriage to the Massingberds who, in 1698, had Bratoft Hall demolished and moved to a new house at Gunby. The moat has moderately steep sides and a largely flat base, and continues to hold water in places. Two small areas of structural remains were identified: a nine metre length of stonework on the inner face of the eastern side of the moat, thought to be the remains of a revetment wall, and an area of brickwork on the southern side of the causeway, which probably formed part of a bridge. The magnetometry survey undertaken on the land within the moated enclosure revealed anomalies associated with the construction and demolition of the hall, including likely wall foundations, yards and rubble spreads. The survey indicated a likely plan of the manorial complex, with the main range of the hall aligned north to south along the western edge of the moat. There was a smaller range along the northern edge of the moat, running into a possible courtyard in the

north-eastern corner of the enclosure. Eight auger transects made across the moat identified the original profile of the moat. It was approximately three metres deep and up to four metres wide at its base when it was first dug. None of the samples recovered were waterlogged or rich in organic remains, suggesting the moat fills have been subjected to repeated wetting and drying.

The earthworks around the remains of Bratoft moat were also surveyed. These possibly represent the remains of an Elizabethan formal garden. The earthworks to the immediate north and east of the moat comprise a number of linear banks and ditches, thought to be the remains of pleasure or kitchen gardens. To the east were two ponds, originally separate, but now joined by a small channel, that may have been fish ponds as well as being ornamental. Substantial earthworks to the south of the ponds possibly represent a later expansion of the formal gardens and comprise the remains of at least one but possibly three small, rectangular ponds and a number of pronounced curvilinear earthworks, possibly representing raised walkways, water-filled canals and prospect mounds.

An area, further to the south-east of the moat of Bratoft Hall, was also surveyed. These earthworks were different in form from those immediately around the moat, and were thought to represent the remains of medieval settlement, including tofts and crofts. These earthworks are characterised by a series of banks and ditches, forming elongated, sub-rectangular enclosures.

Burgh-le-Marsh: Hall Lane, TF 5008 6457. Report No.R4954 in the HER.

Two trial trenches were excavated by PCA. Within the topsoil of one of the trenches, four flints were found, three flakes and one scraper. The scraper may be a late Upper Palaeolithic tool. Also a whetstone, possibly Roman, was found in the topsoil of this trench. An east to west aligned ditch was revealed containing two sherds of a mid fifth- to ninth-century jar and two animal long bones. There was, in addition, an undated gully and a sherd of late thirteenth- to fifteenth-century pottery. Archive at LCNCC, Accn no.2013.204.

Careby, Aunby and Holywell: Holywell Quarry, SK 9889 1625. Report No.R4959 in the HER.

A field walking survey was conducted by University of Leicester Archaeological Services to the north of the present stone quarry. The survey recorded a broken flint knife of likely Neolithic/Bronze Age date (though it may possibly be of earlier Palaeolithic date) and a small concentration of fire-cracked stones that were also probably prehistoric. There were, unusually, no sherds of medieval pottery and only one sherd of post medieval pottery found during the field walking. This suggests that the land had not been ploughed and manured regularly and had been used as pasture for a considerable length of time. Archive at LCNCC, Accn no.2012.57.

Colsterworth: Woodlands Drive, SK 9323 2431. Report No.R4885 in the HER.

A magnetometry survey was undertaken by APS. The magnetic anomalies that were found were interpreted as two possible enclosures with related ditches and a series of pits in a linear alignment. These features were overlain by medieval ridge and furrow.

Croft: The Hollies Solar Park, TF 4958 6341. Report Nos R482 and R5061 in the HER.

A magnetometry survey was conducted by Archaeological Services WYAS and afterwards twenty-one trial trenches were dug by the same company to evaluate the site. A small quantity of prehistoric flints were found. All were residual and comprised two cores, a scraper and four flakes.

The survey work identified a plethora of linear and curvilinear anomalies, relating to a Roman settlement. The trial trenching investigated these anomalies and confirmed that the site was an extensive later Iron Age and Roman settlement, including numerous ditches, pits and enclosures. The quantity and alignments of the features suggest continued use of the site over a long period, with the recutting of many of the ditches and enclosures, and the addition of new areas of activity. A considerable quantity of late Iron Age and Roman pottery was recovered, and comprised an extremely wide variety of vessels, ranging from coarse wares to imported Samian and dating from the late Iron Age to the late third century. Fragments of a near complete possible lamp or crucible were also recovered. Metal artefacts recovered from the ditches included two brooches, an iron knife, an iron tumbler-lock slide-key and several small iron nails and fittings. A considerable quantity of animal bone was also recovered, comprising mostly cattle but including horse, pig, sheep, dog and chicken bones. The finds indicate a modest rural settlement. Analysis of environmental samples taken during the evaluation have indicated a mixed cereal economy of wheat, oats and barley, focussing on spelt wheat.

To the north of this Roman site, the magnetometry survey confirmed the existence of a large, almost square-shaped enclosure that had been seen as a cropmark in aerial photographs. The trial trench evaluation confirmed this was a medieval enclosure, with several ditches and pits being excavated. A large assemblage of animal bone was recovered from the medieval deposits, including cattle, horse, pig, sheep, dog and chicken bones, though dominated by the sheep remains, indicating a possible focus on wool production. A small assemblage of medieval pottery sherds was also recovered, indicating a date for this activity between the eleventh and early to mid thirteenth century.

Archive at LCNCC, Accn no.2013.118.

Crowle: Brunyee Road, SE 772 128. Report in the HER at NLC.

Four trial trenches were excavated by PCA. The results indicated a sequence of buried soil horizons and domestic pits. A steep-sided circular pit containing pottery of the twelfth to fifteenth centuries was the earliest cut feature on the site. An environmental sample from the fill contained charred fenland plants, probably from peat burning for fuel. There was also a posthole that contained thirteenth- to fourteenth-century pottery. A series of seventeenth- and eighteenth-century features including pits, post holes and a brick wall-footing were found, and there was also a clay layer with a large round stone set into it which was interpreted as a post pad for a building. This suggested that the clay layer may have been a building platform for a late eighteenth-century structure. Environmental samples from the site contained a combination of barley, rye and bread wheat grains, typical of medieval and post medieval domestic waste. There were also later nineteenth- and twentieth-century features. Some of these features probably relate to buildings facing out onto Brunyee Road.

Archive at NLM, Accn code CWCZ.

Crowle: The Manor gardens, SE 7712 1288. Report in the HER at NLC.

A watching brief was undertaken by APS. Two large ponds or hollows in the west of the site were recorded. They were filled with late medieval and post medieval deposits including, in the first pond, the partial remains of several seventeenth-century leather shoes. It is possible that these ponds were used as retting pits for soaking flax plants as part of flax processing but in the environmental samples that were taken the evidence for retting was inconclusive.

Archive at NLM, Accn code CWDE.

Eagle and Swinethorpe: Whisby Quarry southern extension, SK 8811 6581. Report No.R5121 in the HER.

A magnetometry survey was undertaken by Bartlett-Clark Consultancy that revealed a linear anomaly, thought to be a former land boundary or drain, and several possible pits, all undated.

Fleet: Lowgate, TF 3970 2588. Report No.R4906 in the HER.

A watching brief was undertaken by APS during the creation of a pond. A scatter of post medieval bricks was revealed, likely representing waste from nearby brick production. Brick kilns are recorded about 300m to the south on the 1888 Ordnance Survey County Series map.

Archive at LCNCC, Accn no.2012.167.

Gainsborough: Court House, Roseway, SK 8153 9005. Report No.R4863 in the HER.

Three trial trenches were excavated by Wessex Archaeology revealing the remains of several former terraced brick buildings fronting onto Church Street, some with tiled floor surfaces and internal foundations, and a number of external yards and outbuildings. The structures correlate well with those depicted on historic

THE HISTORIC ENVIRONMENT IN LINCOLNSHIRE 2012

mapping of the site, and are thought to be the remains of nineteenth- and twentieth-century housing, demolished prior to the construction of the Magistrates Court. The excavation did not reach beyond these post medieval and early modern structures.

Archive at LCNCC, Accn no.2012.134.

Heckington: St Andrew's Church, TF 1427 4410. Report No.R4949 in the HER.

A watching brief was undertaken by APS. Two ditches and a posthole were excavated. These features were sealed by a dumped deposit which contained a fragment of fourteenth- to seventeenth-century floor tile which suggests that the features probably date from the medieval period. The dumped deposit pre-dated a nineteenth-century path which had been resurfaced at least once. Some residual medieval pottery was found during the watching brief. Also found were a sherd of late Anglo-Saxon Stamford ware pottery and a possible seventeenth-century pit. An iron, post medieval, chisel was recovered from the topsoil.

Archive at LCNCC, Accn no.2012.145.

Horncastle: Foundry Street, TF 2629 6919. Report No.R5045 in the HER.

Five test pits were dug by PCA. A number of archaeological features were revealed including several ditches and gullies containing animal bone fragments and first-century pottery sherds of both late Iron Age and Roman date. This evidence shows that the area was part of the extensive Iron Age and Romano-British settlement at Horncastle early in the Roman period.

Archive at LCNCC, Accn no.2012.170.

Horncastle: Banovallum House, Manor House Street, TF 2572 6953. Report No.R4856 in the HER.

A watching brief was undertaken by Neville Hall. Human bone fragments from at least three individuals were found. These appear to have come from disturbed formal inhumation burials and may have originated from Roman roadside burials outside the west gate of the Roman walled enclosure at Horncastle.

Archive at LCNCC, Accn no.2011.420.

Lincoln: Zone D, Brayford Campus, University of Lincoln, SK 9710 7104. Report Nos R4818 and R4857 in the HER.

Test pitting was undertaken by AAL. Four prehistoric pottery sherds, a fragment of fired clay, four worked flint flakes and a burnt pebble were found. Later in the year an auger survey was carried by the same company to recover palaeoenvironmental samples from which radiocarbon dates were taken. The Brayford pool area was utilised from the later Mesolithic until the mid Bronze Age when rising water levels inundated the ground and humans abandoned the area. The area continued to be open marsh until the railway line was built in the Victorian period.

Archive at LCNCC, Accn no.2012.93.

Lincoln: Brayford Wharf East, SK 9733 7096. Report No.R4884 in the HER.

Trial trenching was undertaken by AAL. Some eighty sherds of pottery dating from the second to the early fifth century were recovered, including Samian, greyware, mortaria and black burnished wares. A layer that may have been a clay floor surface of a domestic building was found within which were two sherds of Saxo-Norman pottery. This was sealed by a further layer that contained a small number of late tenth- to late eleventh-century pottery sherds. A ditch was revealed also with late tenth- to late eleventh-century pottery as well as hearth or oven waste. This ditch may have been a bedding trench for sill beams from a wooden structure which had burnt down. A medieval feature was uncovered, that was possibly the remains of a wall, sealed by a layer containing fifteenth- to sixteenth-century pottery. Nearby there was a possible floor surface associated with early sixteenth- to seventeenth-century pottery.

Archive at LCNCC, Accn no.2012.120.

Lincoln: Museum of Lincolnshire Life, Burton Road, SK 9721 7219. Report No.R4903 in the HER.

An evaluation was undertaken by FAS. The layers and surfaces of the original militia parade ground were revealed.

Archive at LCNCC, Accn no.2012.123.

Lincoln: new cemetery, Long Leys Road, SK 9608 7321. Report Nos R4974 and R5111 in the HER.

Further excavation was conducted by AAL on this site following an excavation by the same company in 2010 when evidence for significant Roman activity in this area was recorded. Since the full excavation report was not available for the archaeological round-up produced for 2010, the discoveries are presented here. The Roman activity is thought to indicate the presence of a country residence of a wealthy family who owned and managed an estate in this area, close to Roman Lincoln.

The earliest phase of activity dated to the mid to late second century, and consisted of a number of large drains and field boundaries probably associated with settlement activity to the west of the site. The small pottery assemblage included sherds of south and central Gaulish Samian ware, indicating the early settlement had access to quality products from the outset. There was an increase in activity during the early to mid third century when some stone buildings were constructed at the west end of the site. The walls of these buildings survived to between one and three courses high. Box flue tiles and iron clamps were also recovered, suggesting that at least one of the buildings had underfloor heating. Cereal production was a key element of the agricultural economy, with significant amounts of burnt cereal grain being recovered. A stone-built corn drier and an oval oven were also recorded, with quantities of dried grass remains indicating a possible fuel. A large amount of pottery was found in the third-century features, including pieces of Nene Valley wares and imported Samian and a considerable collection of animal bone was also recovered, with a bias towards cattle, with some sheep or goat bones present. Other finds included a cable-type bracelet of typical late third-century date, several fragments of vessel glass and part of a small bronze bull statue.

The settlement continued throughout most of the fourth century until the site was abandoned towards the end of the century. The stone buildings were demolished at some point in the second half of the century, and the presence of burnt limestone and charcoal perhaps indicates that they burnt down. A large quantity of roof tile and hypocaust tile was also recorded. The large amount of pottery associated with this period suggests that the estate continued to function throughout most of this century. The animal bone remains continue to indicate a preference for cattle although a significant quantity of pig bones was also found. Sheep/goat, horse, dog, red deer and domestic fowl bones were also present. A finger ring, bracelet and disc brooch were also recovered. Medieval ridge and furrow which lay above the Roman remains was also recorded.

The excavation conducted in 2012 was to the immediate west of the area previously excavated. The earliest remains identified on the site were those of a Roman building, probably constructed in the second century. This would slightly pre-date the structures identified in the previous excavation. Fragments of painted plaster were found on the interior, and a small assemblage of late second-century pottery was recovered, including a sherd from an East Gaulish Samian ware bowl. To the north-east of the building was an alignment of three postholes with pottery of the same date as the building, probably representing a fence line.

A second possible building was found with a wall of roughly hewn limestone blocks, indicating a late third-century redevelopment of this part of the settlement. A rectilinear grid of boundary and drainage ditches, containing late third- to early fourth-century pottery, was revealed very close to the buildings. The excavator suggested that these ditches were not contemporary with the buildings and were an indication of changes to the organisation of the settlement, with habitation moving away from this area.

The final phase of activity included a much larger boundary ditch containing fourth-century pottery and also included the stone foundations of a building with associated demolition deposits dating to the late fourth century. This demolition evidence supports the late fourth-century date for the general abandonment of the site with little further activity being recorded, other than the creation of a small number of pits of uncertain function.
Archive at LCNCC, Accn no.2011.52.

Lincoln: Church of St Nicholas with St John, Newport, SK 9769 7246. Report No.R5300 in the HER.

A watching brief was carried out by PCA. A stratified layer of clayey sand containing sherds of third- to fourth-century Roman pottery was recorded. Fragments of disarticulated human bone were also identified in the layer. The layer was cut by the rubble remains of a limestone structure of unknown date. Also identified was a limestone rubble layer, thought to relate to the construction of the church in 1839.
Archive at LCNCC, Accn no.2009.102.

Lincoln: Wellington Street, SK 9678 7156. Report No.R4787 in the HER.

A watching brief was undertaken by AAL. A few sherds of early to mid thirteenth-century pottery and tile pieces were recovered several of which were misfired. This suggested that there was possibly a medieval pottery and tile production site in the vicinity. Similar misfired tiles had been found in Depot Street nearby in 2002.
Archive at LCNCC, Accn no.2012.4.

Mablethorpe: Mablethorpe Care Home, Alford Road, TF 4911 8464. Report No.R4869 in the HER.

Two trial trenches were excavated by AAL on a site where aerial photographs show cropmarks of a medieval moated site and associated settlement remains. The trenches revealed a layer of material which was probably deposited in the medieval period. It may have been dumped during the digging of the moat to create an island for high status buildings. Fifteenth-century pottery and animal bone was also recorded. A sequence of medieval pits and ditches containing brick fragments and roof tile as well as late medieval and early post medieval pottery and a medium amount of animal bone was also found. The domestic refuse found shows the site was occupied during the late medieval period. The finds from the pits and ditches suggest that a building on the site was demolished, probably in the mid sixteenth to seventeenth centuries.
Archive at LCNCC, Accn no.2012.106.

Manton: churchyard survey, Church of St Hybald, SE 934 026. Report in the HER at NLC.

A churchyard survey was undertaken by staff of the North Lincolnshire HER prior to the transfer of the grave markers to the edge of the property. The churchyard plans that were produced were deposited with Lincolnshire Archives, monumental inscriptions section. A full electronic archive remains with the North Lincolnshire HER.

Manton: Manor Farm, SE 936 028. Report in the HER at NLC.

The excavation of nine trial trenches was undertaken by PCA. On the higher ground to the east of Manor Farm, a large, early Bronze Age, cordoned urn was uncovered within a circular pit. The urn had scored and slashed decoration and although it was fragmentary it was largely complete. The urn contained the cremated remains of two individuals aged between twelve and sixteen. It was clear that the bone fragments had been carefully collected from the funeral pyre. The cremation pit lay on the south-west side of a large ditch that ran north-west to south-east. This ditch contained small quantities of charcoal (elm, oak and, perhaps, pine), a few charred cereal grains and a charred tuber of false oat-grass. This species is often found associated with Bronze Age cremations and related features. The ditch may be of a similar early Bronze Age date.

Various later linear features and other small features were excavated indicating an enclosed, cultivated landscape of the Romano-British period. The excavated features contained mid first- to mid second-century Roman pottery including a piece of Samian ware dated to about AD120. A single pit was uncovered that contained undated evidence of ironworking in the area. A ditch and earthwork features associated with medieval agriculture was recorded immediately to the west of Manor Farm.
Archive at NLM, Accn code MTBO.

Manton: Robin Hill, Messingham Quarry, SE 927 028. Report in the HER at NLC.
Twelve trial trenches were excavated by Archaeological Survey and Evaluation Ltd. Earlier work had identified a slag mound on the site and one trench was positioned directly across the slag mound. Some fifty-nine kilograms of iron slag and bog iron (natural ore) was retrieved. Samples of charcoal were taken for radiocarbon dating and dates of 2430 bp and 2445 bp (uncalibrated) (late fifth century BC) were obtained, placing this deposit in the early Iron Age. Other samples contained hammerscale, indicating that iron smithing as well as iron smelting was taking place on the site. This mound is slightly later than the early Iron Age slag mounds identified within other parts of Messingham Quarry. The radiocarbon dates for the slag mounds at Messingham Quarry are amongst the earliest dates for ironworking sites in Britain.
Archive at NLM, Accn code MTBM.

Marton and Gate Burton: Littleborough Lane, SK 833 823. Report No.R5071 in the HER.
Excavation was undertaken by APS as part of a community project to examine part of a known Roman settlement on the Roman road leading to the crossing of the Trent and the Roman town of *Segelocum* which is on the opposite bank of the river in what is now Nottinghamshire. The excavation was targeted on two intersecting Roman ditches that were likely to be property or field boundaries. A sequence of features were identified, mostly dating to the Roman period, including pits and ditched enclosures. These features included a high volume of butchery waste and pottery. The pottery recovered during the investigation was predominantly of the second to the third centuries, although there were some later Iron Age transitional types, which may be first century in date,

and there was also fourth-century material. The coins recovered from the site were mid third to early fourth century in date.
Archive at LCNCC, Accn no.2010.174.

Newton-on-Trent: water treatment works, SK 823 737. Report No.R4838 in the HER.
Twenty trial trenches were excavated by OAE and a ditch containing Roman pottery and a fragment of slag was found. The ditch may be part of a Roman field system associated with the known Roman fort that stands beside the River Trent here. A further contour survey of the area by the same company mapped a portion of the medieval ridge and furrow that, in part, overlies the Roman fort and its outworks.
Archive at LCNCC, Accn no.2011.51.

North Killingholme: Hornsea Offshore Wind Farm cable route (phase one), TA 147 182, TA 148 177. Report in the HER at NLC.
Two trial trenches dug by PCA targeted geophysical anomalies identified during earlier evaluation. A series of ditch features dating to the middle to late Iron Age were revealed. On the first site (TA 147 182), the western ditch of a square enclosure was investigated. It may have had a bank on its western side. Much mid to late Iron Age pottery was found in the ditch fills, along with animal bone, metalworking slag and fired clay. To the east of this ditch was a curvilinear feature, recut on its inner side. Iron Age pottery was found inside the feature and it may have been one edge of a circular structure located inside the square enclosure. The oldest feature within the enclosure was a narrow gully that was dated to the middle Iron Age. This gully was cut by a wider ditch that also contained middle Iron Age pottery, as well as fuel ash slag, animal bone, fire-cracked stones and fired clay. This ditch was superseded by a third ditch of the mid to late Iron Age. The mixture of finds suggests that this square enclosure had a domestic use, rather than being purely for livestock, and that metalworking and crop processing took place.

On the second site (TA 148 177), a large north to south aligned ditch was examined containing mid to late Iron Age pottery. The upper fills contained three fragments of poor quality iron ore and late Iron Age pottery. A further sequence of ditches recorded were in a north-north-east to south-south-west orientation. Two narrow, parallel ditches were thought to be the opposing sides of a rectangular enclosure. They were undated, but an adjoining feature contained thirty-nine sherds of mid to late Iron Age pottery, along with animal bones. Nearby were three intercutting ditches on the same alignment. The earliest was sealed under a natural flood deposit. The boundary had been re-established after the flooding, using two successive ditches of a similar depth and profile. There was no dateable pottery, but the ditches were maintained over a long period.

North Killingholme and South Killingholme: Able UK Ltd Marine Energy Park, TA 167 183. Report in the HER at NLC.

An extensive evaluation of land in advance of a proposed marine energy park was carried out. Field walking and trial trenching by AAL followed geophysical surveys by GSB Prospection and Headland Archaeology. Evidence for an extensive Iron Age and Roman settlement was found. The results of the geophysical surveys includes a groups of conjoined rectangular enclosures with a north to south orientation. The western edge of the settlement appeared to be defined by a series of up to five parallel curvilinear ditches. In the south of the settlement there were rectangular enclosures arranged on either side of a broad rectangular open area, perhaps a courtyard. There were also two double-ditched trackways running east to west at either end of this main complex. Several of the smaller rectangular enclosures contained strong discrete responses, consistent with kilns or hearths. Overall the geophysics results indicated a settlement covering about six hectares. Field walking over these fields collected Roman pottery as well as some Iron-Age-style grit-tempered wares. Later trial trenching identified a number of enclosure and trackway ditches containing Roman pottery. There was some evidence for crop processing and iron smithing in the vicinity but evidence of structures was sparse. The pottery assemblage extended from Iron Age type wares to late Roman period coarse greywares. The field walking also recovered a small amount of worked flint and small quantities of medieval and post medieval pottery.

Archive at NLM, Accn code NKBE.

Sleaford: Waste Transfer Site, Pride Parkway, TF 0732 4680. Report No.R4853 in the HER.

Following trial trenching in 2010 on a known late Iron Age and early Roman site (see *LHA*, 46 (2011), p.63) an excavation was undertaken by APS. Late Iron Age features were found and included a ditch that appeared to define an enclosure. The enclosure would have measured some 21m by 16m with a possible entrance towards its northern corner. It may have functioned as a small livestock paddock. Romano-British deposits were spread across the site but mainly concentrated towards the east. The features, ditches and two pits, contained little in the way of cultural material which suggested to the excavators that the area was used for agriculture rather than being close to a settlement. The Romano-British deposits date from the first to the second century with no deposits or finds clearly of third- to fourth-century date. Finds included late Iron Age pottery, sherds of Roman greyware and fineware and a stone muller from a saddle quern which may be of Iron Age date. A number of undated ditches, pits and post holes were also recorded some of which may well be associated with this Iron Age and Roman site. These excavation results indicate a change in the agricultural regime at the site during the late Iron Age to Roman period with the amalgamation of fields into larger areas that were no longer being managed from dispersed farmsteads but rather from an estate centre, such as a villa, in the neighbourhood.

Archive at LCNCC, Accn no.2012.70.

South Cockerington: St Leonard's Church, St Leonard's Lane, TF 3814 8873. Report No.R4881 in the HER.

A watching brief was undertaken by Neville Hall in the churchyard. Two inhumation burials, one an infant and one an adult, were revealed but left in situ at the bottom of the trench. Wooden coffin remains and disarticulated human remains were also identified.

Archive at LCNCC, Accn no.2011.9.

South Elkington: Acthorpe Farm, Acthorpe Lane, TF 3078 8934. Report No.R4876 in the HER.

A watching brief was undertaken by Neville Hall. An east to west aligned ditch was identified which contained late fourteenth- to mid sixteenth-century pottery, two sherds of residual late Iron Age or Roman pottery and two sherds of eleventh- or twelfth-century pottery. In addition a north to south aligned ditch, a possible pit and a gully, all undated, were also found.

Archive at LCNCC, Accn no.2012.80.

South Killingholme: Hornsea Offshore Wind Farm cable route (phase one), TA 148 164. Report in the HER at NLC.

A number of trial trenches were excavated by PCA around and within the moated site at Blow Field. The earliest archaeological deposits found were associated with a probable Romano-British settlement. There were indications that this settlement had late Iron Age origins. One trench contained eight pit and ditch features that produced late Iron Age and early Roman pottery. Much of the pottery was utilitarian shell-gritted ware, typical of the late Iron Age to Roman transition in North Lincolnshire. A further trench some 60m to the north-east produced a distinctively late Roman pottery assemblage of the third to fourth century AD. A soil sample from this area was found to contain twenty hobnails, coal, cinders and charred plant remains. Another ditch close by contained third- to fourth-century pottery in the lower fill and fourth-century pottery in the upper fill. Both fills contained metalworking residue, fired clay fragments, oyster shells and animal bone.

Later activity was associated with the moated enclosure. A shallow pit contained ninth- to tenth-century pottery, as well as a fragment from a fired clay loomweight. A trench located within the northern central section of the moated enclosure contained a complex series of intercutting features representing two phases of activity. The first phase included three pits, that appeared to be of a similar date, containing late tenth- to twelfth-century pottery. There was also a possible ring-gully of mid eleventh- to thirteenth-century date although a sherd of the mid ninth to tenth century was found in one pit. The later phase was characterised by parallel features running north to south. The largest had a channel in the base of the ditch, which may have carried a fence or palisade. The most substantial fill of this ditch dated to the mid twelfth to fourteenth century. A second ditch in this phase contained twelfth- to mid fourteenth-century pottery, with significant amounts of charred bread wheat and fuel materials. Several flood deposits overlay all the cut features in this trench.

The evaluation established that this was the site of late Iron Age and Roman occupation, overlain by a settlement with late Anglo-Saxon origins that continued into the fourteenth century. The range of finds from this site appear to indicate that it may be one of the three manors associated with Killingholme at Domesday. The moated enclosure appears to have been dug at some time in the twelfth century.

South Killingholme: Greengate Lane, TA 1469 1639. Report in the HER at NLC.

Six trial trenches were excavated by Archaeological Research Services Ltd. A large ditch aligned north to south was found; its width varied between 2.4m and 1.9m. There was also a second, narrower north to south aligned ditch recorded. The common alignment of these ditches suggested a shared purpose, perhaps as part of a double-ditched trackway or enclosure. Both ditches were sealed beneath a layer that contained medieval pottery and so were thought to be of Romano-British date, probably part of the complex identified to the north (see previous entry).

A large medieval ditch was recorded, orientated east to west and some six metres wide. The upper fill contained plastics indicating that it was still a landscape feature in recent times. A fragment of charcoal from the ditch was radiocarbon dated to between 1154 and 1255. There was a small assemblage of thirteen-century pottery from the site. The ditch and pottery are probably associated with the former medieval moated site to the north (see previous entry).
Archive at NLM, Accn code SKAL.

Spalding: Westerly Way, Wygate Park, TF 2340 2354. Report No.R4878 in the HER.

An archaeological excavation undertaken by APS identified a series of ring-ditches and curvilinear ditches, two of which were dated to the later medieval period whilst the more recent were dated to the nineteenth century. There were a number of other features in close association with these, including enclosure ditches, pits and post holes. At first some of these features were interpreted as bird traps used in pewit drives but, following excavation, the lack of bird remains found in the ditch fills suggested that that these features were more likely to be the remains of stack stands. The animal bones that were recovered were all from cattle or other large mammals. A series of post medieval dumped deposits were recorded associated with the construction and maintenance of the adjacent drains.
Archive at LCNCC, Accn no.2011.375.

Stenigot: proposed water main, Stenigot to Benniworth, TF 2461 8101. Report No.R4907 in the HER.

A geophysical survey was undertaken that identified geophysical anomalies indicative of pits and ditches or enclosures in the west of the parish.

Sturton-by-Stow: off Tillbridge Road, SK 8933 8017. Report No.R4888 in the HER.

An earthwork survey of medieval ridge and furrow was undertaken by AAL. Two adjacent sections of ridge and furrow were recorded, one broadly orientated north to south and the other east to west. A relatively prominent bank between the two sets of strips is probably the remains of a headland.
Archive at LCNCC, Accn no.2012.104.

Tetney: land at Bishopthorpe Farm, TA 3284 0389. Report No.R4939 in the HER.

Twenty-four trial trenches were excavated by AAL following an earlier auger survey conducted by the same contractor that had identified buried land surfaces and former palaeochannels on the site. The trenching found a dumped deposit containing a high quantity of fired clay, charcoal and other burnt material. The fired clay fragments were identified as briquetage, mostly being pieces of hearth structure. The site is in an area of medieval salt making and a medieval date is most likely. Buried land surfaces and former palaeochannels were also recorded across the site and the ready access to saltwater and firm ground at this location would indicate an area that was very conducive to salt making.
Archive at LCNCC, Accn no.2012.105.

Tetney: wind farm development, Newton Marsh, TA 3284 0389. Report No.R4871 in the HER.

A magnetometry survey was undertaken by AAL. A number of magnetic anomalies indicating likely archaeological features were recorded, including features interpreted as palaeochannels, linear boundaries and several possible pits or infilled ponds. The former channels appeared to correlate well with previously identified cropmarks of medieval salterns and the anomalies are probably related to the salt-making process.

Thornton Curtis: Thornton Abbey, TA 1183 1907. Report in the HER at NLC.

A programme of evaluation involving earthwork survey, geophysical survey and trial trenching was undertaken by the University of Sheffield, Department of Archaeology, as part of a five year programme of investigations in partnership with English Heritage (see LHA, 47 (2012), p.81). Resistivity survey undertaken within, and south of, the central precinct recorded a number of high resistance demolition spreads, probably clearance deposits from the church. One feature may have been a building close to a small medieval culvert. Strongly marked linear anomalies east of the church were the paths of a post medieval formal garden, as was verified by the discovery of a cobble path during later trial trenching. A mound south-west of the church showed archaeological features, including later cuts through the mound, but the origin of the mound is yet to be established.

A magnetometer survey carried out in the same area recorded two parallel linear features running east to west through the centre of the church. These are possibly indications of the stone foundations that would have supported the load-bearing pillars within the church, but it is more likely that they were the outer walls of the original church, which was reused as footings for new pier bases when the church was rebuilt and extended. The remains of terraced banks were visible extending east to west, directly to the east of the Skinner mansion, the seventeenth-century house that later occupied the site of the abbey. These were part of formal post medieval gardens, a section of which was excavated in 2011. There were also similar anomalies to the south of the plot that were represented on the ground by a number of linear earthworks. These banks, given their magnetic signature, are likely to be constructed of tile or brick. The north-west corner of the plot showed two areas of magnetic disturbance that match earthworks plotted on the Ordnance Survey map. Subsequently, following excavation, these proved to be of modern date. The final feature identified was a circular anomaly some twenty metres east of the Skinner mansion; this may represent the remains of an industrial feature, such as a kiln or furnace.

Six trial trenches were excavated to target particular features on the site. East of the church a trench recorded a medieval floodbank with nineteenth-century dumped layers overlying it. A trench was located across the northern edge of the Skinner mansion, joining a 2011 trench to create a continuous section across the building. This area was labelled as a parlour on the early seventeenth-century John Thorpe plan. All the internal and external foundations were absent. There was a north to south aligned, stone-coursed wall present within the parlour, but this was part of a fourteenth- to fifteenth-century monastic outbuilding recorded in 2011 and not part of the later Skinner mansion foundations. A further trench, in the central precinct, revealed a wall and internal floor surface beneath demolition rubble. This belonged to a post-dissolution bakehouse, with an oven and possible dough trough. Elsewhere in the trench was a small hearth that had been used for melting lead in the immediate post-dissolution period.

Torksey: land adjacent to St Peter's Church, SK 8372 7894. Report No.R5232 in the HER.
A watching brief was undertaken by OAE after human remains were encountered during the repair of a leaking water main on the roadside by the churchyard. A large quantity of disturbed human remains was recovered representing multiple individuals. Two human burials were also recorded. The remains belonged to the adjacent churchyard that has been in use since the medieval period; it seems that the original churchyard has been encroached upon by the widening of Main Street probably during the post medieval period.
Archive at LCNCC, Accn no.2012.107.

Wilsford: service trenches at St Mary's Church, TF 0064 4302. Report No.R5311 in the HER.
A watching brief was carried out by Witham Archaeology. The articulated remains of five burials were identified in the churchyard of St Mary's Church. The burials comprised two adults and three juveniles. A quantity of disarticulated bone and a horizontally laid stone slab, possibly a re-used grave cover was also recovered. Neither the burials of the stone slab could be closely dated, though several sherds of unstratified medieval pottery were retrieved from the surrounding topsoil.
Archive at LCNCC, Accn no.2012.74.

Winteringham: land at Eastfield Farm, Composition Lane, SE 941 218. Report in the HER at NLC.
Fifteen trial trenches were excavated by PCA following on from earlier work (see *LHA*, 44 (2009), p.62). Two prehistoric flint scrapers were found. The excavations revealed an early Roman east to west aligned ditched trackway situated towards the north of the site that appeared to have been re-cut several times. The ditches defined a similar trackway, extending southwards of this, and were associated with two enclosures one of which was double-ditched. There was good evidence from the pottery record that this trackway system was not in use over a long period (less than a hundred years), and was confined to the first century AD. The trackways seem to have been used for moving sheep and cattle between fields and enclosures. The double ditched enclosure was of the same date and there was no evidence for use in the second century AD. Both enclosures were thought to have been animal enclosures. The double ditched enclosure could have been for larger cattle or valuable breeding stock.

Most of the pottery dated to before the Roman conquest and was mainly late Iron Age locally produced coarse wares, although some imported wares (Terra Nigra and Gallo-Belgic White Ware) suggested that the site was linked to trading networks in the middle of the first century AD. The settlement seems to have spanned the conquest period, as a Samian sherd and a few wheel-made Roman coarse wares were also present. The environmental evidence indicated local crop production and crop processing, mainly of spelt wheat and hulled barley.
Archive at NLM, Accn code WGMDG.

Winteringham: potato store, Eastfield Farm, SE 9445 2118. Report in the HER at NLC.
The construction layers of a road dating to the early Roman period were discovered and two linear features were tentatively interpreted as possible roadside ditches. There were also the remains of the Roman *agger* (the raised causeway for a Roman road). Other Roman features and deposits were also identified, and there was a small amount of pottery dating to the Neronian period, AD54 to AD68. The finds and environmental samples indicated that, near to the road, there was probably some domestic habitation and the keeping of domestic animals. Archive at NLM, Accn code WGMDE.

Wragby: All Saints' Church and churchyard, TF 1358 7766. Report No.R4819 in the HER.
A geophysical survey was undertaken by Grid 9 Geophysics and AAL on behalf of the Wragby Heritage Group. Anomalies recorded during the survey were identified as the nave, chancel and tower on the site of the former church. Also visible were features that may be the north transept. It is known that most of the church was dismantled in 1836.

Wragby: field walking in the parish. Report pending in the HER.
Field walking was carried out in the parish by the Wragby Heritage Group as part of a continuing project (see *LHA*, 47 (2012)). A further site to the north-west of the village was recorded with a dense scatter of Roman pottery of the second to fourth century including hypocaust tile, roof tile and other artefacts. This scatter may be associated with the high status Roman farmstead to the north identified in 2011. Further north in the parish there was another dense scatter of Roman pottery of the second to fourth century with finds including hypocaust tile and a single fragment of painted wall plaster. The pottery was mostly local grey wares, but with an occasional fragment of imported and regional fine ware and an amphora sherd from southern Spain. This too is likely to be a farmstead. There was a further scatter of Roman pottery of the same date from an area covering about seventy metres by forty metres to the north of Wragby village. (For further details on these sites see, Pete Wilson, 'Roman Britain in 2012, I. Sites Explored, 4. Northern England. Lincolnshire', *Britannia*, 44 (2013), pp.302-04.)

Historic building recording in Lincolnshire 2012

by Mark Bennet

Alford: The Workshop, Commercial Road, TF 4519 7596. Report No.R4872 in the HER.
A building survey of a complex of light industrial buildings was carried out by PCA. The buildings comprised a series of adjoining structures of the mid to late nineteenth century, typical of other light industrial complexes of this age. Although considerably altered and remodelled throughout its history, the complex represents a rare survival of these once commonplace structures. Archive at LCNCC, Accn no.2012.76.

Burgh-le-Marsh: 69 High Street, TF 5036 6505. Report No.R4781 in the HER.
An historic building survey was undertaken by PCA. The buildings on the site were constructed in red brick after 1842 and before 1888 and consist of a former malthouse, outbuildings, stables and wagon storage. The site became a bottling plant and, after the First World War, was converted to a motor garage. During the Second World War the building was requisitioned as the headquarters of the local Auxiliary Fire Service but was used as a garage again after the war. Archive at LCNCC, Accn no.2012.6.

Gainsborough: an outbuilding at 1 Morton Terrace, SK 8138 9037. Report No.R4794 in the HER.
An historic building survey was undertaken by MAS. The building dates from the late nineteenth century and is contemporary with 1 Morton Terrace. The buildings are not present on the 1885 town map of Gainsborough but are present by 1905. This two storey building is built of red brick with a pantile gabled roof with an end stack. The surviving windows are Yorkshire sashes under segmental heads. It was probably originally for housing a horse and a trap with associated tack. One ground floor room would have had a small stove or fireplace as there is a flue and chimney. The upper storey, a single long room, was most likely used for the storage of bedding and feed, and there is a pitch-hole at the south end facing Bayard Lane. Archive at LCNCC, Accn no.2012.42.

Gosberton: Woodbine Farm, Beck Bank, Gosberton Clough, TF 1916 3101. Report No.R4883 in the HER.
Historic building recording was undertaken by Witham Archaeology. Woodbine Farm is an evolutionary farm which developed around three sides of a cattle yard which is open to the south. The farm probably dates to the early nineteenth century, initially with a barn, stables and probably a granary. One of the earliest buildings still standing on the site is the granary/threshing barn. The westernmost of the two storey structures in the north range is also an early building. It is red brick with a gabled pantile roof supported by tumbled-in bricks. The structure has undergone much alteration but it is likely that, originally, it was a multi-function barn; its location within the cattle yard suggests that it could have been used as shelter with the first floor being used for storage of grain or other foodstuffs. This north range was extended later in the nineteenth century with a hipped roof, this extension may have initially been conceived as stables and for cattle sheds. At some point, prior to 1889 (as indicated on historic maps), the west range was extended to accommodate a root house. In the late nineteenth century a separate cart shed was built and the cart shed was amalgamated with pigsties, a meal house and fowl house. This is slightly unusual as often the

pigs and poultry were located close the farmhouse. In the twentieth century the shelter in the north range was converted into a cow house and there are still fragmentary remains of stall divisions.
Archive at LCNCC, Accn no.2012.155.

Hagworthingham: mud and stud barn at Willow Farm, TF 3453 6965. Report No.R4775 in the HER.

An historic building survey was undertaken by R. J. Design Architecture. The threshing barn dates from the mid to late seventeenth century but has, over time, been modified significantly. The barn is of typical mud and stud construction with riven ash laths nailed to rails and earth/straw daub walling. Only four mud and stud barns are known to survive in Lincolnshire. The timber frame largely survives along the north and the south walls. The original frame would have included four principal frames dividing the building into three bays. The inner two frames survive in their entirety and the timbers are elm which is relatively rare for Lincolnshire mud and stud. The bracing for the main frames is an unusual form of ladder bracing with two parallel braces between the tie beam and post that has not been found in any other building locally. The barn was originally built on a foundation of field-stones bedded in an earth mortar. This foundation was well built under the south wall, but elsewhere, where the ground is at a higher elevation, the structure of the barn was simply erected on pad stones. This might have been done because the building stands on a slope with the stone plinth under the south wall acting as a retaining wall to bring the interior level of the barn up to a level. The barn has a brick floor. It is possible that major work on the barn took place in 1818 as this date has been recorded on a timber beam within the barn. The building was re-roofed in the twentieth century.

Lincoln: Oxford Hall, Oxford Street, SK 9768 7093. Report No.R4852 in the HER.

A photographic building survey was undertaken by AAL prior to the building's demolition. The building developed from a group of mid nineteenth-century houses, 2 to 5 Norman Street, which in the late nineteenth century became two hotels. In the 1960s The Oxford Hotel and The Grand Hotel merged into a single establishment. There were also a range of nineteenth-century outbuildings to the north. By 2004, it had been developed into student accommodation.
Archive at LCNCC, Accn no.2012.88.

Long Sutton: The Crown and Woolpack, High Street, TF 4320 2301. Report No.R4976 in the HER.

A photographic survey was undertaken of this reasonably typical Georgian coaching inn of the mid to late eighteenth century. The building is listed and has had various alterations during the nineteenth and twentieth centuries. The original frontage was painted white in the nineteenth century but the upper floors now show the brickwork and limestone dressings.

Long Sutton: 15 High Street, TF 4322 2299. Report No.R4899 in the HER.

An historic building survey was undertaken of this listed house which was constructed in the very late eighteenth century, or the turn of the nineteenth century. It is rendered brick and has a slate roof with two gable stacks. This building is reputed to be that in which the infamous highwayman, Dick Turpin, lived, or stayed, in the early eighteenth century. The present building may have replaced an earlier house on the site as there appears to be a house on the site on a 1706 map. After 1842 but by 1888 the building was used as a shop with accommodation above. The house was considerably altered in the twentieth century.

Manton: Cleatham Hall, SE 9335 0164. Report in the HER at NLC.

A photographic survey of parts of Cleatham Hall was carried out by AAL prior to its conversion to a hotel. The listed Hall was originally eighteenth century but was rebuilt in 1855, perhaps by J. M. Hooker of Tunbridge Wells. The report includes detailed descriptions of internal and external architectural features.
Archive at NLM, Accn code MTBP.

Saxilby-with-Ingleby: Mill Farm, Mill Lane, Saxilby, SK 8987 7564. Report No.R4783 in the HER.

An historic building survey recording was undertaken by MAS. A complex of farm buildings built of red brick and dated from the mid nineteenth century was recorded. The outbuildings all had pantile roofs although the farmhouse had modern tiles. A second stable was added after the last quarter of the nineteenth century. The second stable stood somewhat awkwardly against the first stable and was probably constructed sometime in the last quarter of the nineteenth century, possibly as a single storey structure and only later having a second storey added. A further store room was added in the mid twentieth century.
Archive at LCNCC, Accn no.2012.49.

Scawby: former sugar refinery, Scawby Brook, SE 9875 0613. Report in the HER at NLC.

A photographic building record of surviving buildings at this former sugar refinery factory was made by PCA in advance of their demolition. A group of twelve structures were recorded that were additional to the main factory, built in 1928, which had already been demolished. The site operated until 1991 and the buildings demonstrated a long period of evolution, beginning with the construction of warehouse buildings in 1934 and 1938. The site developed with the addition of offices, stores and warehousing during the 1950s and 1960s, while the weighbridge and security building were built during the reorganisation of the access to the site in the 1980s.

Scothern: The Old Barn, 5 Back Lane, TF 0372 7744. Report No.R4793 in the HER.

A photographic record of was undertaken by Cathedral Design Ltd. The barn was constructed in the early nineteenth century with later additions in the third quarter of the same century. It is built of brick and stone and has a pantile roof. The west elevation in stone is probably early nineteenth century. At the south end, a there is a stone stable that is probably part of the original build. The thatched brick and stone farmhouse associated with the barn on the opposite side of the road was demolished in the 1970s.

Searby-cum-Owmby: Searby Top Farm, Searby Wold Lane, TA 0878 0720. Report No.R4784 in the HER.

An historic building survey was undertaken by Witham Archaeology. The farm dates from the second quarter of the nineteenth century probably originally established as a satellite component of a village-based farm. The buildings are of red brick and of limestone with red brick dressings. There is a combined barn with granary constructed in the period between about 1825 to 1850 and an attached shelter shed was probably built soon after the barn. In about 1850 another shelter shed and probably the cartshed (attached to the west of the barn) were built. At the same time the original stables were built but these were demolished some time between 1923 and 1956. New stables were constructed between 1907 and 1923 and became an office at a much later date.
Archive at LCNCC, Accn no.2012.55.

Skegness: Church Farm, Church End, Winthorpe, TF 5607 6576. Report No.R4908 in the HER.

Photographic building recording was undertaken by PCA. The farmhouse was built in 1755, while the outbuildings were extensively remodelled in the second half of the nineteenth century, adopting their present layout by 1887. The farm buildings occupied the north, east and west sides of a crew yard, with a two-storey barn and cartshed with hay and grain storage above forming the north range, and stabling and cattle accommodation forming the single-storey east and west ranges. They were built of brick with slate roofs, a departure from the locally traditional pantiles, and suggestive of a date towards the end of the nineteenth century.

South Reston: The Chapel, Main Road, TF 4040 8313. Report No.R4809 in the HER.

A building survey was undertaken by Archemi Architecture. The Wesleyan Chapel was built in 1879 and it appears that the worship room and rear schoolroom may have been built at the same time. The porch and rear store were added later. The chapel closed in 2006. The building is of red and yellow brick and has a gabled roof. The windows have rubbed-brick pointed-arches with stone hood mouldings and gothic glazing bars. There are decorative buttresses with pinnacles and a finial. Underneath the front central window there is a blind arcade of three gothic arches.

Spridlington: barn at Elm House, TF 0087 8436. Report No.R5180 in the HER.

A brief photographic survey was conducted by Ward Cole following the partial collapse of part of this barn.

The building is a late eighteenth-century, two storey structure, built of limestone and with a pantile roof. The eastern third of the building had suffered storm damage and several roof timbers were rotting. The damaged part of the building had to be demolished.

Sutton St James: 2 Chapel Gate, TF 4001 1847. Report No.R4777 in the HER.

Historic building recording was undertaken by APS prior to the building being demolished. Originally this was a pair of two storey cottages dating to approximately 1800 constructed in red brick with a pantile roof. The cottages were possibly L-plan in form with one large room and one small room at ground floor level. It is also possible that the two cottages were made up of three rooms and that the central room may have been held in common by both properties. This is further supported by the presence of doorways on the first floor which make the central room accessible from both properties. The building was then, at some point, converted into a single house.
Archive at LCNCC, Accn no.2012.33.

Thimbleby: outbuildings at The Old Rectory, Main Road, TF 2410 7006. Report No.R4962 in the HER.

A photographic recording exercise was undertaken by MAS of a small group of buildings dating to the last half of the nineteenth century including stables, a tack room, a coach house and a cart store. They are built in red brick with slate roofs and were clearly designed and built as a single integrated unit. The original buildings are reasonably preserved. They retain their context with the Old Rectory and their original planned layout.
Archive at LCNCC, Accn no.2012.147.

Thornton Curtis: stables at Burnham Manor, TA 0561 1713. Report in the HER at NLC.

A photographic survey was made by CAC of the brick built stable range at Burnham Manor. These early nineteenth-century stables had, when built, three southern doorways and two northern doorways. There were two windows on the northern side giving light to the ground floor. The upper floor or loft was probably used as a granary and was accessed by an external stair against the west wall. Later an engine house was built against the west wall and so a new external stair, and a door, was built on the south wall. Marks on the floor indicated that the stables would have had timber loose boxes, accessible from both south and north, as well as a central room for fodder and tack. It seems likely that the horses were used for pleasure, riding in Burnham Park to the north. Later the southern doorways were widened, perhaps to accommodate larger working horses.
Archive at NLM, Accn code TCAL.

Torksey: Torksey Castle, SK 8362 7877. Report No.R5046 in the HER.

A building survey was conducted by FAS which identified that a significant loss of fabric from the upper levels had occurred since the second half of the twentieth century with cracking and loss of stonework, especially to the western elevation. Torksey Castle dates to about 1560 and the house is associated with the Jermyn family. It was not they who had the house built, however, as the Will of Sir Robert Jermyn (died 1614) states that he inherited the house from his father who had purchased it from the Thorpe family. During the English Civil War, the house was badly damaged by fire and although the property remained with the Jermyn family it was in a ruinous state by the time it was illustrated by Samuel Buck in 1726. In 1810 Torksey Castle passed to the Cust family with whom it remained throughout the nineteenth century. By the late nineteenth century pretty much only the western facade of the building survived on the flood plain of the River Trent.

Willingham: Willingham Methodist Church, SK 8751 8456. Report No.R4761 in the HER.

An historic building survey was undertaken by PCA. The original building was built in 1811 but was rebuilt in 1885. In 1915 additional buildings were constructed on the site including a schoolroom. The building is built of red brick with yellow brick dressings and has a distinctive yellow brick and blue pamment string course. The chapel closed in 2010.

Archive at LCNCC, Accn no.2011.519.

Finds reported to the Portable Antiquities Scheme in 2012

Compiled by Adam Daubney

The following objects have been reported to the Portable Antiquities Scheme (PAS) during 2012. In some cases the objects were found in previous years but only reported to the PAS during 2012. Details of all finds recorded by the PAS can be obtained from The Department of Portable Antiquities and Treasure, British Museum, London, WC1B 3DG. The finds described here are only a selection of the more important of the Lincolnshire finds. In total 7050 finds (in 5614 records) from Lincolnshire have been recorded by the PAS during this period. Unless otherwise noted the finds have been recorded by Adam Daubney the Lincolnshire Finds Liaison Officer (FLO). Full descriptions of all finds recorded by the PAS are available on the PAS website at www.finds.org.uk.

Brigg: late Bronze Age hoard, found while metal-detecting. PAS record nos NLM-F5AEB0, NLM-B31E53, NLM-B39215 and NLM-B34183 (Treasure reference no.2012 T619).

A hoard of late Bronze Age objects, dated approximately to between 1000BC and 800BC, comprising two incomplete swords and two rings. The first item to be found was the upper blade and ricasso from a sword of Ewart Park type, found as two separate fragments in the plough soil. They were found close to each other, but several months apart. The fracture surfaces on the two fragments appear fresh, suggesting that the object had recently been broken by the plough. Subsequent metal-detecting revealed that further items were located *in situ* at the same place. A small scale excavation took place to investigate the findspot led by the North Lincolnshire FLO. The excavation revealed a second, near-complete, late Bronze Age sword also of Ewart Park type, and two copper-alloy rings, deposited in the bed of what was once an active spring. Sandy soil had accumulated over both rings and also around the sword, indicating that the spring remained active, or intermittently active, after the deposition. It has been suggested that during this ritual deposition the sword was first metaphorically 'killed', by the breaking of the hilt, and then laid in the spring on top of a belt with a metal ring at each end. The sword, possibly in a scabbard, was laid down flat over the belt and between the metal rings, its weight helping to keep the belt in place. Modern ploughing had clipped, bent, and lifted, the tip of the sword blade, and this was probably the first disturbance the deposit had suffered since its placement. Recorded by Martin Foreman (North Lincolnshire FLO).

Crowle: Roman enamelled copper-alloy bowl, found while metal-detecting. PAS record no.FAKL-9900E3.

Fragments of a cast copper-alloy bowl dating to the second century. Three fragments survive and one, bearing the remains of the rim, is folded back on itself. All three fragments join but are distorted making it impossible to determine the original dimensions of the vessel. Nevertheless, it is clear that it was originally globular and small, with a diameter comparable to that of other bowls in the series. The bowl is decorated with *champlevé* enamel; most of the enamel is now missing but the *champlevé* cells show the decorative scheme to have consisted of a series of 37mm diameter circular panels set around the circumference. Each of these contained a three-armed whirligig, their arms open to contain enamel. These arms are linked to the centre via a hollowed joint.

This vessel is the third example of its kind to be recorded by the PAS, the first, and best known is the 'Staffordshire Moorlands pan' (PAS record no.WMID-3FE965) which bears, in addition to its 'Celtic' decoration, a list of some of the Roman forts along Hadrian's Wall. A further example was found at Winterton, North Lincolnshire (PAS record no.NLM-F50443) some fifteen kilometres to the east of Crowle. The Winterton bowl bears a geometric design consisting of square panels inlaid with *champlevé* enamel, a feature that it shares with the Rudge cup, although the Winterton find lacks both an inscription and the 'crenulations' seen on the Rudge cup.[1] The decoration on the Crowle bowl resembles that seen on the Moorlands pan, in that both are 'Celtic' and laid out in circular panels (eight in the case of the Moorlands pan). The decoration on the Moorlands pan is more fluid than the Crowle find and all panels touch, rather than some being linked by horizontal bars. All four bowls (Crowle, Rudge, Moorlands and Winterton) share the same pallet of enamel colours, have similarly shaped rims and are likely to be products of the same workshop. Enamel decorated vessels were being made at Castleford, South Yorkshire and, while most of the material produced there bore geometric or leaf designs some 'Celtic' designs were being used. An actual vessel fragment from Castleford, while bearing leaf-motifs, has some stylistic similarity to the Crowle find. [2] Recorded by Kevin Leahy (National Finds Advisor).

Notes
1. John Horsley, *Britannia Romana or the Roman Antiquities of Britain* (1732); M. Henig, *The Art of Roman Britain* (1995).
2. H. E. M. Cool and C. Philo, *Roman Castleford Excavations 1974-1985*, volume 1: the small finds (Exeter, 1998), no.474, pp.98 and 219, Fig.95.

East Keal: medieval seal matrix, found while metal-detecting. PAS record no.LIN-6E7508.

A medieval copper-alloy seal matrix (Fig.1). The seal is pointed oval and depicts St Peter standing, robed, holding the book of the Gospels in one hand and a pair of keys in another. At his feet is a kneeling figure looking up to St Peter with hands together in a prayerful or pleading position. The inscription surrounding reads: +S' ROBERTI VICARII DE SCHORNE, translated as 'Seal of Robert, vicar of the church of Schorne'. It is possible that the 'Schorne' referred to is Shorne in Kent, for which a 'Robert, vicar of the church of Schorne in Kent' is recorded in the records of the Exchequer in the year 1269.[1]

Note
1. *A Descriptive Catalogue of Ancient Deeds in the Public Record Office*, volume 3 (1900), D47, p.410.

Honington: Anglo-Saxon inscribed silver-gilt object, found while metal-detecting. PAS record no.PAS-6F2DA2 (Treasure reference no.2012 T295).

A silver-gilt object similar to a pair of tweezers, in form, but one of the arms is broken off shorter than the other and both tips are missing. It consists of a tightly folded strip (or possibly two strips riveted together) of silver tapering towards the remaining ends and close to the head it appears to have been pierced through by a copper rivet, traces of which survive. Traces of a circular outline round the rivet stubs on both sides suggest the rivet may have had a domed head on each end of it. The arms are bowed and the head end is slightly bent down at the point where the arms meet.

Both arms are lightly incised with inscriptions in Anglo-Saxon runic letters. The inscription is within incised linear borders on each arm, although parts of the surface have been lost or obscured by corrosion resulting in the loss of some details. Nevertheless, Professor John Hines has been able to identify the runes successfully and provide a reading of the texts. Side A: + *þecblætsigubilwitfæddæ*. Side B: *ondwerccagehwelchefænondecla*.

Hines observes that the texts are remarkably close to a passage of three lines of verse in the Old English poem known as 'Azarias', translated as 'Let the glories of the created world and everything made, the heavens and the angels, and the pure water, [and all the power of creation upon Earth], bless Thee, kind Father'. The lines in turn represent a vernacular paraphrase of part of the Book of Daniel, 3:51ff. about the three youths in the fiery furnace.

The form of the object is only very broadly comparable with a pair of tweezers from Reculver, Kent, dating to the eighth or ninth century.[1] But, on the basis of linguistic and runographic parallels, Professor Hines proposes a date range around AD725 to AD825 for the inscription. The exact function of the object is a little uncertain in view of the ancient damage, although the inscriptions suggest it may possibly have had an ecclesiastical purpose, perhaps as tweezers or candle-snuffers used in church rituals. Identified and recorded by John Hines (University of Cardiff), and Barry Ager (British Museum).

Note
1. D. M. Wilson, *Anglo-Saxon Ornamental Metalwork 700-1100 in the British Museum, Catalogue of Antiquities of the Later Saxon Period*, volume 1 (1964), p.161, no.62, pl.28, 62.

Fig.1. East Keal: medieval seal matrix.

Fig.2. Kirkby-la-Thorpe: Anglo-Scandinavian trefoil brooch.

Kirkby-la-Thorpe: Anglo-Scandinavian trefoil brooch, found while metal-detecting. PAS record no.LIN-56D731.

An incomplete Anglo-Scandinavian or Viking copper-alloy trefoil brooch, dating approximately to between AD850 and AD950 (Fig.2). The brooch is in excellent condition with minor damage on one lug. The brooch is flat, has three arms with rounded terminals and is decorated with a triangle in the centre delimited by a deep perimeter groove. A ring-and-dot motif is located within the centre of the triangle, and further ring-and-dot motif is located on each corner of the triangle. The three arms are bounded by a pair of deeply cut grooves enclosing a foliate design. On the reverse are two integral lugs facing one another, one of which contains iron corrosion from the pin. Trefoil brooches are known from the East Midlands, however it is unclear whether they are Scandinavian in origin or are local copies in Scandinavian style. Similar examples bearing stylised leaf decoration are known from Lincolnshire, from Lenton, Keisby and Osgodby parish (PAS record no.LIN-16CB00), Washingborough (PAS record no.LIN-87E516), and Lusby with Winceby (PAS record no.DENO-E9A0F5). The latter example is almost identical and includes the ring-and-dot motifs less commonly seen on these items.

Kirton-in-Lindsey: late Roman or fifth-century penannular brooch, found while metal-detecting. PAS record no.SWYOR-EC09E8.

A silver penannular brooch.[1] The brooch has zoomorphic terminals that may represent stylised horses' heads. Small zoomorphic penannular brooches such as Fowler's type E are considered to date to between about AD300 and AD600, spanning the Roman and Anglo-Saxon periods. Recorded by Amy Downes (South West Yorkshire FLO).

Note
1. Elisabeth Fowler, 'The origins and development of the penannular brooch in Europe', *Proceedings of the Prehistoric Society*, 26 (1960), pp.149-177, type E.

Near Louth: Anglo-Saxon iron bell, found while metal-detecting. PAS record no.LIN-B17DA7.

A small iron bell plated with copper-alloy using the 'fusion-plating process', of Bourke's class 1 (Fig.3).[1] The bell is corroded but appears to be made from a single piece of iron that has been folded in two. The seam, which is located to the side, is now open and it is unclear whether it was once riveted or simply joined with the copper-alloy brazing metal which also covers the body. The base forms a distorted circle and the body tapers to a rectangular apex. A ring was set in the top of the bell which served both as a handle and to suspend the clapper.

The bell is smaller than, but similar in form to, one discovered in the grave of an Anglo-Saxon smith at Tattershall Thorpe, Lincolnshire, dated to about AD660 to AD670.[2] The condition of the Tattershall Thorpe bell suggested that it was already old at the time of deposition, and the location of the item in the grave demonstrated that it belonged with other tools rather than with the scrap metal. Bells have been found accompanying males, females and children, and the majority of examples can be dated to the seventh or early eighth centuries.[3] Iron bells have also been found in association with tool hoards at Flixborough[4] and Mastermyr in Gotland.[5]

Braized bells are well known in Ireland where many have been discovered on monastic sites.[6] The Scottish series of brazed iron bells – which are also assigned a seventh- or eighth-century date – have a greater size range, from 60mm to 326mm tall[7] and have been interpreted as evidence for the activity of Columban monks and the influence of the Columban (or Irish) Church.[8] The use of bells within Christian contexts is also well documented in this period where particularly the larger bells may have been used for summoning people to prayer.[9]

In England, Anglo-Saxon bells demonstrate a greater range of sizes than those from Ireland and Scotland, particularly at the lower end where one example from York stands just 17mm tall. At the other end, examples from Repton and Tattershall Thorpe stand over 100mm tall.[10] The present example falls somewhere in between at 37mm. The form of copper-alloy brazed iron bells remains fairly consistent across Ireland, Scotland and England however.

Notes
1. Cormac Bourke, 'Early Irish hand-bells', *The Journal of the Royal Society of Antiquaries of Ireland*, 110 (1980), pp.52-66.
2. David A. Hinton, *A Smith in Lindsey: The Anglo-Saxon Grave at Tattershall Thorpe, Lincolnshire*, Society for Medieval Archaeology Monograph Series, no.16 (2000), pp.44-47, Fig.30.
3. D. Hinton, *A Smith in Lindsey*, pp.45-47; H. Geake, *The Use of Grave-Goods in Conversion Period England*, c.600-c.850, British Archaeology Reports, British Series, no.261 (Oxford, 1997), p.102.

Fig.3. Near Louth: Anglo-Saxon iron bell.

4. P. Ottaway, 'The Flixborough tool hoard' in *Life and Economy at Early Medieval Flixborough* c.*AD600-1000: The Artefact Evidence* edited by D. H. Evans and Christopher Loveluck, Excavations at Flixborough volume 2 (Oxford, 2009), pp.256-66, esp. p.256.

5. Greta Arwidsson and Gösta Berg, *The Mästermyr Find: A Viking Age Tool Chest from Gotland* (Stockholm, 1983), pp.28-29.

6. C. Bourke, 'Early Irish hand-bells'.

7. C. Bourke, 'The hand-bells of the early Scottish church', *Proceedings of the Society of Antiquaries of Scotland*, 113 (1983), pp.464-68, esp. p.464.

8. *Ibid.*, p.466.

9. Patrick Ottaway, 'The products of the blacksmith in mid-late Anglo-Saxon England' (1995), part 2, p.5, available on the PJO Archaeology website, at http://www.pjoarchaeology. co.uk/academic-consultancy/anglosaxon-ironwork.html, accessed 14 June 2012.

10. P. Ottaway, 'The products of the blacksmith', part 2, p.7.

Near Louth: diminutive Anglo-Saxon lead tablet, found while metal-detecting. PAS record no.LIN-66AD26.

A diminutive lead tablet, probably complete, with maximum measurements of 57mm in length, 41mm in width and 10mm in thickness. It is undecorated apart from some lettering and small incised crosses. One face of the tablet contains a text, which gives the Old English female personal name Cudburg.[1] The letters are incised in insular script without framing lines and read horizontally:

+ / **CUDBUR** / + / **G** / **E** / + / +. The back of the tablet contains three incised lines, starting on the left side towards the top and finishing on the right side near the bottom. However the lines appear to be non-continuous in the middle. It is unclear whether or not these lines are original. The lower edge of the tablet apparently contained further lettering. There are three possible letters, followed by a blank space, and then two possible crosses: [. I S] [+ +]. A number of inscribed lead crosses and lead plates dating from the Anglo-Saxon period are known, and on the basis of these parallels it seems likely that the present tablet was used in a funerary context.[2] The evidence from the letter-forms seems consistent with a date preceding the early tenth-century emergence of square minuscule as the manuscript hand.[3] A date between about AD700 and AD900 is suggested. Recorded by Elizabeth Okasha.

Notes

1. Elisabeth Okasha, *Women's Names in Old English* (Farnham, 2011), pp.28, 70.

2. Elisabeth Okasha, 'A third supplement to hand-list of Anglo-Saxon non-runic inscriptions', *Anglo-Saxon England*, 33 (2004), pp.225-81, esp. pp.229-30.

3. Elisabeth Okasha, 'The non-runic scripts of Anglo-Saxon inscriptions', *Transactions of the Cambridge Bibliographical Society*, 4, part 5 (1968), pp.321-38, esp. p.332 and Table 1b.

Navenby: silver *denarius* of King Juba, found while metal-detecting. PAS record no.DENO-A89103.

A silver *denarius* of King Juba I of Numidia, North Africa, dating to the period 60BC to 46BC (Fig.4). The obverse reads 'REX IVBA' , and depicts the diademed and draped bust of Juba facing right, with a sceptre at the shoulder. The reverse has a neo-Punic script to either side of a temple. Recorded by Charlotte Burrill (Derbyshire and Nottinghamshire FLO).

Fig.4. Navenby: denarius *of King Juba of Numidia.*

Nettleton: Roman figurine of Mercury, found while metal-detecting. PAS record no.LIN-25CC02.

A near-complete copper-alloy figurine of Mercury (Fig.5). The figure is naked except for a *paenula* (a cloak similar to a poncho) draped over the left shoulder and left arm. He stands facing, with legs apart and left leg bent slightly forward. His head is turned slightly to his right. He has curly hair and wears a cap with two wings. The facial features are worn but appear somewhat provincial in style. His arms are bent forward. In his right hand he holds a money-bag. His left hand is incomplete but is semi-circular in section and most probably once held a *caduceus* (a staff entwined with a serpent). The figurine does not stand up on its own.

Redbourne: Roman miniature altar, found while metal-detecting. PAS record no.YORYM-9E8875.

An incomplete, enamelled, copper-alloy, model altar. This would originally have been one of a tier of similar items. The altar is square in plan with a flat top, hollow base and four small worn knops projecting from each corner of the upper surface which would have allowed the stand to secure into holes in the legs of an upper tier. The sides of the object are decorated with a recessed square with a saltire cross, the resulting cells of which are in-filled with enamel. These stands are usually decorated with enamel and have a circular opening at the top, and they come in groups of decreasing size.[1] They have been variously interpreted as miniature tables, stools or altars, but Butcher has suggested they may have been used to hold candles; each tier could be removed as the candle burned down, perhaps as the candle was used to measure time or mark the different stages of a ritual.[2] Such objects

are often associated with temples and forts. Recorded by Rebecca Griffiths (North Yorkshire FLO).

Notes
1. Philip Kiernan, *Miniature Votive Offerings in the North-West Provinces of the Roman Empire, Mentor, Studien zu Metallarbeiten und Toreutik der Antike, band 4*, edited by Reinhard Stipperich and Richard Petrovsxky (Wiesbaden, 2009), pp.173-75.
2. S. A. Butcher, 'Enamels from Roman Britain' in *Ancient Monuments and Their Interpretation. Essays Presented to A. J. Taylor* edited by M. R. Apted, R. Gilyard-Beer, and A. D. Saunders (1977), pp.41-70.

Roxby-cum-Risby: Roman copper-alloy finger-ring inscribed '*TOT*', found while metal-detecting. PAS record no.NLM-AA76B4.

A Roman copper-alloy finger-ring of Henig Type IX.[1] The bezel contains a crude border comprised two rows of punched dots either side of the relict ridge. Within the border are the letters *TOT*, an abbreviation for the Celtic god-name *Toutatis*. Silver rings bearing the inscription *TOT* are well known finds from the East Midlands, especially in Lincolnshire.[2] Recorded by Martin Foreman (North Lincolnshire FLO).

Notes
1. M. Henig, *A Corpus of Roman Engraved Gemstones from British Sites*, British Archaeological Reports, British Series 8 (second edition, Oxford, 1978).
2. A. Daubney, 'The cult of Totatis' in *A Decade of Discovery: Proceedings of the Portable Antiquities Scheme Conference 2007*,

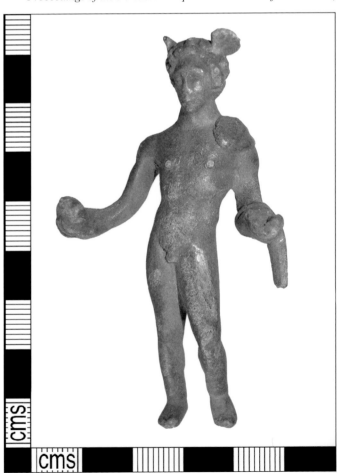

Fig.5. Nettleton: Roman figurine of Mercury.

edited by S. Worrell, K. Leahy, M. Lewis and J. Naylor, British Archaeological Reports, British Series, 510 (Oxford, 2010), pp.109-20.

Winteringham: four Roman copper-alloy finger-rings found together, found while metal-detecting. PAS record nos DUR-AED1B2, DUR-AE8882, DUR-AE2975, DUR-AE2975.

Four complete Roman copper-alloy finger-rings found in the same place. All are of Henig type Xb, which dates to the second or third century.[1] All have decorated bezels; the first depicts a crouched stag, the second depicts what are probably two ducks, one behind the other. The final two both depict a cup containing a plant, possibly corn ears. Recorded by Emma Morris (Finds Liaison Assistant).

Note

1. M. Henig, *A Corpus of Roman Engraved Gemstones from British Sites*, British Archaeological Reports, British Series 8 (second edition, Oxford, 1978).

Book Reviews

This section aims to review some of the more important volumes relating to the county published since the last issue of this journal was produced. The bibliography aims to include all the titles that the Reviews Editors became aware of relating to Lincolnshire. The majority of these titles, if still in print, are available at the Society's Bookshop, Jews' Court, Steep Hill, Lincoln LN2 1LS.

BENNETT, Nicholas. *Lincolnshire parish clergy, c.1214-1968: a biographical register: Part 1: The Deaneries of Aslacoe and Aveland.* Lincoln Record Society [and] Woodbridge, The Boydell Press, 2013. xxxviii, 472pp. ISBN 978 0 901503 96 1. (Lincoln Record Society publications, Vol.103). £30 hbk.

Perhaps because of its flat landscapes and low horizons Lincolnshire's churches seem to be an ever-present feature. Spires and belfries punctuate the fields, wolds and farmlands of a mainly rural county and a view which does not contain a church must be a rare one indeed. Nicholas Bennett tells us that on the eve of the First World War there were some 700 Anglican churches in the diocese and though there has since been some decline, the vast majority still perform an important role in their communities. For those interested in the history of these buildings it is relatively easy to visit them. In so doing we can immediately gather information about them by gazing at their walls, windows and artifacts. But the fabric of our churches tells us little about those who served them. Bennett urges us to go beyond the buildings themselves and explore the lives of the people who used them, and in parish churches he adds, 'we must begin with the parson'.

This handsome volume is the first in a planned series which will eventually provide a biographical register of all the Lincolnshire parishes starting at 1214, when Bishop Hugh of Wells began what was to be the first episcopal register of its kind in Western Europe. Nicholas Bennett, the general editor of the series was, until his recent retirement, Vice-Chancellor and Librarian at Lincoln Cathedral. Ideally placed for such a project he has drawn on the bishops' registers and other sources in order to compile a beautifully crafted biographical registry of the first two alphabetically placed deaneries; namely Aslacoe and Aveland. Parish by parish he lets us know who the priest was, when they were inducted as well as providing intriguing glimpses of a fascinating group of people. Along the way we learn that Richard Laminge of Caenby in 1566 'understands Latin; but [is] little versed in sacred learning'. Education of clergy was clearly a priority in Elizabethan

England and just a year later at Cammeringham we hear that their incumbent has the opposite problem being, 'ignorant of Latin; moderately versed in sacred learning'. The reader has a strong urge to ask the residents of the respective parishes which they consider worse.

In Snitterby in 1908, Revd John Swalwell received an 'Order of Affiliation' (who knew such things existed?) for the maintenance of the bastard daughter of Mary Wright. His appeal was unsuccessful. It is perhaps more gratifying to read that in the same parish in 1921 the priest, Graeme Maurice Elliott was the author of, *Angels seen To-day*. Also, and with an even more felicitous title, *A Modern Miracle: being the story of how a little girl was saved by an Angel*.

This volume is not only a treasury of insights into seven centuries of Lincolnshire parish life it is also an important tool for historians and scholars. Thanks to eighteenth- and nineteenth-century antiquarians others counties have long been in possession of such catalogues. By an accident of history this has not been the case in Lincolnshire and this volume fills a significant lacuna. The editor has set himself a herculean task. The diocese of Lincoln has, at one time or another, possessed twenty-two deaneries, with a further four in Stow. This first volume has set a very high standard and the completion of the whole biographical registry will make an enormous contribution to local, national and ecclesiastical history.

Dr Jack Cunningham, Bishop Grosseteste University.

ESSICK, John Inscore. *Thomas Grantham: God's Messenger from Lincolnshire.* Mercer University Press, 2013. 246pp. ISBN 978 0 88 14646 1 0. £24.50 hbk.

The Baptist leader, theologian and polemicist, Thomas Grantham (1633/34-1692) was probably born in the village of Halton near Spilsby. His family seemed to have been well established, though a contemporary tells us that they lost much for the King's cause during the English Civil Wars. Perhaps for this reason he was apprenticed to a tailor though, fortuitously for English Baptists, on completing his service he gave himself over to study and became 'proficient in learning'. Just how successful he was as an autodidact is apparent in the writing that he went on to produce. In this he demonstrated an ability to systematize a dissenting theology (no easy task) whilst underpinning his deliberations with references not only to Scripture, but also to an array of patristic writing from the first 500 years of Christianity.

After turning to God in his teenage years Grantham was baptized in the Baptist Church in Boston at around the age of nineteen. Only three years later he had his own congregation which grew to such a size that he was eventually provided with his own chapel. Life was not easy for his particular branch of dissenters and even in the Interregnum, when the Lord Protector was generally tolerant of Protestant sectarians, they continually ran into trouble. Grantham tells us himself that they were often brought before the judgment seat for not worshipping like Cromwell, and their goods were confiscated.

Nor did the situation improve at the Restoration. In 1660 Grantham signed *A Brief Confession* that petitioned the newly returned Charles II: a year later he was petitioning once more but this time from Lincoln gaol. Several more incarcerations followed including six months in Louth, but by 1666 he was elected 'Messenger' for the General Baptists. This is an interesting role and one that this present volume does much to shed light on. The Messenger was a travelling minister based on what the General Baptists saw as an important functionary in the early Church. Without being tied to a particular parish they were free to provide a peripatetic service preaching and helping to organize regionally. John Inscore Essick has convincingly argued that Grantham's role as Messenger, at a time when the office was coming into being, was crucial in the development of this ministry.

Even more importantly, in his role as Messenger, Grantham seems to have considered it incumbent upon himself to engage in many controversies often with figures in the established church, sometimes with other denominations, and occasionally even with fellow Baptists. His *magnum opus* was *Christianismus Primitivas* (1678) that runs to over 600 pages and is probably key to the author's assertion that Grantham is the first systematic theologian among the Baptists. This work presents a unified vision of a Church that is based on the spirituality and ecclesiology of the early Christian movement. Grantham's Baptist faith is 'General', as opposed to 'Particularist' which means that he subscribed to the belief that Christ died for all people and not just the elect. This furnished him with a warm perspective and in his polemics Grantham was generally polite, though also not entirely incapable of being abrasive. *A Friendly Epistle* (1680) is an irenic plea for better relations between dissenters and the Church of England, a view he would not have shared with many Baptists, nor indeed does it represent the tendency of the population in general in England during this much divided century. Inscore Essick introduces his readership to these works and other works; in addition, he makes additional good use of some previously unknown texts that together produce an excellent overall summary of Grantham's theology. He also brings to our attention Grantham's private letters which do much to offer us a glimpse of a man who was capable of deep friendships that extended beyond the boundaries of his own religious communities.

Grantham was a great man, a leader of spirit, an organizer with energy and a theological mind well worth our time to consider. There has never been a book on him before and this volume is more than able to fill that void. It is organized well, written clearly and it provides us with an important introduction to the man and his

works. In this capacity it not only offers an insight into Baptist history but also a fascinating glimpse into the Lincolnshire and East Anglia of the early modern period. For such a handsome hardback volume it is also pleasingly affordable, I highly recommend it.

Dr Jack Cunningham, Bishop Grosseteste University.

KLEINEKE, Hannes and STEER, Christian, editors. *The Yorkist age: proceedings of the 2011 Harlaxton Symposium.* Donington, Shaun Tyas and Richard III and Yorkist History Trust, 2012. [xix], 488pp. and 28 plates. ISBN 978 1 907730 22 1. (Harlaxton Medieval Studies, Volume XXIII). £49.50 hbk.

How to suggest in a brief note the range of the papers here and the wealth of research and reference they demonstrate? The Harlaxton Symposium is now a very well-established forum for the dissemination of new thoughts on all aspects of our medieval history. The latest volume, finely produced as always by a Lincolnshire publisher, maintains the quality of the series.

The Yorkist Age offers a wider remit than has usually been the case and twenty-five scholars presented papers covering many aspects of that troubled period. There are four main groupings of the papers: The Royal house of York; War, Kingship and Governance; Drama and Literature in the Yorkist age; and, Death and Commemoration in the Yorkist age. Within these groupings are pieces on piety, Richard III's charters to his towns, the wars in the Low Countries, Theatricals in York during the fifteenth century and two pieces on Fotheringhay church in Northamptonshire but a good deal more.

The presentation of papers came too late for the news of the discovery of Richard III's burial place in Leicester but they provide a great deal of extra background reading to the present discussions surrounding the discovery. There is, perhaps, a special significance in the final paper in which Dr Alexandra Buckle discusses the rarity of accounts such as the one she retells of the re-burial of Richard Beauchamp, Earl of Warwick in 1475; it/he had to await the consecration of the chapel in which he was to be interred. She discusses in detail the varying dates suggested in the past for that event.

A very comprehensive bibliography supplements the texts and there is a fine collection of plates at the end to enhance further the book's appeal.

R. A. Carroll, Bourne.

ROBINSON, P. *Lincoln's excavators: the Ruston-Bucyrus years, 1970-1985.* Wellington, (Somerset), Roundoak Press, 2013. 336pp. and over 500 illus. ISBN 978 1 871565 58 4. (History of Ruston/Bucyrus, Volume 4). £36.95 hbk.

This is the final volume in the monumental four-volume series on Lincoln's excavators. The author, Peter Robinson, was eminently suited for the task. He was born in Lincoln, served a student apprenticeship with Ruston-Bucyrus Ltd, qualified as a design draughtsman, and was employed in R-Bs engineering department. for seventeen years. He then had a career change when he took an honours degree in education and became a teacher in art and design technology.

In retirement, Peter Robinson took up his hobby of 'excavators' and produced a great collection of quality scale models of Ruston excavators. His fertile mind was, meanwhile, fermenting the idea of writing a serious account of Lincoln's excavator industry. Perhaps the millennium spurred him on, because it was at that time that he started work on the ambitious project.

The author set out, in his own words, to 'create traditional reference books that will serve as a lasting text for the enthusiast or researcher', and that they would be 'a testament to Lincoln's great industrial past when the skills, craftsmanship and dedication of its work-force carried the words "Made in Lincoln" to every corner of the world'.

Each volume in the series has lived up to these aims, and the whole set will always be seen as a classic work on its subject. This final volume shows the author's great knowledge of all the machines that he writes about. They are all illustrated with many first-class photographs showing production, assembly and working machines. The text is enlivened by frequent anecdotes involving the machines and the men who designed, built and worked with them. The machines are written about by an author who was obviously part of the team that produced them. The men were written about as colleagues and comrades.

This volume covers the Ruston-Bucyrus years from 1970 until the end of the company in 1985. It is divided into chapters – some giving in-depth accounts of individual machines, and others on significant events or eras in the company's history. The first chapter deals with the RB-71 – an excavator of robust design that became a popular choice for removing the 'overburden' in opencast coal mining. Production of this successful machine was maintained until the closure of the company in 1985. The next chapter moves into a different league, describing the development and role of the 725-ton RB-48W walking dragline. Two of these giant machines were ordered for work in a German opencast coal site. Many photographs and drawings are used to illustrate the design, production, transport and assembly of the RB-48W machines. Further chapters give similar accounts of the 61-RB excavator, the RB 195-B mining shovel, and the 380-W walking dragline.

This period saw a big surge in the demand for cranes in the construction industry. Ruston-Bucyrus met this demand very readily, commencing with the 22-RB heavy-duty lifting crane, mounted on crawlers. It was employed in large numbers installing the hundreds of

miles of pipelines for the distribution of the new supplies of North Sea gas. A range of transit cranes followed – to meet a growing demand for mobile cranes. The early rope machines were later replaced by hydraulic machines with telescopic booms.

Throughout this period, the reader is told about the pressure from Bucyrus Erie for the Lincoln factory to build machines to American designs. This was often unsuitable for machines sold in the European market, and a considerable amount of re-design work had to be carried out by the Lincoln engineers at Ruston-Bucyrus.

In the final chapters the author describes the circumstances that led to the Lincoln share of the company being sold to Bucyrus Erie and how the remaining operations in Lincoln became split into two new companies: Bucyrus Europe (mining machinery) and RB (Lincoln) Ltd (construction excavators and cranes).

Volume 4 is a fascinating and exciting read, provided by a very well informed writer. It deserves a place on the bookshelf of all enthusiasts of earth-moving equipment and cranes alongside the three previous volumes.

Ray Hooley, North Hykeham.

SEATON, Keith. *The River Welland: shipping & mariners of Spalding*. Stroud, The History Press, 2013. 192pp. ISBN 978 0 7524 9449 9. £16.99 pbk.

Keith Seaton was attracted to the River Welland from an early age, crossing it via a bridge every day as he walked to school (p.7). A Lincolnshire lad, born and bred in Spalding, his love of the area is evident by his anecdotal commentary. Yet, he maintains that the commercial importance of Spalding, once a thriving port, is neglected in terms of its maritime history. He argues the area is now more commonly associated with its agricultural links. Thus, he takes a sentimental journey inspired by his research into his own family history to help recapture Spalding's shipping heritage and ensure it is recorded for prosperity in this his inaugural book.

Seaton begins by successfully combining descriptive narrative and historical photographs to introduce the reader to the River Welland. He details the river's history from Roman times through to the nineteenth century. Paintings, sketches and detailed technical information, which vividly illustrate the type of vessels that commonly used the Port of Spalding are included. Fuelled by his own interest in sailing, Seaton unearths past seafaring connections within his own ancestry. Whilst interrogating the census and local directories he also discovers other important Spalding mariners. He skilfully paints a rich picture of life in the area particularly when recounting the memories of Spalding residents and stories from local newspapers. Listing Boston Ships' Registers (1824-92) and material from both the census and merchant marine census, he creates a comprehensive record of local maritime life. Extracts also include the shipping news from local newspapers including, for example, that the *Wellington Johnson* arrived with linseed cakes on 4 September 1819 (p.138). He also devotes a chapter to the Spalding Shipwrecked Society, which highlights the importance of such a charity to the local community demonstrated by records of its accounts. He effectively utilises census and directory sources when researching the occupation of boatbuilding and those industries such as rope-making that depend on the maritime association. Seaton observes life as Spalding moves into the twentieth century and notes the decline of sailing vessels on the river. Sources throughout the book include maps, photographs, sketches, newspaper reports, census records and directory entries which result in an eclectic collection of historical information which combine to become an important reference book of Spalding's nautical heritage.

A particular strength of the book proves to be stories of local mariners and their families, which pertinently conveys their colourful characters. One such individual is Edwin Goute, who had to threaten his crew with pistols to gain order in a storm. Yet he 'bashed his leg to pulp' because of barrels rolling loose on deck in the chaos (p.132). Nevertheless, after returning to England to have his leg amputated he once again returned to sea. Another story that aptly illustrates how times have changed with regard to health, safety and welfare is that of seaman Jonathan Turner. He was aboard HMS *Discovery* which ran aground returning from the Pacific. On 6 August 1792 whilst trying to refloat her, he fractured his arm. His debilitating injury no doubt contributed to his falling overboard some months later whilst moving heavy goods. However, being rescued did not invoke sympathy as he was then flogged as punishment. Poor Turner appears again in the ship's log in March 1793 when he received 'twenty-four lashes for neglect of duty' (p.67). This illustrates the life of a seaman was not for the fainthearted!

On a lighter note, there was another 'notorious character' named Mrs Payne who acted as mate on her husband's ship (p.130). She always put up her umbrella when it rained and was a remarkable sight for children who rushed to see her in charge of the tiller clutching her umbrella.

To conclude, what started out for Seaton as a personal interest in his family history has resulted in a valuable record of life in a local seafaring community, the record of which otherwise may have been unpublished. This book will not only appeal to those interested in all things nautical but also those who are keen to discover there is much more to the local history of Spalding than may first appear.

Rachel Maxey, history undergraduate, Bishop Grosseteste University.

SPENCER, Andrew. *Nobility and kingship in medieval England: the Earls and Edward I, 1272-1307*. Cambridge University Press, 2013. 317pp. ISBN 978 1 10 702675 9. (Cambridge Studies in Medieval Life and Thought, Fourth Series). £65 hbk.

'Edward I preferred masterfulness to the art of political management'.[1] One of the central objectives of Andrew Spencer's new book is to reappraise this conclusion of K. B. McFarlane's influential 1965 article on Edward I's relations with his earls, which was highly critical of what McFarlane perceived as Edward's domination of, rather than co-operation with, his magnates; conclusions which have done much to influence subsequent interpretations of Edward's reign. Spencer, in the course of this volume, offers a fundamental reassessment of Edward's style of kingship and while taking a frank look at Edward's relationship with his mightiest subjects, presents a nuanced picture of the earls and their interactions with the king at various stages of the reign.

One of the greatest strengths in this volume is Spencer's engaging style and the admirable clarity of expression. The result is that this is an easy book to read, even for those less familiar with the subject matter. This is not another biography of the king, however, and it presumes the reader possesses a degree of familiarity with not only the reign of Edward but those of his father, son, and to a lesser degree, his grandson. The discussion is based around three parts; first, an examination of the relationship between the king and his earls; second, an important study of the role of the earls in local society; and, third, the engagement of the earls in the politics of the reign. These are preceded by a discussion of the comparative wealth of the various earls and their lands. The result is a systematic and thematically cogent examination of the earls and Edward's relationship to them that presents Edward, in contrast to McFarlane's portrayal, as maintaining a close and mainly positive relationship with these men for most of the reign and which Edward sustained with unusual success even after the death of the men of his own generation. In this study, Spencer builds well upon the pre-existing examinations of particular comital families by Altschul, Morris and Maddicott, and offers important fresh work on the earls of Lincoln, Lancaster and Cornwall. Henry de Lacy, earl of Lincoln's career (1272-1311) and important relationships with both Edward and the earls of Lancaster, the latter to whom Lacy was linked through the marriage of his daughter, are well explored here, particularly the considerable degree of reliance that the king placed on Lacy, who was the longest serving of all Edward's earls. Of particular interest is Spencer's original research on the composition of the affinities of Lincoln, Lancaster and Cornwall. While Spencer highlights the regular appearance of the Lincolnshire knights as Lacy's charter witnesses, he contends that Lacy's comital following does not seem to have penetrated 'very deeply into the great pool of gentry families' either there or in his other seat of power in south Yorkshire (pp.126-27). Included in the appendices are very useful calendars compiled by Spencer of the surviving *acta* of Lincoln, Lancaster and Cornwall for the reign, drawn from a variety of sources including the National Archives.

This book is an extremely valuable contribution to the scholarship of the late thirteenth century, but where there is perhaps a question mark is Spencer's decision to frame the second part of the book, on the earls in local society, around the bastard feudalism debate. Spencer explains his reasons for doing so as cogently as ever, the bit of 'necromancy' he performs, as he puts it, is 'to explain something of how and why she came into existence' (p.100). This in itself is not problematic and he provides a useful historiographical account, but Spencer continues to use 'bastard feudalism' as a concept throughout Part II where 'bastard feudal' and 'feudal' patterns in the earls' behaviour are contrasted with each other. Spencer's decision is, of course, partly influenced by the historiography, and particularly the debates of Cox, Carpenter and Crouch regarding the possible origins of this in the twelfth and thirteenth centuries. One feels though that Spencer would have benefited from following through with his deconstruction of the issues surrounding this nineteenth-century term in order to drop its use altogether for the subsequent analysis. Clarity of meaning is not assisted by phrases like 'bastard feudal rewards' or 'a feudal mindset' (p.134).

This book is an important revisionist account of the reign of Edward I and helps provide a far deeper understanding of the operation of local society and the development of royal government, including the earls' growing role in this, over the late thirteenth century. As such this is a valuable read for political historians of both the thirteenth and fourteenth centuries and those interested in the role and history of some of the great comital families, like the Lacys of Lincoln.

Note

1. K. B. McFarlane, 'Had Edward I a Policy towards the Earls?', *The Nobility of Later Medieval England* (Oxford, repr. 1980), pp.248-267, at 267.

Fergus Oakes, PhD student,
University of Glasgow.

John Smith, lately Director of Stamford Museum, has written an extensive paper that will be of interest to students of the county's eighteenth-century history. Stukeley (born in Holbeach) was Vicar of All Saints Church in Stamford from 1730 to 1747; John Smith has delved into Stukeley's life and activities in the town during that period, in particular trying to identify all his various homes and the ways his gardens reflected his religious

beliefs and antiquarian interests. The paper appears in *Antiquaries Journal* (Volume 93 for 2013), pages 353-400 and is entitled: 'William Stukeley in Stamford: his houses, gardens and a project for a Palladian triumphal arch over Barn Hill. Access online to this article is through:

http://journals.cambridge.org/abstract_ S0003581513000267

This is a valuable precursor to volume 104 in the Lincoln Record Society (LRS) series. This deals with the correspondence of Maurice Johnson, founder of the Spalding Gentleman's Society (SGS) in 1710, with the noted antiquary William Stukeley, covering the years 1714 to 1754. The volume has been edited by Diana and Michael Honeybone. The Honeybones were the editors of an earlier volume (number 99 in the LRS series and issued in 2010). Then they used the SGS archives to produce a record of early correspondence held there for the years 1710 to 1761.

Bibliography

This list aims to include as many titles as possible that came to the attention of the Reviews Editors and were published since the last volume of *Lincolnshire History and Archaeology*. There may be the odd addition from 2012 for titles that came in after the volume for 2012 went to press. Titles that are reviewed in the preceding pages of this annual volume are printed in bold type; titles that have received shorter reviews in the Society's quarterly journal *Lincolnshire Past and Present* are shown with the relevant issue number in brackets at the end of the entry. Not all the works listed were actually sent in for review purposes.

BENNETT, Nicholas. *Lincolnshire parish clergy, c.1214-1968: a biographical register: Part 1: The Deaneries of Aslacoe and Aveland*. Lincoln Record Society [and] Woodbridge, The Boydell Press, 2013. xxxviii, 472pp. ISBN 978 0 901503 96 1. (Lincoln Record Society publications, Vol.103). £30 hbk.

BOURN, Hugh. *From humble beginnings: the autobiography of Hugh Bourn, OBE*. [The author, 2013]. 176pp. ISBN 978 0 9569729 5 8 unpriced hbk; 978 0 9569729 6 5 £14.99 pbk.

BOYCE, Rosalind. *'Forever young': Harold Tennyson RN, the poet's grandson*. Tennyson Society, 2013. 29pp. ISBN 978 0 901958 63 1. (Occasional Paper, 13). £3.50 pbk (or £4 by post from the Society, Central Library, Free School Lane, Lincoln LN2 1EZ). (*LP&P*, 93).

CHILDS, Darron E. *The last baronets of old Gainsborough: featuring Sir Charles Henry John Anderson, 9th and last Baronet of Lea and Sir Henry Hickman Beckett Bacon, Premier baronet and last Lord of the Manor of Gainsborough*. [The author, 2013]. [4]. 103pp. No ISBN. £20 hbk (post free from The Delvers, 3 Willingham Road, Lea, Gainsborough DN21 5EH). (*LP&P*, 92).

CHISHOLM, Michael. *In the shadow of the abbey: Crowland.* Coleford (Glos.), Douglas McLean Publishing, 2013. 240pp. ISBN 978 0 946252 90 9. £15.99 pbk. (*LP&P*, 94).

CLAPSON, Rodney. *A Lincolnshire shipyard – New Holland.* Barton-on-Humber, The author, 2013. [4], 55pp. ISBN 978 0 9557444 1 9. £7.50 pbk (or £9.75 by post from the author, 16 Whitecross Street, Barton-on-Humber DN18 5EU). (*LP&P*, 94).

ESSICK, John Inscore. *Thomas Grantham: God's Messenger from Lincolnshire.* Mercer University Press, 2013. 246pp. ISBN 978 0 88 14646 1 0. £24.50 hbk.

FANTHORPE, Rod and FANTHORPE, Jean. *Fanthorpe – people & places: how a worldwide family developed from its Lincolnshire locative roots in its social & economic* context, Lincoln, The authors, 2013. ix, 322pp. ISBN 978 0 9927243 0 0. £30 hbk (postage extra from the authors, 1 Neile Close, Glebe Park, Lincoln LN2 4RT).

FISKERTON HISTORY & ARCHAEOLOGICAL GROUP. *Fiskerton then & now, [by Sally Scott and Dave Willey].* The Group, 2013. 84pp. No ISBN. £7 pbk.

FORD, Avril. *Going home the long way round: how a very ordinary little girl from Kent grew up to become one of the first women priests in Lincolnshire, and her adventures on the way.* [The author, 2013]. 95pp. ISBN 987 0 9569729 7 2 [sic]. Unpriced pbk. (*LP&P*, 94).

GOODHAND, Bill and BURKETT, Molly. *Will, the boy from Welbourn, Sir William Robertson.* Barny Books, [2013]. 48pp. ISBN 978 1 906542 46 8. £4.95 pbk. (*LP&P*, 97).

HIGHAM, N. J. editor. *Wilfrid: Abbot, bishop, saint: papers from the 1300th Anniversary Conference.* Donington, Shaun Tyas, 2013. xxvi, 390, [14]pp. ISBN 978 1 907730 27 6 - £35 hbk; 978 1 907730 29 0 - £19.95 pbk.

HILL, Nick and ROGERS, Alan. *Guild, hospital and alderman: new light on the founding of Browne's Hospital, Stamford, 1475-1509.* Bury St Edmunds, Arima Publishing, 2013. 62pp. ISBN 978 1 84549 582 4. £10 pbk. (*LP&P*, 93).

JAMES, Maureen. *Lincolnshire folk tales.* Stroud, The History Press, 2013. 190pp. ISBN 978 0 7524 6640 6. £9.99 pbk.

JONES, Robin. *Lighthouses of the East Coast: East Anglia and Lincolnshire.* Wellington (Somerset), Halsgrove, 2013. 144pp. ISBN 978 0 85704 167 8. £16.99 hbk. (*LP&P*, 93).

KING, Gemma. *Haunted Boston.* Stroud, The History Press, 2013. 95pp. ISBN 978 0 7524 8624 6. £9.99 pbk. (*LP&P*, 97).

KIRK, Tom. *A doctor's war: the diary of Dr Tom Kirk,: 1939-1945; edited by Geoffrey F. Bryant, Nigel*

D. Land [and] Stephen J. Wright. Barton-on-Humber, Barton Civic Society and Fathom Writers Press, 2013. [6], 222pp. ISBN 978 0 9555950 9 7. (Barton remembered, 1939-1945: Part Four). £10 pbk (or £13 by post from either Wilderspin School, Queen Street, Barton-on-Humber DN18 6QP or Fathom Writers Press, The Ropewalk, Barton-on-Humber DN18 5JT). (*LP&P*, 95).

KLEINEKE, Hannes and STEER, Christian, editors. *The Yorkist age: proceedings of the 2011 Harlaxton Symposium.* Donington, Shaun Tyas and Richard III and Yorkist History Trust, 2012. [xix], 488pp. and 28 plates. ISBN 978 1 907730 22 1. (Harlaxton Medieval Studies, Volume XXIII). £49.50 hbk.

LEACH, Terence and PACEY, Robert. *Lost houses of Lincolnshire, Volume 2; [new re-issue].* Lincoln, Society for Lincolnshire History & Archaeology, 2013. 80pp. ISBN 978 0 90358 28 5. £8.95 pbk.

LUDLAM, A. J. and ELDRIDGE, P. J. *Gone but not forgotten.* Ludborough, Lincolnshire Wolds Railway Society, 2013. [4], 45pp. ISBN 978 0 9926762 0 9. £7.95 pbk. (plus £1.10 postage from the LWRS, Ludborough Station, Station Road, Ludborough DN36 5SQ). (*LP&P*, 95).

[MENNELL, Gary and MENNELL, Brian]. *Slightly below the glide path II: RAF Waddington...* York, Fox 3 Publishing, 2013. 101pp. ISBN 978 0 9566319 2 3. £7.99 pbk. (*LP&P*, 93).

MITCHELL, Vic and SMITH, Keith. *Nottingham to Lincoln [including the Southwell branch].* Midhurst, Middleton Press, 2013. [c.60pp]. ISBN 978 1 908174 43 7. £16.95 hbk. (*LP&P*, 95).

OGDEN, R. J. *Brief history of Horncastle.* Tattershall, Scrivelsby, Somersby, etc. Burgh le Marsh, Robert Pacey, 2013. 77pp. No ISBN. £4.99 pbk (a reprint of a work first published in 1913 by W. K. Morton of Horncastle; postage extra from Dr R. Pacey, Old Chapel Lane, Burgh le Marsh PE24 5LQ). (*LP&P*, 97)

OTTER, Patrick. *1 Group swift to attack: Bomber Command's unsung heroes.* Barnsley, Pen & Sword Aviation, 2013. xvi, 368pp. ISBN 978 1 781590 94 2. £25 hbk. (*LP&P*, 95).

PAINTER, Bill. *The transportation of 135 female convicts from Lincolnshire to Australia, 1787-1851: 'to a land beyond the seas'.* [The author], 2013. [5], 88pp. No ISBN. £8.95 pbk. (*LP&P*, 95).

POPE, Margaret. *The history of Theddlethoirpe, Gayton-le-Marsh, Burwell and Walmsgate.* [The author, 2013?] 25pp. No ISBN. 90pp. pbk. (*LP&P*, 94).

REED, John. *Ruskington as I remember it: a few of the memories...* [Ruskington], jrr publishing, 2013. ix, 143pp. No ISBN. £6.99 pbk. (*LP&P*, 96).

REID, William. *The history of Lincoln Fire Brigade*. Waddington, The author, 2013. 110pp. ISBN 978 0 9043270 8 3. £15 pbk. (*LP&P*, 94).

ROBINSON, P. *Lincoln's excavators: the Ruston-Bucyrus years, 1970-1985.* **Wellington, (Somerset), Roundoak Press, 2013. 336pp. and over 500 illus. ISBN 978 1 871565 58 4. (History of Ruston/Bucyrus, Volume 4). £36.95 hbk.**

ROTHERHAM, Ian D. *The lost Fens: England's greatest ecological disaster*. Stroud, The History Press, 2013. 207pp. ISBN 978 0 7524 8699 4. £17.99 pbk.

ROWORTH, Peter and ROWORTH, Janet. *Spirit of Lincoln*. Wellington (Somerset), Halsgrove, 2013. 64pp. ISBN 978 0 85710 080 1. £4.99 hbk. (*LP&P*, 94).

RYHALL C. E. PRIMARY SCHOOL and HADEN, John. *Robert 'Troublechurch' Browne of Tolethorpe and the separatist movement, by the pupils of Ryhall... and John Haden*. Tollerton (Notts.), Barny Books, 2013. 79pp. ISBN 978 1 906542 61 0. £5.99 pbk (postage extra from the publisher, 76 Cotgrave Lane, Tollerton, Notts NG12 4FY). (*LP&P*, 95).

SALTER, Mike. *Medieval walled towns*. Malvern, Folly Publications, 2013. 224pp. ISBN 978 1 871731 96 5.

£15 pbk. (*LP&P*, 92).

SEATON, Keith. *The River Welland: shipping & mariners of Spalding.* **Stroud, The History Press, 2013. 192pp. ISBN 978 0 7524 9449 9. £16.99 pbk.**

SPENCER, Andrew. *Nobility and kingship in medieval England: the Earls and Edward I, 1272-1307.* **Cambridge University Press, 2013. 317pp. ISBN 978 1 10 702675 9. (Cambridge Studies in Medieval Life and Thought, Fourth Series). £65 hbk.**

The Victorian façade, 1859-1918: William Watkins and Sons, architects, Lincoln. [University of Lincoln, 2013]. 50pp. ISBN 0 9516340 0 3. £7.50 pbk. [A reprint of the original 1990 publication with two new forewords]. (*LP&P*, 94).

WALKER, Andrew, editor. *Boultham and Swallowbeck: Lincoln's south-western suburbs*. The Survey of Lincoln, 2013. 72pp. ISBN 978 0 9538650 8 6. (The Survey of Lincoln booklet series, 9). £6.95 pbk. (*LP&P*, 95).

WILLIS, Steven. *The Roman roadside settlement and multi-period ritual complex at Nettleton and Rothwell, Lincolnshire*. Canterbury, Steve Willis and Pre-Constuct Archaeology Ltd and the University of Kent, 2013. xx,

----

Erratum

In the article by Rob Wheeler, 'The rise of Clayton and Shuttleworth' in the last *LHA* journal, 47 (2012), pages 61-71, figure six (on page 70) was inadvertently published with errors. The correct version of this figure is reproduced below with apologies for the error.

	1856	1857	1858
Austria			
Wolff	7	20	0
Vienna Establishment			21
Other	1	4	1
Hungary			
Erkory	2	8	0
Pest Establishment			3
Other	2	1	6
Vienna for Pest			2

Note. Engines shipped to Moravia or Galicia are excluded.

Fig.6. Destinations of engines shipped to Austria and Hungary, 1856-58 (source, MERL TR 3 MAR/1).